ORGANIZATIONS AS LEARNING SYSTEMS

'LIVING COMPOSITION' AS AN ENABLING INFRASTRUCTURE

ADVANCED SERIES IN MANAGEMENT

Series Editor:
Professor Ron Sanchez
Copenhagen, Denmark and Lund, Sweden

The intent of the Advanced Series in Management is to produce foundational books for a new era of management theory that will be long-lived in serving future generations of management researchers and practitioners. To this end, the Advanced Series in Management has three goals:

1. publishing volumes that develop new conceptual foundations for management theory;
2. countering the trend towards increasing fragmentation in management theory and research by developing a new theory base for management that is interconnected and integrative;
3. developing new management theory that has clear, direct usefulness for the practice of management.

The volumes in the Advanced Series in Management are intended collectively to elaborate a broadened and more integrated theory base for understanding and addressing the challenges facing contemporary managers. Volumes in the Advanced Series in Management therefore seek to stimulate and shape the development of management thought in ways and directions that reach beyond the content and perspectives of established management theory. The Advanced Series in Management intends to be, in effect, the series of academic management books that is willing to break away from the pack and to publish titles that advance new frameworks for management thinking.

Related Publications:

Number 1: MORECROFT, SANCHEZ, HEENE
Systems Perspectives on Resources, Capabilities, and Management Processes

Number 2: SKÖLDBERG
Tracks and Frames: The Economy of Symbolic Forms in Organizations

Number 3: HEDBERG, BAUMARD, YAKHLEF
Managing Imaginary Organizations: A New Perspective on Business

Forthcoming titles include:

SANCHEZ
Beyond the Boundaries of the Firm: Integrating Theories of the Firm and Theories of Markets

Related Elsevier journals

Business Horizons
European Management Journal
Journal of Management
Leadership Quarterly
Long Range Planning
Organizational Dynamics
Scandinavian Journal of Management

ORGANIZATIONS AS LEARNING SYSTEMS

'LIVING COMPOSITION' AS AN ENABLING INFRASTRUCTURE

MARJATTA MAULA

ELSEVIER

Amsterdam • Boston • Heidelberg • London • New York • Oxford
Paris • San Diego • San Francisco • Singapore • Sydney • Tokyo

Elsevier
The Boulevard, Langford Lane, Kidlington, Oxford OX5 1GB, UK
Radarweg 29, PO Box 211, 1000 AE Amsterdam, The Netherlands

First edition 2006

British Library Cataloguing in Publication Data
A catalogue record for this book is available from the British Library

Library of Congress Cataloging-in-Publication Data
A catalog record for this book is available from the Library of Congress

ISBN-10: 0-08-043919-5
ISBN-13: 978-0-08-043919-8

For information on all Elsevier publications
visit our website at books.elsevier.com

Printed and bound in The Netherlands

06 07 08 09 10 10 9 8 7 6 5 4 3 2 1

Working together to grow
libraries in developing countries
www.elsevier.com | www.bookaid.org | www.sabre.org

ELSEVIER   BOOK AID International   Sabre Foundation

Contents

About the Author

D.Sc. Marjatta Maula is a Professor of Knowledge and Information Management at the Institute of Business Information Management, Tampere University of Technology, Finland. She holds a D.Sc. (Economics and Business Administration) degree in international business from The Helsinki School of Economics, and an M.Sc. degree in computer sciences from The University of Tampere, Finland. Earlier she has been an Associate Research Professor at the Copenhagen Business School, a management consultant in several international management-consulting firms, a technology and development director, and a systems manager and analyst. She has written about multinational knowledge-intensive firms as learning and evolving systems, change processes, knowledge management, and ICT.

Contact information:

Professor Marjatta Maula, D.Sc., M.Sc.
Lindforsinkatu 21 A 3
FIN-33720 Tampere, Finland
Mobile: +358 40 8490224
E-mail: marjatta.maula@tut.fi

Introduction to the Advanced Series in Management

The intent of the Advanced Series in Management is to produce foundational books for a new era of management theory that will be long-lived in serving future generations of management researchers and practitioners. To this end, the Advanced Series in Management has three goals:

1. publishing volumes that develop new conceptual foundations for management theory;
2. countering the trend towards increasing fragmentation in management theory and research by developing a new theory base for management that is interconnected and integrative;
3. developing new management theory that has clear, direct usefulness for the practice of management.

The volumes in the Advanced Series in Management are intended collectively to elabo-rate a broadened and more integrated theory base for understanding and addressing the challenges facing contemporary managers. Volumes in the Advanced Series in Management therefore seek to stimulate and shape the development of management thought in ways and directions that reach beyond the content and perspectives of established management theory. The Advanced Series in Management intends to be, in effect, the series of academic management books that is willing to break away from the pack and to publish titles that advance new frameworks for management thinking.

The Series introduces new conceptualizations for management theory that rise above any single or dominant theoretical perspective. In essence, the defining theoretical sensibility of the Series is a new perspective on management that includes essential dynamic, systemic, cognitive, and holistic aspects of managing organizations and that seeks to treat these aspects theoretically as an interconnected whole. A key focus in this new approach to building management theory is therefore elaborating the dynamics of the interactions between the multiple aspects of the management processes that thus far have not been — and indeed cannot be — adequately addressed through the theoretical lens of a single discipline.

The Advanced Series in Management takes as a given that *change* is the normal state of the world that managers face — and that management theory must therefore address adequately the dynamics of markets, technologies, organizations, and society that managers must contend with. Understanding the disequilibria in the environments of contemporary organizations and how managers can respond to them is thus a central concern of the Series.

The Series also holds firmly to a view of organizations as *human systems* in which the multiple interactions and interdependencies of all participants must be explicitly recognized and reconciled in theory as well as in practice. The systemic view of organizations and the management process is intended to provide a conceptual framework that is receptive to inputs from both established theory and new theoretical perspectives and that is capable of more balanced and thus more realistic representations of organizations in theory.

The Series also advances a cognitive perspective in which imperfect information, bounded rationality, and the resulting cognitive limits of managers are not assumed away for the sake of building elegant theory, but rather are seen as "core constraints" in the management process that must be directly addressed by new management theory. In plain language, the Advanced Series in Management is not an outlet for yet more management theory that pretends that managers — or observers of managers — have information and understanding that no one can actually have in the complex and uncertain environments managers actually work in. Rather, the Series intends to establish new management theory that is consistent with the actual cognitive processes and limitations of human managers and researchers.

A final sensibility of the Series is the belief that management theory must recognize the full set of interrelated stakeholder interests (employees, suppliers, customers, communities, debt holders, and shareholders) that interact in organizations. New theory developed in the Series will recognize and explore the identification, weighing, and balancing of multiple stakeholder interests that are fundamental to the management process.

Our expectation is that this volume and the other volumes in the Series will form a collection of foundational books that will be long-lived in providing theoretical impetus to both current and future generations of management academics and practitioners.

Each volume in the Series must meet the dual requirements of achieving conceptual clarity and theoretical coherence, while yielding useful recommendations for improving management practice. Each volume in the Series has the mission of advancing our thinking about management in ways that:

- connect management theory with management practice by refocusing management theory and research on the actual problems and concerns of contemporary managers;
- link together the currently fragmented areas of management theory by elaborating new concepts that can connect and integrate the theory bases of relevant disciplines — and do so in ways that more effectively address the real concerns of managers;
- introduce new theory that is not currently established in the management disciplines, but that can be used to represent management problems more fully and realistically.

To meet these criteria, development of volumes for the Series is guided by thefour principles of inclusiveness, connectedness, theoretical grounding, and applicability.

Inclusiveness means that the volumes in the Series include many disciplines, perspectives, and approaches, both established and new, that offer useful improvements in our understanding of the problems and processes of managing. What the Series will not do, however, is proliferate volumes that apply a single theoretical perspective to a wide range of management issues and topics — i.e., a single theoretical hammer treating every management problem as if it were a nail. Thus, the Advanced Series in Management is not just another collection of "the usual suspects" — a marketing perspective, an operations title, an advanced organization behavior perspective, etc. — that have no evident theoretical connection with each other. While conceived as a collection of volumes that is intendedly broad in its theoretical scope, the Series nevertheless requires each volume to make a definable, significant, and coherent contribution to developing management theory that embraces and integrates multiple perspectives on managing.

Connectedness means that each volume in the Series must develop clear conceptual connections to other perspectives developed in existing or planned volumes in the Series. While each volume must develop well an approach to studying management that is distinctive in its own emphases, it must also establish theoretical connections with the themes developed in other volumes. In this way, the volumes in the Series are intended to weave a web of interconnected concepts and theories that will in time collectively define a new theory base for management. What we want to achieve through connectedness is nexus of ideas — each volume not only bringing its own useful ideas for understanding management, but also linking its ideas to ideas in other volumes in the Series to compose an interconnected view of the multiple aspects of the management process.

Theoretical grounding means that each volume must develop a perspective that is carefully grounded in actual management processes and built up from a well defined and carefully elaborated conceptual framework for representing and analyzing those processes. What we wish to avoid in the Series is theoretical rigidities and narrowness that make us blind to important management realities. What we wish to achieve in the Series is the progressive development of concepts and theories that are understandable to both academics and managers. Thus each volume starts with a statement of fundamental concepts and basic presumptions and then moves on to comprehensible theoretical propositions, clear applications to important management contexts, and useful suggestions for both practice and further theory development.

Applicability means that each volume in the Series must meet a test of clear applicability to actual — not imagined or posited — management problems and concerns. To meet the criterion of applicability, each volume must have a well stated, theoretically developed set of ideas that it applies directly to a well defined and important set of management concerns. What the Series will avoid is volumes that are laden with theory but short on useful applications, on the one hand, and volumes that approach important management problems with inadequately developed concepts or flawed logic, on the other. In essence, what the Series intends toachieve is volumes that advance ideas about managing that have both theoretical clarity and demonstrable usefulness to managers.

If successful in meeting these goals and norms, the Advanced Series in Management will play an important role in shaping the direction of management theory and practice in the next decade — and in the decades to follow as well.

Ron Sanchez, Series Editor
Copenhagen, Denmark and Lund, Sweden

Series Editor's Introduction

The 'four cornerstones' that define the fundamental orientation to management in the *Advanced Series in Management* are *dynamic, systemic, cognitive, and holistic* perspectives on the management process. Although the main emphasis in the volume is on learning processes — a key cognitive activity of organizations — the study of learning in organizations by Marjatta Maula presented in this volume effectively embraces all four of these fundamental perspectives on managing organizations.

In this volume, Professor Maula develops a conceptual model of the essential elements and processes in organizational learning — a model that she refers to as a 'Living Composition' model of organizations — and validates and supports the application of the model through empirical studies of organizations that have demonstrated significant capacity for organizational learning. Her model elaborates in considerable detail the fundamental cognitive processes of sensing, interpreting, responding, reflecting, and learning that must be developed in organizations if they are to be capable of surviving in changing environments.

Professor Maula also examines organizational approaches to making those activities effective. A centerpiece of her representation of organizational approaches to learning is the representation of organizations as systems in which interactions of all essential elements of sensing, interpreting, responding, reflecting, and learning must be managed with a clear goal to achieving learning. Professor Maula provides in this volume a detailed guide to a comprehensive model of how organizations can learn — and thereby survive — in dynamic environments. Her emphasis on systematic approaches to managing these processes also reflects an awareness of the holistic nature of organizations, and the resulting need to attend to multiple stakeholder interests in managing learning processes.

Professor Maula's study draws on a number of theoretical approaches to understanding organizations, and makes extensive use of several concepts from chaos and complexity theories to characterize how organizations interact with their changing environments.

In a field of study in which institutional incentives increasingly draw researchers into ever more finely focused studies, Professor Maula's study offers an exceptional — and essential — integrative view of approaches to managing organizations in ways that can sustain high rates of learning in rapidly changing environments. It is a privilege to be able to include this important work in the *Advanced Series in Management*.

Ron Sanchez, Series Editor
Copenhagen, Denmark and Lund, Sweden

Acknowledgments

This book is the result of a long research process. It is based on cooperation with several persons and organizations to whom I would like to express my warmest gratitude.

Professor Ron Sanchez, Copenhagen Business School and Lund University, has provided insightful advice for transforming the ideas of my academic research report into a book for managers, academics, and consultants. His contribution to this book is invaluable. I want to present my warmest thanks to him for his patient and wise way of commenting on various ideas in the manuscript.

Heather A. Hazard, PhD, Associate Professor at Copenhagen Business School, has been an excellent advisor for the earlier research project that is the basis for this book. She encouraged exploration among new approaches and aimed at innovative research results. Professor Reijo Luostarinen provided the possibility to conduct the research project at Helsinki School of Economics and helped it to reach its academic objectives.

The empirical material was collected from four management consulting firms. Because of turbulence in the industry, some of the firms have merged or changed name, and many of the interviewees have moved to new positions or other firms. The managers at Arthur Andersen (Business Consulting), Arthur D. Little, Inc. (Europe), Ernst & Young (Management Consulting), The KaosPilots/KaosManagement, PBS (Danish Payment Systems Ltd.) and Progrès A/S made this project possible. I want to thank Robert J. Hiebeler, Carsten Dalsgaard, Nils Bohlin, Maurice Olivier, Kamal Saad, Philippe Alloing, Ralph W. Poole, John G. Peetz, Knud Musaeus, Michel Constant, Uffe Elbaek, Marianne Egelund Siig, Per Ladegaard, Erik Nørgaard, Jane Blichmann, Sven Klint Bergh, and many other directors who expressed genuine interest in the topic of this book and provided important information and comments. I express my warmest gratitude to all other persons who contributed to the study and to this book by providing access to the case firms and investing their time in the interviews. The complete lists of the interviewees are included in Appendices 5–8.

The methodological analysis of the empirical material was carried out at the European Centre for Analysis in the Social Sciences (ECASS), the University of Essex. The work was supported financially by The European Commission Training and Mobility of Researchers — Access to Large Scale Facilities Programme. The following sources and foundations supported the research project financially: Nordisk Forskerutdanningsakademi NorFA, the Finnish Science Academy/FIGSIB, Helsinki School of Economics, Helsinki School of Economics Foundation, The Danish Research Academy, Foundation for Economic Education, Yrjö Uitto Foundation, Marcus Wallenberg Foundation, Alfred Kordelin Foundation, and Seinäjoki Polytechnic. Feedback from colleagues and students at the Tampere University of Technology has been very inspiring during the finalization stage of this book.

The final editing of this book has been a demanding task. I want to express my warmest thanks to Karen A. Liu for her skillful work. She has checked and corrected the text and helped to transform my expressions into better English.

Finally, I want to thank my friends and family, especially my children, young academics and students Markku, Mikko, Katri, and Kirsti for their knowledgeable comments and encouraging attitude during the research process.

Marjatta Maula
January 2006

PART I

PRELIMINARIES ABOUT UNDERLYING STRUCTURES AND DYNAMICS

Part I of this volume discusses the need to explain the underlying structures and dynamics of organizations and takes the first step in analyzing alternative approaches. After the preliminary introduction to the living composition model (Chapter 1), Part I continues with a review of literature about learning and renewal (Chapter 2) and about underlying structures and dynamics (Chapter 3). Organizations as systems will be discussed in the light of well-known system theories and models, and some principles of complexity theories will also be presented (Chapter 4).

Thus, the definition of the model and necessary theoretical background will be presented first in this part, and detailed analysis of the selected theory and exact definitions of concepts of the developed model will be presented in subsequent parts. The objective is that with this preliminary insight and definition in mind, it will be easier for the reader to follow the analysis that is needed to develop and specify the living composition model. Definitions of the key concepts can be found in the glossary in Appendix 1.

Chapter 1

Introduction

This chapter will present an overview of the 'living composition', the model of living organizations, which explains the processes of learning and renewal that drive and are based on continuous co-evolution and self-production of an organization. The chapter then introduces the reader to challenges that organizations face as they attempt simultaneously to operate efficiently, to learn and renew themselves, and to co-evolve with their complex, globalizing environment. It also presents the tension between creativity and efficiency and specifies five dilemmas of learning organizations that have several managerial implications. The dilemmas concern underlying structures of organizations and can be derived from two 'worldviews', which also have implications for knowledge and learning. (A third view that is based on the living composition model and helps to reframe these dilemmas will be presented in Chapter 17.) Finally, this chapter provides a guide to reading the remainder of this book.

1.1 A Structured Model of Living Composition: The Goal of this Book

The theory of living, self-producing systems (autopoiesis theory) was developed by Humberto Maturana and Francisco Varela (1980, 1987). It belongs to a broader group of theories called complex adaptive systems (CAS). The ideas of this book are based on an academic study that resulted in a new interpretation of autopoiesis theory in the context of organizations, the living composition model (Maula, 1999, 2000a).

The model of living composition is based on the principles of complexity and especially on the theory of self-production (autopoiesis). The model is a new, original interpretation about an organization as a self-producing, living system. The main propositions implicit in the living composition model are:

1. The evolutionary capability of a living organization is derived from the functioning of its living composition.
2. A successful organization is likely to have found ways to utilize the complexity phenomena of self-organization and emergence through its living composition.

A living organization improves its chances for co-evolving with its complex environment within its business ecosystem by creating and utilizing boundary elements.

The definition of the living organization and living composition:

> **The living composition model** specifies the essential characteristics of living organizations. A living organization is a self-producing (autopoietic) system that is composed of 10 different non-physical strategic components. Boundary elements are included as one component type. The living

composition model describes the 'structure' of a living organization in which the strategic components and their interrelationships determine an organization's evolutionary capability. An organization evolves by continually producing its strategic components as simultaneous tracks with a pattern of interactions. The production and interaction of the components and their relationships facilitate sensing (interactive openness) and memory (organizational/internal closure) in an organization. Sensing and memory are simultaneous and interconnected phenomena. They enable both an organization's current efficiency and its capability to learn, to renew itself, and to co-evolve with its changing environment within its larger business ecosystem.

In this book, the theory of living, self-producing systems will be applied only to human, social organizations. The central idea is that organizations are living systems that may learn and renew themselves continually, thereby improving their chances of survival and success. The living composition model attempts to explain the structure and behavior of organizations. The assumption is that the living composition constitutes an internal enabling infrastructure of an organization. It is composed of 10 strategic components that are continually produced by the organization. The model also distinguishes two major kinds of knowledge flows — sensing and memory. *Sensing (a condition for interactive openness)* means that the organization interacts, co-evolves, and coordinates its activities with its changing environment. An organization can create new knowledge by using its various kinds of boundary elements, such as roles and functions through which it interacts reciprocally with its environment. *Memory (self-referentiality, a characteristic of internal closure)* means that the organization 'understands itself' and has access to its own accumulated knowledge. The organization is internally closed in the sense that it utilizes its existing knowledge resources and may thereby operate efficiently. Sensing and memory help an organization to make distinctions that then become embedded in its internal structure. The continual production of the 10 strategic components and their interconnections as well as sensing and memory enable the functioning and continual renewal of the organization. The living composition facilitates the efficiency, creativity, learning, and renewal of an organization, as well as its co-evolution with its environment. Figure 1.1 illustrates the two major knowledge flows and their relationship.

In the living composition model, an organization produces its own non-physical strategic components and boundary elements in a continuous manner. The components and their relationships as well as major knowledge flows constitute a living composition that can emerge as a result of drift, through organizational design, or as a result of both.

Because organizations are complex systems and evolve continually as both a theoretical and practical matter, it may be difficult to decide where and how to start improvement initiatives. In a systemic entity, small changes may cause large and complex effects over time. Efforts may fail, independent of their magnitude, if their role in the systemic processes is not understood. Understanding the composition and major knowledge flows of an organization may help in planning improvement initiatives. For this reason, this book also develops consistency/intentionality platforms and evolution models that help managers, consultants, and researchers to determine where an organization currently stands and how to improve its ability to successfully co-evolve with its changing environment.

LIVING COMPOSITION

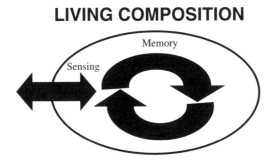

Figure 1.1: The living composition — the two major knowledge flows generated by strategic components.

Through multiple cases, this book also provides ideas about how competent learning organizations are composed in practice and how they can be designed. The concepts of the living composition model have, in effect, been tested empirically from 1997 to 1999 in four management consulting organizations: Arthur Andersen (Management Consulting), Arthur D. Little (Europe), Ernst & Young (Business Consulting), and The KaosPilots and KaosManagement. The management consulting industry was selected because it has globalized rapidly, the consulting firms are knowledge-intensive, and many of them have invested considerably in knowledge management and information and communication technology (ICT) solutions. The case firms differ by their orientation, age, and size. Three of the subject companies are large, multinational, knowledge-intensive firms, and one is a very small networked organization. This book uses the experiences of the case firms to develop the model of living composition further. The model suggests that the improvements observed in these companies can also be obtained in other organizations, including small organizations and those in other industries and the public sector. In general, the principles of the model can be applied to small and large, fast and slowly growing as well as high- and low-tech organizations. Moreover, the results are scalable and can also be applied to subunits of an organization.

This book will illustrate how the 10 strategic components and two knowledge flows can be identified in an organization and describes how they explain its learning and renewal capability in theory and practice. The cases demonstrate how the structured model of living composition enables systematic and structured analysis of complex and dynamic social organizations. The model also helps to describe an organization's current state, to prioritize the targets for improvement, and to compare the compositions of different kinds of organizations.

The specific contributions of this book are as follows.

- The definition of living organization and formulation of the living composition model, including the specification of 10 strategic components and two major knowledge flows that facilitate an organization's learning and renewal in co-evolution with its environment. The model depicts the underlying structures and dynamics of organizations and facilitates their systematic analysis and development.

- From a theoretical perspective, the book provides a new, original interpretation of selected concepts of complexity theory, and especially of the theory of self-production (autopoiesis) in an organizational context.
- The analysis of the role of boundary elements for simultaneous openness and closure of an organization. They help in understanding the interconnectedness of structures that facilitate creativity and efficiency.
- The empirical application of the living composition model to four case organizations.
- The formulation of consistency/intentionality platforms and evolution models. An organization's method to evolve can be positioned, evaluated, and developed further by using consistency/intentionality platforms and evolution models.

This book is intended for practicing managers, management consultants, researchers, and teachers. The experiences indicate that the living composition model is useful for organizational analysis and development, as well as for research and teaching purposes. The cases serve as a basis for teaching because they illustrate how different kinds of organizations can be analyzed by using the model. These implications will be discussed at the end of this book.

1.2 How to Improve Survival and Success? The Question of Creativity and Efficiency

Many organizations operate in an environment that is characterized by globalization, competition, and non-linear changes. Achieving the required efficiency often involves increasing control and streamlining, for example by implementing ICT systems to enable better control of processes and activities. Simultaneously, globalization and competition require creativity, which may be associated with emergence, self-organization, diversity, and reduced control. Some approaches that are related to knowledge creation relax the assumption of control and emphasize creative chaos,[1] crisis, revolution, empowerment, and self-organization (Itami & Roehl, 1987; Nonaka & Takeuchi, 1995). Thus, there seems to be contradicting pressures. However, self-organization, emergence, and related concepts need not necessarily mean 'laissez-faire' in the organization. Instead, these concepts can be reframed in a productive way in the larger context of living composition.

The question of simultaneous creativity and efficiency is controversial and is generally regarded as difficult to solve. Equally, the problems of simultaneous freedom and control or exploration and exploitation (March, 1991) are difficult in theory and practice. These questions are approached in this book through the organization's composition and knowledge flows and its capability to learn and renew itself.

Organizations co-evolve with an increasingly global, complex, dynamic, and turbulent environment. Some organizations have better capabilities to survive and succeed than others, but it is often difficult to explain why. As a result, it often seems problematic to improve an organization's chances of success. Even the best research results and consulting advice are usually fragmented and address only parts of the puzzle that managers must solve.

The development of knowledge, competences, and learning capability, as well as information and communication systems, are central concerns of managers. However, it is not clear how they are related to each other and to the organization's capability to renew itself. Moreover, these aspects are often seen as isolated from the larger organizational context. It is difficult to understand the logic behind the complex fabric of various organizational aspects.

According to Doz and Prahalad (1993), it is not clear how organizational components should be coordinated so that efficiency and creativity can be achieved simultaneously. Therefore, managers, consultants, and academics would benefit from a theory and model that could depict the underlying structures and dynamics that enable the learning, renewal, coevolution, survival, and success of an organization. Doz and Prahalad claim that there is need for an approach that could reframe the phenomena of learning and renewal. First, there is a need for positive theory development and understanding these phenomena. Second, normative prescriptions are needed that could support the development and implementation of organizational strategies, structures, and practices.

Based on this reasoning, there is a need for a framework that explains the underlying dynamics of organizations, including both the drives to achieve fit among organizational components and to pursue inconsistent strategies. More generally, there is a need for a structured theory that explains how learning and evolution occur in organizations. According to Doz and Prahalad (1993), it is necessary to progress beyond the static resource-based views, to transcend the structural dimensions, and to analyze the underlying processes that enable continual change in organizations. More important than the formal structure of an organization are the informal flows and networks of information. The emphasis should be shifted from physical infrastructure and resource deployment to information-processing networks and resource mobilization. Managerially relevant midrange concepts are needed to model the strategic and organizational behavior of complex organizations. Studying large numbers of relatively similar organizations may lead to generalizable theories, but such theories often treat organizations as 'black boxes' and do not develop detailed knowledge of organizational functioning. Doz and Prahalad claim that from a managerial research standpoint, there is a need for a robust conceptual model of how a learning organization[2] really works.

Knowledge creation, learning, and competence development are relevant issues for managers, consultants, and academics interested in understanding the challenges of environmental turbulence and competition. Emergence and self-organization have become popular concepts in this context. These concepts deviate from the conventional strategy emphasis of seeking fit among organizational components, and their relationships need to be clarified and conflicts resolved to develop new insights into processes of creativity and renewal that are essential in a learning organization.

There is an unsatisfactory shortfall in prevailing explanations of learning and renewal. Conventional models of organizations are often overly simplistic compared to the actual complexity of organizations. Increasingly refined models and theories have been developed to depict and explain organizational structures and processes. However, the increasing level of detail in these models often does not help us to understand the essential processes of learning and renewal better.

Also, the strategic role of knowledge in organizational renewal and co-evolution remains largely uncovered. However, an organization may nevertheless improve the effectiveness of its knowledge management activities if they are organized within a theoretically sound and organizationally shared view of the organization's behavior. In response to this need, this book develops a living composition model to represent the composition and functioning of living, learning organizations, and the crucial role of knowledge flows.

The living composition model helps to reframe the controversy between control and autonomy, between efficiency and creativity, and between exploitation and exploration. The model helps to align strategic components so that there are better opportunities to achieve these objectives simultaneously.

1.3   Five Dilemmas of Learning and Knowledge: The Importance of Underlying Structures

This section illustrates the importance of underlying structures in organizational strategy and daily practices. For this purpose, it presents five dilemmas that managers may face in their daily work. According to Dodgson (1993), organizational learning and evolution are characterized by conflicts and dilemmas. Not surprisingly, then, our understanding of renewal, creativity, learning, and knowledge is based on several conflicting assumptions that have pragmatic implications for strategic management and organizational design. These dilemmas illustrate the need to understand better the underlying structures and conditions for sustainable organizational evolution. The five dilemmas of learning and knowledge presented in this section are reframed in the light of the living composition model in Chapter 17.

Dilemma 1: The goal: knowledge, or learning and renewal?

View 1: Knowledge (asset) is the goal. Learning facilitates the production of new knowledge. Knowledge is an asset and the desired output of a learning process. Organizations should improve their learning capability so that they can produce knowledge that increases their intellectual capital.

View 2: Learning and renewal are the goals. Knowledge facilitates continuous learning and renewal in the changing environment. Organizations should improve their knowledge flows so that they increase their learning and renewal capability and thereby improve their adaptability and chances of survival and success.

Dilemma 2: Is knowledge objective or subjective?

View 1: Knowledge is objective. Knowledge represents the reality 'out there'. Knowledge is 'objective' and independent of people. Knowledge can reside in explicit form in documents and databases. The purpose of knowledge management is to exploit individuals' knowledge efficiently by converting it from tacit into explicit form. Knowledge management is the process of classifying, storing, and accessing knowledge.

View 2: Knowledge is subjective. Knowledge is subjective and context sensitive. It resides in people who create and interpret it continually. Knowledge cannot be acquired, accumulated, stored, distributed, or retrieved. Only data can be processed. The purpose of knowledge management is to facilitate the creativity of individuals and to develop individual skills, group level capabilities, and organizational competences. The main processes for knowledge management are communication and sharing among individuals.

Dilemma 3: Is knowledge located in an organization or in several brains?

View 1: Knowledge is located in an organization. An organization has a superior, more enduring role than individuals. It employs people who may come and go, while the organization itself remains. An organization's role is to acquire and utilize knowledge resources by designing and implementing appropriate structures and processes.

View 2: Knowledge is located in several brains. Organizations consist of people, of 'several brains'. People create new knowledge and construct their worlds through communication and interaction — i.e. by being social. Moreover, people in knowledge-intensive industries are often more loyal to their profession than to their organizations. Self-actualization has a higher position in their motivation hierarchy than economic rewards. Therefore, it is important to create favorable learning conditions for individuals to ensure that they learn at the individual level and stay in the company.

Dilemma 4: Control, order, and efficiency, or autonomy, freedom, self-organization, emergence, and creativity?

View 1: Control, order, and efficiency. Efficiency is the most important precondition for competitiveness. Control, order, standards, rules, and well-defined structures and processes enable efficiency. Strategy, organizational structure, and environment should therefore fit together. Efficient accumulation, storing, retrieval, and sharing of knowledge therefore have high priority. Information technology plays a key role in controlling the organization and monitoring its environment.

View 2: Autonomy, self-organization, emergence, and creativity. Creativity is the most important precondition for competitiveness. Organizations should encourage autonomy, freedom, self-organization, and emergence of new ideas. Empowerment is one example of increasing autonomy in organizations. Some researchers even recommend 'chaos', revolution, and crisis for organizations to facilitate their capability to learn, innovate, create, and change. Overlapping and conflicting ideas and informal communication fertilize innovativeness. A flat and flexible organization facilitates communication. It is necessary to connect people and to remove unnecessary rules and standards. Open and shared ICT solutions, such as the Internet, facilitate creativity and reduce the need for hierarchical control.

Dilemma 5: Detailed long-term planning or chaos and revolution?

View 1: Detailed long-term planning. A competent organization can be built up and its evolution can be conducted by implementing a well-defined, detailed, long-term plan and related control mechanisms. Investments in integrated solutions involve the whole organization. Information and communication systems require coordinated planning and carefully defined responsibilities.

View 2: Chaos and revolution. The world is emerging, and we do not know what the future will be. Real changes in an organization only happen through crisis, chaos, and revolution. Therefore organizations have to abandon planning and control. If a crisis is not at hand, a competent organization can evolve incrementally by experimenting and learning from errors.

These five dilemmas can be summarized roughly into two contradicting worldviews that represent significantly different philosophical paradigms and relationships to knowledge.

They have practical managerial implications for strategic decisions, organizational design, knowledge and information management, and competence development. These two worldviews can be identified in various forms in management books, consulting methodologies, and the applications of ICT (Table 1.1).

The first worldview is based on a realism that assumes that knowledge is objective and explicit, represents existing reality, is located in the organization independent of individuals, and can be engineered. It is associated with control, efficiency, rational approaches to decision-making, and an emphasis on technical solutions. Control, order, structure, and standards are highly valued. The major objective of knowledge management is to exploit individuals' tacit knowledge by transforming it into explicit form and sharing it. Progress occurs through detailed planning.

The second worldview is based on an idealism that emphasizes ideas, subjectivity, and the constructed nature of knowledge. It is associated with learning, creativity, innovation, and renewal. Socio-technical approaches and personal competencies are highly valued.

Table 1.1: Five dilemmas, two worldviews and knowledge.

The five dilemmas	Worldview 1	Worldview 2
Dilemma 1: The goal: knowledge, or learning and renewal?	Realism: objective world Empiricism: observation Knowledge (asset) as a goal	Idealism: ideas Learning and renewal as goals Knowledge as a tool
Dilemma 2: Is knowledge objective or subjective?	Knowledge: objective From tacit knowledge to explicit, shared knowledge	Knowledge: subjective, constructed From data to information and further to wisdom (= tacit knowledge)
Dilemma 3: Is knowledge located in an organization or in several brains?	Knowledge: in the organization Organizational effectiveness, rational decision-making Knowledge engineering	Knowledge: in the brains Human creativity, innovation, learning 'Soft' human approach, skills, capabilities
Dilemma 4: Control, order, efficiency, or autonomy, self-organization, emergence, and creativity?	Control, order, 'fit' and efficiency Exploitation	Autonomy, freedom, self-organization, emergence, and creativity Exploration
Dilemma 5: Detailed long-term planning or chaos, crisis, and revolution?	Detailed long-term planning Control mechanisms	Chaos, crisis, and revolution Learning from errors Abandoning of planning

Knowledge is assumed to be tacit by nature and located in individual people. Low hierarchies and abandoning of structures, rules, and standards facilitate self-organization and emergence of new solutions. Development occurs through 'chaos', crisis, and revolutions. The major objective of knowledge management is to make data and information available in an organization so that people can increase their personal tacit competencies and wisdom.

In managerial situations, it may be difficult to choose among these contradictory approaches and to justify the choice of one approach over the other. However, reframing these dilemmas and seeing them from a new perspective can help us to make more appropriate choices. The approach to managing living, learning organizations developed in this volume attempts to reframe these contradictions into a more comprehensive, coherent, and satisfactory worldview. The resulting third worldview will be presented in Chapter 17.

1.4   Guide to Reading This Book

This book is divided into four parts. Part I discusses the need to explain the underlying structures and dynamics of organizations and takes the first step in analyzing the alternative approaches. Chapter 1 has introduced the main ideas of this book. Chapter 2 reviews literature about learning and evolving organizations. The analysis reveals several trends that indicate the need for a more dynamic approach to knowing and change. Chapter 3 discusses the importance of underlying structures and dynamics for organizations and their learning and renewal capability. It starts by reviewing literature about control, self-organization, and emergence, and continues by analyzing structural aspects of strategy. The chapter ends with the preliminary formulation of the living composition model and discussion about consistency between components. Chapter 4 investigates an organization as a system. It presents selected system theories and analyzes how they explain organizational learning and evolution.

Part II of the book develops the living composition model in full detail. In Chapter 5 the book elaborates how to apply the principles of self-production (autopoiesis) to organizations. It discusses the assumptions about reality and knowledge in autopoiesis theory and compares them to conventional philosophical paradigms. The analysis clarifies how autopoiesis theory can be applied in an organizational context. In Chapter 6 the living composition model will be defined. Chapters 7–9 provide further analysis, conclusions, and implications of the model. Chapter 7 identifies and analyzes the strategic components of a living organization. The two major knowledge flows that enable the sensing and memory of an organization are introduced in Chapter 8. Chapter 9 analyzes the four knowledge processes.

Part III of the book will present the empirical cases. After discussing the characteristics of the management consulting industry in Chapter 10, the living composition model is applied empirically to the case organizations in Chapters 11–14. Chapter 15 summarizes the findings of the case firms, focusing especially on the components and major knowledge flows.

Part IV presents conclusions and implications. Chapter 16 discusses opportunities to proactively improve organizations through applying the model. It develops concepts of consistency/intentionality platforms and evolution models, and defines a process for systematically identifying and prioritizing improvement activities. Chapter 17 summarizes the findings of the earlier chapters by revisiting and reframing the concepts of control, self-organization, and emergence in the light of the model and empirical evidence. Finally, it presents theoretical implications and suggestions for further research. Additional material, including a glossary, literature reviews, a description of the research process and method, and facts about the case companies are included in Appendices 1–8.

1.4.1   About the Terminology

Key concepts and terms are marked with single quote marks at least when introduced for the first time. Some concepts, such as 'organization' and 'structure' have specific meanings in autopoiesis theory that differ from their conventional meanings in business contexts. In order to avoid confusion, these specific terms will be marked with single quote marks.

The terms 'self-producing', 'autopoietic', and 'living' are taken here to have equivalent meanings and are used interchangeably.

This book makes a distinction between the terms 'information' and 'knowledge', although in organizations they are often used interchangeably.

The term 'evolution' is used here with a specific meaning that is interchangeable with 'continuous renewal'. 'Co-evolution' is used when it is necessary to emphasize an organization's mutual interaction with the business environment.

1.5   Summary

This chapter introduced the reader to the main ideas of the book. The main propositions implicit in the living composition model are:

1. The evolutionary capability of a living organization is derived from the functioning of its living composition.
2. A successful organization is likely to have found ways to utilize the complexity phenomena of self-organization and emergence through its living composition.
3. A living organization improves its chances for co-evolving with its complex environment within its business ecosystem by creating and utilizing boundary elements.

The chapter also introduced the reader to challenges and dilemmas that organizations face as they operate efficiently and simultaneously learn, renew themselves, and co-evolve with their complex, globalizing environment.

Notes

1. Chaos refers to confusion or a confused mass of formless matter and infinite space, supposed to have existed before the ordered universe; or any mixed mass, without due form or order — from Greek chaos, empty space, abyss. The term 'chaos' is often used metaphorically in the organizational context. Chaos is not identical to complexity.
2. In particular, a distributed multinational corporation (DMNC).

Chapter 2

Learning and Evolving Organization

There is clear distinction between learning organization and organizational learning. 'Learning organization' emphasizes structural and other aspects that make learning processes possible. 'Organizational learning' deals with the learning process and its stages and characteristics. The focus of this book is on learning organization.

Some researchers claim that learning only occurs when a change in behavior can be identified. However, the relationship between learning, change, and organizational evolution is not self-evident. According to Hildén (2004), *changes improve organizational functionality* and may have broad implications on organizational processes, networks, and individual working conditions. However, frequent changes may also reduce the learning capability. An organization may create adaptation mechanisms that help to implement frequent changes, but that also neglect the intentions of managers.

According to Doz and Prahalad (1993), analysis of current organization theories[1] shows a gap between the highly abstract theories and the concrete, descriptive, and empirical research. There is a lack of knowledge concerning the structures, forces, and dynamics that influence firms' functioning, learning, and evolution. Only organizational learning theory and part of institutional theory focus primarily on change and development. Moreover, only contingency theory and some recent developments in institutional theory operationalize theories into a model or a framework in other than statistical terms.

This chapter will first review learning and renewal as a source of strategic advantages. Thereafter, selected models about organizational learning and renewal will be presented. They illustrate different aspects of adaptation, incremental learning, and imitation. The main focus will, however, be on selected literature about learning organization. Learning organization can be seen as an interpretation system and as a system of knowing. Also the ideas of the resource- and competence-based views will be discussed because they provide necessary insight about the relevance of knowledge as a resource for continual learning. Some approaches emphasizing the evolutionary nature of a learning organization will be presented under the title of organizational ecology.

2.1 Learning as a Source of Strategic Advantages

Organizational learning is a source of strategic advantages. 'Learning' is a dynamic concept that emphasizes the continually changing nature of organizations. In a global learning economy, learning is based on joint development and worldwide sharing of knowledge.

According to Dodgson (1993), organizational theory often regards learning as an adjustment to external stimulus. The management and innovation literature regards it as an attempt to retain and improve competitiveness, productivity, and innovativeness in uncertain technological and market circumstances. Most economists' research about organizational learning is limited to descriptive analyses of the outcomes of cumulative experience. Dodgson claims that it is necessary to progress beyond static views of organizations as bundles of resources. Learning is a dynamic concept that is defined as enhanced organizational capability and has thereby broad analytical value. It emphasizes the continually changing nature of organizations. It is an integrative concept that can unify various levels of analysis: individual, group, and corporate.

The outcome of learning may include quantifiable improvements in activities (economists' viewpoint), sustainable comparative competitive efficiency (management and business literature), or improved innovative efficiency (innovation literature). Learning can also be defined as a *change in the state of knowledge* within the organization (Lyles, von Krogh, Roos, & Kleine, 1996). On the other hand, learning can be defined as a *process* that changes the state of knowledge of an individual organization. Learning also changes the level of mastery at which the firm knows and applies its knowledge (Sanchez & Heene, 1997).

Learning improves the organization's efficiency and its capability to adapt in the changing environment, which increases the probability of survival. Successful learning is generally measured by useful outcomes, the changed and better ways to perform. Several factors in the environment, such as rapid and turbulent technological change, increasing complexity, and the shortening of product life cycles, increase the need for organizational learning. The rate of environmental change influences an organization's capability to compete, especially when the changes are related to the market situation and technological basis of production. According to Burns and Stalker (1994), a turbulent environment may favor organizational forms that have the capacity to respond quickly to new opportunities. A changing environment contributes to organic management, such as constant alteration of a firm's expectations and resetting the decision framework, while a relatively stable environment leads to a mechanistic and bureaucratic management system. However, firms' capabilities to recognize significant changes in the environment may vary. Rapid industry transformations require that managers learn to change their dominant logic and the recipes that they have grown with (Prahalad & Hamel, 1994).

Theories about multinational companies and internationalization emphasize learning and capability to change. The sources of competitive advantages include location-specific advantages that are based on exploiting local differences, and firm-specific (global) advantages that consist of economies of scale and scope (Prahalad & Doz, 1987). According to Kogut (1993), multinational firms learn in the context of what they can know. Learning is determined by their position in the industrial network and by the structure of national and international social relations. In a multinational company, learning is transferred across subsidiaries that are responding and adapting to different environmental pressures.

On a broader scale, a learning economy may mean that worldwide learning is based on joint development and worldwide sharing of knowledge. Building a learning economy requires a shared vision and individual commitment (Bartlett & Ghoshal, 1989). In the knowledge society, knowledge supplements the traditional economic resources of capital, natural resources, and labor. Organizations should build systematic practices for innovating continually as an organized process. Knowledge demands continuous learning because it constantly changes itself (Drucker, 1992).

2.2   Adaptation, Incremental Learning, and Imitation

Organizational learning occurs under ambiguity and is interconnected to individual learning. Conventionally, learning has been regarded and depicted as a cyclic action that facilitates incremental learning and helps adaptation by correcting errors. Learning may also involve consideration of why and how to change.

Earlier research in organizational learning is based on Simon's (1991) ideas of bounded rationality. However, organizational learning occurs under ambiguity. Some organizations may benefit from incremental learning characterized by layered feedback structures that detect and correct errors. Incremental learning is based on the assumption that adaptively rational systems learn from their experiences and involve adaptive processes at all levels of the organization. The inferences from history are encoded into routines that guide behavior. While some researchers regard organizational learning as a metaphor that is derived from our understanding of individual learning, others claim that individual learning and organizational learning are distinct processes that are interconnected to each other. Behavioral learning links individual beliefs, individual action, organizational action, and environmental response into a cycle.[2]

Learning can be regarded as a cyclic action that starts from concrete experience and continues by reflective observation, abstract conceptualization, and active experimentation. These again produce experiences to be utilized in the next learning cycle (Kolb, 1984). Argyris and Schön's (1996) model of single-, double-, and deutero-loop learning was originally developed for explaining the learning processes of individuals, but it is useful in the context of organizations as well. *Single-loop learning* reflects the behavior of a thermostat. If an error occurs, it will be corrected. The governing variables, such as goals, values, plans, rules, and strategies, are taken for granted and only action strategies that will work within the governing variables are considered. This means that the governing variables are operationalized rather than questioned. *Double-loop learning* causes changes in the governing values. *Deutero-loop learning* (learning to learn, triple-loop learning,) indicates that an organization knows how to carry out single-loop and double-loop learning. Learning takes place only when new knowledge is translated into new, different behavior that is replicable. In Dodgson's (1993) words, single-loop learning involves adding to the knowledge base, firm-specific competences, or routines without altering the nature of the activities. Double- and deutero-loop learning involve consideration of why and how to change, and they imply that cognitive strategies and attitudes change.

Learning can also refer to the capability to avoid errors. It may occur by acquiring insight and knowledge, by learning relevant habits and skills, and by emotional conditioning and learned anxiety. However, avoidance behavior does not help to determine what the correct response could be, and it does not encourage learning by trial and error (Schein, 1993).

Imitation, such as inferring best practices, can affect the rate of adaptation and also the selection of goals. However, both the adaptive and selection views on learning ignore the guided learning from others either by imitation, consultancy, or cultural institutions such as schools (Kogut, 1993).

2.3   Learning Organization

Learning organization has become a relevant concept among large organizations. However, there is no consensus about how to define a learning organization: should it be defined as a learning entity as such, or through its individual members? Kim (1993) assumes that organizations learn via their individual members, and the learning process is fundamentally different at individual and organizational levels. This book will regard organization as a learning entity and focus on an organization as a system. A learning organization facilitates the learning of all its members and continually transforms itself. According to Sanchez (2001a), a competent organization manages five learning cycles that connect the knowledge of individuals, groups, and an organization.

According to Boisot (1995), there are two kinds of theories about learning organizations. The neoclassical theories explain the 'war of position' and Schumpeterian theory explains the 'war of movement'. Neoclassical theories of learning favor retentive strategies and lead the firm to accumulate its technological assets. Learning is based on the codification and diffusion of knowledge about objective reality. Schumpeterian learning is based on subjective apprehension of reality. Innovations occur through creative destruction. The interpretations of reality are not fully shared. Schumpeterian learning emphasizes the absorption of knowledge (learning by doing, internalizing of tacit knowledge) and scanning (integrating codified and uncodified knowledge). A learning organization is 'a Schumpeterian animal, a creative destroyer that is forever destabilizing markets'. This book will focus on 'war of movement'. This approach can be identified in an extreme form in D'Aveni and Gunther's (1994) idea of 'strategic maneuvering'. It involves disrupting the market and status quo and eroding and destroying an opponent's advantage by making it obsolete, irrelevant, or non-unique. It implies that companies should abandon the objective to establish fit between environment, mission, strategy, and organizational characteristics,[3] because 'fit' implies permanence and predictability that is easy to read by competitors.

2.4   Organization as an Interpretation System

An organization can be regarded as an interpretation system that consists of 'several brains'. On the other hand, an organization itself can be regarded as a cognitive system such as a brain or an information processing system that is characterized by holographic design. Organizations should know their interpretation processes; for example, the process of translating events and developing shared understanding and conceptual schemes among upper management. Lateral rigidity reduces a firm's capability to learn.

The cognitive sciences have provided new understanding about the cognition of individual persons and organizations. Burrell and Morgan (1979) have analyzed the paradigms that can be used in analyzing organizations. The interpretive approaches to learning belong to the broader interpretive sociological paradigm of organizations.[4] They assume that the social world consists of 'several brains'. It is a construction of individuals who create and sustain a social world of intersubjectively shared meaning by developing and using common language. The social world is, therefore, in a continuous process of reaffirmation and change.

On the other hand, an organization itself can be regarded as a cognitive system. Organizational thinking can be seen as something more global than the aggregate of individual cognitions (Ginsberg in von Krogh & Vicari, 1993). Nevis, DiBella, Gould (1995) share the same idea and claim that learning is a systems-level phenomenon because it stays within the organization, even if individuals leave.

According to Morgan (1986), a learning organization can be compared to a brain or an information processing system that is characterized by holographic design, the capability to learn to learn, minimum critical specification, and redundancy of functions, which refers to excess capacity and room for maneuver. It is also characterized by requisite variety,[5] which suggests that close attention must be paid to the boundary relations between the organizational units and their environments. The following principles of holographic design facilitate self-organization in an organization: (1) get the whole into the parts, (2) create connectivity and redundancy, (3) create simultaneous specialization and generalization, and (4) create the capacity to self-organize.

Daft and Weick (1984) regard an organization as an interpretation system, as a process of translating events and developing shared understanding and conceptual schemes among upper management. The assumption is that organizations are open social systems that process information about the uncertain environment.

According to Pfeffer and Salancik, an organization must base its action on its information about its environment. It must develop information processing mechanisms that can detect relevant trends, events, competitors, markets, and technological developments. Moreover, organizations should know their interpretation processes. "Since there is no way of knowing about the environment except by interpreting ambiguous events, it is important to understand how organizations come to construct perceptions of reality" (Pfeffer & Salancik, 1978, p. 13).

Organizational learning is constrained by barriers. Cultural dysfunctions, fragmentation, competition, and reactiveness affect organizational life and learning (Kofman & Senge, 1993). Lateral rigidity and forward elasticity influence strategic decision-making. Lateral rigidity reduces a firm's capability to learn. It is caused by limited perception of international business impulses, restrictive reaction to the impulses, selective search for international business alternatives, and confined choice of the alternatives. What is usually needed to change lateral rigidity to forward elasticity is a strong trigger signal that may be based on a crisis or discontinuity, or an exceptionally tempting profit inducement in foreign markets (Luostarinen, 1979). These conclusions emphasize an organization's perception of its environment, and the internal cognitive and organizational capabilities needed to react to trigger signals.

2.5   Organization as a System of Knowing

Learning depends on the continuous creation of conflicts between old and new knowledge. New knowledge that does not fit the existing knowledge challenges productivity and facilitates learning. Firms have institutional capabilities that allow them to integrate and protect knowledge.

Dodgson (1993) suggests that a learning organization can be defined as one that develops its learning capability proactively. This means that it moves beyond natural learning, beyond mere adaptation to a changing environment. Instead, a learning organization attempts to develop constructive or generative mental functions that are reflected in its strategies and structures.

A company can be regarded as an institution that integrates individuals' specialist knowledge (Grant, 1996). Firms also have institutional capabilities that allow them to protect knowledge from expropriation and imitation more effectively than by using market contracting. They can unify the ownership of knowledge and other assets of the firm, thereby reducing employee mobility (Liebeskind, 1996).

A learning organization is skilled at creating, acquiring, and transferring knowledge, and at modifying its behavior to reflect new knowledge and insights (Garvin, 1993). Also Dodgson (1993) suggests that an organization's uniqueness can be defined by its knowledge bases and the processes of acquisition, articulation, and enhancement of the knowledge over which it has control. Organizational learning presupposes that knowledge is communicable, consensual, integrated, and distributed across the organization (Duncan & Weiss, 1979).

There is a transition from theories of knowledge to theories of knowing (Blackler, 1995). The increasing dependence on conceptual skills and cognitive abilities means moving from knowledge-routined organizations (machine bureaucracies) and expert-dependent organizations (professional bureaucracies) toward communications-intensive organizations (adhocracies) and symbolic-analyst-dependent organizations (knowledge-intensive firms).

Choo (1998) and Spender and Grant (1996) suggest that the firm is a system of knowing activity rather than a system of applied abstract knowledge. It is essentially organic and inherently inexplicable. The knowledge-based theory of the firm means moving toward a more agricultural notion of management. It refers to the intervention in and husbandry of the natural knowledge-creating processes of individuals and collectives. Spender and Grant suggest that a synthesis should be made of socio-technical systems theory and self-regulating biological systems that depend on emergent internal closure.

Current theories about knowledge in organizations are largely based on connectivism, codability, transferability, and diffusion across borders. They assume that knowledge represents external reality. With few exceptions, organizational theorists have adopted a positivist theory of knowledge that takes little account of the debate concerning the problematic nature of human knowledge (Spender, 1996). Network models of organization are often based on the connectionist notion of knowledge implying that complex organizational patterns can be created by rich connections of simple units (von Krogh & Roos, 1995).

A multinational corporation can be regarded as a social community that specializes in the creation and internal transfer of knowledge. It is a superior organizational vehicle by which one can transfer knowledge across borders. Theory about knowledge in multinational companies is based on the codability and transferability of knowledge. Multinational companies have a general tendency to codify knowledge and thus to destroy its competitive value (Kogut & Zander, 1993). However, the very process of codifying the constituent elements of a core competence makes the knowledge more diffusion-prone, thus eroding its scarcity value for the firm (Boisot, Griffiths, & Moles, 1995).

2.6 Resource-, Knowledge-, and Competence-Based Views of Learning and Renewal

Resource-, knowledge-, and competence-based views emphasize different aspects and also have different implications for organizational learning and renewal. In the *resource-based view*, the nontradable, nonimitable, and nonsubstitutable asset stocks are the central concern. In the *knowledge-based view*, knowledge accumulates into intellectual capital. However, the process of 'knowing' may become an increasingly important aspect of the knowledge-based view. The *competence-based view* has earlier focused on the identification and development of core competences. New holistic, cognitive, systemic, and dynamic approaches to competences characterizes organizations as open systems that are embedded in larger systems, such as markets (Sanchez & Heene, 2004).

According to Barney (1991), sustained competitive advantage necessitates a resource-based view. Resources are internal and include all assets, capabilities, organizational processes, firm attributes, information, knowledge, and other physical, human, or organizational capital resources. They are strengths that firms can use to conceive of and implement their strategies. Internal resources and competences supplement the earlier focus on firms' external contingencies (Rumelt, 1974; Wernerfelt, 1984; Dierickx & Cool, 1989; Teece & Pisano, 1994; Peteraf, 1993).

Asset stocks are strategic to the extent that they are nontradable, nonimitable, and nonsubstitutable. They are the central concern of the resource-based theory. These assets are largely tacit and socially complex and they are born of organizational skill and corporate learning. They are immobile (bound to the firm), and their development is path-dependent.

The knowledge-based view of organizations emphasizes the specific nature of knowledge among other resources. Knowledge is classified as tacit and explicit, and knowledge conversions enable a spiral-like creation and improvement of knowledge (Nonaka & Takeuchi, 1995). The 'consumption' of knowledge does not follow the models that are typical for many other kinds of resources. For example, efficient distribution and utilization of knowledge may increase the opportunities to create new knowledge. Knowledge accumulates into intellectual capital (invisible assets, intangible assets, knowledge assets) that is a characteristic of the knowledge-based view of organizations. However, recent discussions indicate that the process of 'knowing' will be an increasingly important ingredient in the knowledge-based view.

Organizational competences are critical for multinational organizations. Core competences result from collective learning and provide competitive advantage (Prahalad & Hamel, 1990). They refer to the coordination of diverse production skills and the integration of multiple streams of technologies.[6]

According to Sanchez and Heene (2004), an organization's competence can be defined as its ability to sustain coordinated deployments of assets and capabilities in ways that help the organization to achieve its goals. In the competence perspective, economic organizations function through systemic processes that, when designed and managed under appropriate strategic logics, create a 'virtuous circle' of value creation and distribution. This means that several key processes must be managed well to create sustained value creation and distribution. These processes are systemically interdependent. Economic organizations sustain their value-creation activities by carrying out resource exchanges and other interactions with their environment. These exchanges include markets for inputs (resources) and outputs (products). Moreover, competence-based management characterizes economic organizations as open systems that are embedded in larger systems (markets). The interaction with the environment occurs through cooperation and competition. Sanchez and Heene also define the theory of competence-based strategic management as integrative strategy theory that incorporates economic, organizational, and behavioral concerns in a framework that is holistic, cognitive, systemic, and dynamic. The competence perspective differs from the evolutionary and dynamic capabilities perspectives by adding to them the fundamental role of managers' own cognitive processes in overcoming the constraints of path dependency, in choosing the best path for developing new capabilities, and in developing the 'corporate imagination'.

2.7   Organizational Ecology

Evolutionary theories are a class of theories, models, or arguments that explain how firms evolve and why successful firms differ from each other. They explain the generation and renewal of variation by random elements and winnowing. Inertial forces provide continuity to whatever survives the winnowing. Many of the economic evolutionary theories assume that individual learning, organizational adaptation, and environmental selection of organizations are going on at the same time (Nelson & Winter, 1982; Nelson, 1994, 1995).

Evolutionary theories can also be regarded as learning theories (Dodgson, 1993). Foss, Knudsen, & Montgomery (1995), attempt to explain technological evolution and competition through a set of variables that is changing over time, as well as the dynamic process behind the observed change. Evolutionary theories are process-oriented and they are based on routines that preserve and stabilize organizational behavior. They focus primarily on intangible resources, whereas the resource-based theory focuses in principle on all resources.

Evolutionary economic theories are consistent with the Schumpeterian evolutionary view of economic process and change. They focus on the dynamic process of social construction, and on the transformation of alternative forms within and across generations of competing organizational routines, forms, and institutions (Nelson, 1994). Evolutionary theories are explanatory process theories, not predictive ones (Van de Ven, 1992). Their level of analysis has conventionally been an industry and the main emphasis has been on firm populations. An evolutionary theory of the firm has been largely lacking (Foss et al., 1995). The new evolutionary literature is sensitive to intraorganization, organization, population, and community evolution (Baum & Singh, 1994a, 1994b; Aldrich, 1999).

Baum and Singh (1994a) write that since the 1960s the open systems model, where the environment locates outside the system, has been the prominent view of organization theory. However, the environment can be treated as exogenous only if the system of variables is in equilibrium. In different conditions, it is more useful to take a co-evolutionary approach and view each variable as influencing the others.

2.8 Summary

Based on the literature about learning organizations and organizational learning, this chapter identified several themes that will be relevant in the later discussion.

- Organizational learning is a source of strategic advantages. 'Learning' is a dynamic concept that emphasizes the continually changing nature of organizations. Organizational learning occurs under ambiguity. In a learning economy, learning is based on joint development and worldwide sharing of knowledge.
- Conventional learning has been depicted as a cyclic action that facilitates incremental learning and helps adaptation by correcting errors. More advanced methods of learning may also involve consideration of why and how to change.
- Learning organizations can be analyzed in terms of neoclassical 'war of position' and Schumpeterian 'war of movement'. The 'war of movement' is closer to the approach of this book.
- There is no consensus about how to define a learning organization: as a cognitive learning entity or as an interpretation system that consists of 'several brains' of individual members. This book will focus on an organization as a cognitive learning entity, i.e. as a system.
- Learning depends on the continuous creation of conflicts between old and new knowledge. New knowledge that does not fit the existing knowledge challenges productivity and facilitates learning. Organizational learning is interconnected to individual learning.
- Firms have institutional capabilities that allow them to integrate and protect knowledge. The firm is a system of knowing activity rather than a system of applied abstract knowledge. It is essentially organic and inherently inexplicable. Firms are increasingly communications-intensive adhocracies and knowledge-intensive organizations.
- The *resource-based view* of organizations is based on nontradable, nonimitable, and nonsubstitutable asset stocks. The *knowledge-based view* focuses on knowledge that accumulates into intellectual capital, and increasingly on the process of 'knowing'. The *competence-based view* emphasizes holistic, cognitive, systemic, and dynamic approaches and characterizes organizations as open systems that interact with the environment. This book has strong affinities with the knowledge-based view and especially with the competence-based view of organization.

Notes

1.
   - *Transaction cost theory* explains choices between institutional forms. It is based primarily on the concepts of self-interest (opportunism) and hierarchy.
   - *Agency theory* explains management control issues in various forms of contractual relationships between principals and agents.

- *Population ecology* (e.g. Hannan & Freeman, 1977) assumes that environmental resources are unequally distributed between 'niches' of the environment, and that inertia *limits strategic redirection.*
- *Institutional theory* investigates (within and between the firms) the adaptation of subunits to differentiated local environments by using the 'organizational field' concept. The interactions, mutual awareness, information, and patterns of competitive and coalitional behavior between organizations are regarded as determinants of their adaptation.
- *Contingency theory* (e.g. Lawrence & Lorsch, 1969) is based on the idea of differentiated responses to diverse environments and integration of action across environments.
- *Power relationship and organizational adaptation theories* explain firms as networks of relationships in which 'actors' play collective 'games' mediated by collectively accepted 'rules', driven by the resources and constraints of the individual 'actors'.
- Organizational learning theories involve adaptive processes at all levels of the firm, and the institutionalization of learning takes place through organizational routines.

2. See, for example, Cyert and March (1963), March and Olsen (1975), March (1991) and Levinthal and March (1993).
3. D'Aveni and Gunther(1994) recommend the new '7-S': (1) superior stakeholder satisfaction, (2) strategic soothsaying, (3) speed, (4) surprise, (5) shifting the rules of competition, (6) signaling strategic intent, and (7) simultaneous and sequential strategic thrusts.
4. The other paradigms are the radical humanist, radical structuralist, and functionalist paradigms.
5. The law of requisite variety means that internal diversity of any self-regulating system must match the variety and complexity of its environment if it is to deal with the challenges posed by that environment. In other words, an organization should embody critical dimensions of the environment with which it must interact, so that it can self-organize to cope with the demands it is likely to face (W. Ross Ashby in Morgan, 1986).
6. The ideas of organizational competences have been developed further in Prahalad and Doz (1987), Bartlett, Doz, and Hedlund (1990), Hamel and Heene (1994), Hamel and Prahalad (1994a, b), Montgomery (1995), Sanchez (2001a, b), Sanchez and Heene (1996, 1997, 2004), Sanchez, Heene, and Thomas (1996).

Chapter 3

Underlying Structures and Dynamics

The perspective developed here suggests that it is possible to reframe the dilemma between control and autonomy and thereby gain better insights into organizational efficiency, creativity, and their underlying dynamics. This chapter reviews prior management literature about control, autonomy, self-organization, and emergence. Thereafter it views underlying dynamics by analyzing structural aspects of strategy. The last section analyzes the underlying dynamics in living composition. It discusses the role of consistency between strategic components. Literature concerning fit, order, consistency, and efficiency is reviewed in Appendix 2.

3.1 Earlier Approaches to Control, Self-Organization, and Emergence

Organizational efficiency can be defined as a characteristic that depends on *control* and achieving a *degree of fit* among organizational and environmental variables. However, control and fit alone are not sufficient to explain the necessary conditions for achieving organizational performance, creativity, innovativeness, learning, and evolution. De Leo observed the persistence of *unfit* strategies across firms within the same industry: "If the underlying economic logic of the industry is given, why there are unfit strategies? Perhaps the inherent goal of the strategy is not to exploit existing asymmetries but to search for and develop new ones" (1994, pp. 36–37).

Renewal is a strategic paradox that arises from conflicting forces for stability and change (Baden-Fuller & Volberda, 1995). This conflict, like that between productivity and innovation, is related to the dilemma between exploration and exploitation of knowledge (March, 1991; Levinthal & March, 1993). The exploitation of the familiar may occur through refinement, production, efficiency, implementation, and execution, whereas the exploration of new possibilities may occur through search, variation, risk-taking, experimentation, play, flexibility, discovery, and innovation. Both these processes are essential for organizations, but they compete against each other for scarce resources. Therefore organizations have to make choices. While exploitation is characterized by certainty, speed, proximity, and clarity, exploration may be uncertain, slow, new, and risky. As a result, many organizations tend to favor exploitation over exploration. Similarly, management research has focused primarily on fit, consistency, efficiency, performance, and control; and less on creativity, learning, renewal, and creating the infrastructure that could facilitate the emergence of new solutions.

During the last two decades, strategic management researchers have explored alternatives to the ideas of 'fit' and 'control'. They have argued that organizations should move from contingency-based strategies to exploration and implement strategies that are characterized by stretch and leverage. Stretch creates, by design, a substantial misfit between resources and aspirations. This deliberate mismatch — pushing away from the equilibrium — may motivate an organization to adapt. Empowerment, decentralization, and deliberate mismatch between organization and environment can help to create a state of tension that facilitates adaptation and learning (Doz & Prahalad, 1993; Prahalad & Hamel, 1994; Hamel & Prahalad, 1993, 1994a,b; Sanchez & Heene, 1996).

According to Nonaka (1988, 1990), firms may purposefully engage themselves in producing crisis to bring about change. This creative chaos is one of the preconditions for knowledge creation. Creative chaos employs ambiguous visions and intentionally created environmental fluctuation[1] within an organization. The breakdown of entrenched habits encourages reconsideration of fundamental thinking, adoption of new perspectives, and questions the validity of familiar attitudes toward the world. In an organization, new knowledge can be created out of the chaos generated naturally through a real crisis. It may also be created intentionally by evoking a sense of crisis. Creative chaos increases tension and focuses the attention of organizational members on defining its problems in a new way, and on resolving crisis creatively (Nonaka & Takeuchi, 1995).

Self-organization is a property of complex adaptive systems and refers to the capability of a system to create order from chaos, for example when pushed to the state that is 'far from equilibrium'. *Emergence* means that coherent new patterns, structures, and behaviors emerge from prior ones. Self-emergent properties provide possibilities for unexpected new solutions (Kauffman, 1993; Holland, 1995, 1998).

Self-organization is sometimes mistakenly used as a synonym for chaos, implying that an organization may achieve new order just by removing control. Self-organization and chaos are, however, based on different theoretical assumptions and also have different organizational implications. Especially in a social context, the application of chaos theory may not be appropriate because humans have cognitive capabilities that enable them to change their rules of interaction (Mitleton-Kelly, 2003). Also, complexity and chaos have sometimes been regarded erroneously as synonyms, but they are based on different theoretical definitions.

Self-organization can be facilitated in an organizational context by applying seven principles: aggregation, non-linearity, flows, diversity, tagging, internal models, and building blocks. A self-organizing organization is not based on detailed planning but rather on careful implementation of these principles to create a platform and infrastructure that facilitate the emergence of new ideas and phenomena (Holland, 1995).

Managers and management researchers have developed several ways of simultaneously achieving control of the organization and facilitating creativity and innovativeness. Examples of these approaches are:

- sequential (periodical) differentiation
- organizational differentiation
- simultaneous strategies
- hypercompetition.

In *sequential differentiation*, periods of control and emergent breakthrough of new ideas and new order follow each other. For example, Itami and Roehl (1987)[2] present as conventional wisdom that an organization's strategy should fit its level of resources and take advantage of the corporate culture. However, a firm should also consciously create deviations from the ideal of static fit among resources and organization. In order to facilitate creative tension, the organization must venture into new fields, reach beyond the limits of consensus, take an unbalanced approach to resource and environmental fit, and consciously select a strategy that does not match the current corporate culture. In the long term, intentional overextension and creation of dynamic imbalance are parts of healthy strategies for living organizations. New overextension strategies should be introduced periodically so that the organization's strategy will alternate between balance and imbalance. The key to success is 'destroy the balance'.

Organizational differentiation means that new emerging activities and an organization's conventional, controlled activities are located *in different organizational units*. For example, research and development of new ideas are often located in a separate R&D unit or a spin-off unit. This solution may guarantee the freedom to generate new ideas and to protect the main organization from disturbance. However, innovation processes may remain tightly controlled.

Simultaneous strategies refer to control and efficiency in the short term, and relaxed control in the long term. Strategy may be incremental in the sense that future steps cannot be predetermined in detail beforehand. Therefore, two kinds of strategies are needed. Strategy as stretch in the long term tolerates uncertainty and should be ready to take risks. In contrast, the short-term perspective is characterized by greater certainty and order, short-term objectives, and near-at-hand resources (Hamel & Prahalad, 1993).

Hypercompetition is a concept defined by D'Aveni and Gunther (1994). It means that management attempts to create dynamic fit within a firm and disruption in a market and within an industry. In contrast, creating equilibrium (a static fit) would cause many risks because it implies a state that is predictable and an easy target for competitors. By creating a static fit, a firm could focus on a single objective but thereby also make itself inflexible and unable to change its strategy. If a company's goal is to sustain advantage, it tries to create an equilibrium in its industry at a point at which it has an advantage. In hypercompetition, however, the company attempts to disrupt the industry, to create new advantages for itself and erode those of its competitors.

In spite of these alternatives, the dilemma of how to simultaneously achieve control and creativity, and exploitation and exploration, remains largely unsolved and requires further investigation. The survival and success of some firms that apply inconsistent strategies suggest that earlier strategy frameworks may be too simplistic and narrow to explain the firms' underlying dynamics (De Leo, 1994). Therefore, the following section discusses structural aspects of strategy that define the enabling infrastructure more systematically.

3.2 Structural Aspects of Strategy

Recent strategic management literature has introduced several concepts that differ from the concept of *strategic management* and address *structural aspects* of organizational strategy. *Strategic management* refers to the *management process* that defines an organization's goals for value creation and distribution and designs the way the organization will be composed, structured, and coordinated in pursuing these goals (Sanchez & Heene, 2004). The concepts that emphasize structural aspects of strategy include 'strategic architecture', 'strategic intent', 'strategic logic', 'competitive strategy framework', and 'strategic puzzle'. Each concept adds to our understanding of the role of underlying structures in capabilities, competences, and organizational learning, and illustrates the importance of organizational structures in organizational evolution.

Strategic architecture is an organization's high-level blueprint for deploying new functionalities, acquiring new competences or utilizing existing ones, and reconfiguring its interfaces with customers. It helps to establish objectives for competence building. Strategic architecture is a road map of the future that helps to identify the needed new competences and to define their constituent technologies (Prahalad & Hamel, 1990; Hamel & Prahalad, 1994a,b).

Sanchez (2001b) suggests that modular architectures provide a framework for integrating an organization's technology and market knowledge. Defining modular product and process architectures can improve the precision and speed of a firm's processes for developing strategically useful technologies. They may also contribute to acquiring new knowledge about customer preferences in the market.

Strategic intent refers to an animating strategic vision. While a strategic architecture helps to point the way to the future, strategic intent provides the emotional and intellectual energy for the journey. Strategic intent is a vision that implies a significant stretch for the organization. Stretch in this case does not emerge by accident, but is a result of conscious design by strategic managers. Strategic intent creates an intentional, substantial misfit between current resources and aspirations for the future (Hamel & Prahalad, 1994a,b).

Strategic logic is an organization's operative rationale for achieving its goals through coordinated deployments of resources (assets and capabilities). Strategic logic expresses the system elements and interactions that are regarded in the organization as essential for achieving the goals of value creation and distribution. Strategic managers guide organizational behavior by perceiving possibilities for new competences, creating new ones, finding new uses for existing competences, and maximizing their benefits. Competence-based competition creates environmental turbulence and uncertainty. Therefore, the essential dynamic of strategic management in competence-based competition will be a process of continuous learning at a conceptual level that leads to qualitative changes in a firm's system elements (Sanchez & Heene, 1996, 2004). In order to maintain the strategic logic and a viable system design for value-creation processes, managers have to identify and understand changes in the macroenvironment, industry environment, and product market.

The competitive strategy framework connects strategic building blocks such as corporate culture and style, organizing, competitive arenas, competences and capabilities, and product/market competition into a multi-layered structure. The relationships between the building blocks are characterized by causality and various kinds of organizational and environmental links (De Leo, 1994).

The strategic puzzle game is a constructional perspective on strategy. It implies a search for fit between strategic components (assets). Proper linking between the components can lead to sustainable competitive positions and collective learning (Bogaert, Martens, & van Cauwenbergh, 1994).

These approaches to strategy are largely concerned with purposely designed organizations. They do not help in understanding emergent organizational phenomena. They do not sufficiently address underlying processes, flows, and networks of information, and the role of knowledge and communication in organizational change. Therefore, a new model of *living composition* will be developed in the following chapters.

3.3 Consistency of Underlying Structure

Literature on organizational strategy introduces several concepts to be coordinated, such as organizational components, strategic building blocks, strategic assets, resources, capabilities, competences, and system elements. As previous analysis shows, there are many structural approaches that concern strategic architecture, logic, and framework.

Consistency is a conventional concept that has been widely used in the context of organizational strategy. Strategy and effective organizational structures are frequently presented as seeking consistency (fit) between various components so that the organization can successfully co-evolve with its environment. Recent literature has, however, also introduced ideas such as stretch, revolution, and chaos that refer to loosening the requirement for fit. The organization's composition and systemic behavior require, therefore, more careful analysis and specification.

This book assumes that the concept of consistency may have explanatory power in the context of living, dynamic, self-producing systems. It can be used for evaluating their underlying structures, and especially the composition of a living organization. As was presented in the definition of living composition, the organizational components and their relationships are defined so that their production and interaction facilitate sensing and memory of the organization. Consistency among the strategic components, or lack of it, largely defines the nature of an organization's composition and evolutionary process.

Figure 3.1 illustrates the role of consistency among the strategic components. The assumption is that alternative forms of consistency also have implications for an organization's learning and renewal capability.

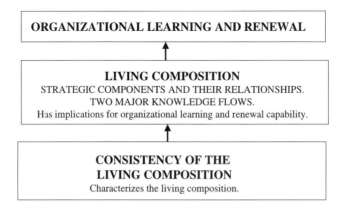

Figure 3.1: The consistency of living composition influences organizational learning and renewal.

Table 3.1: Four types of consistency, i.e. relationships between strategic components measured by the degree of consistency and intentionality of the composition.

		INTENTIONALITY	
		Intended	**Unintended**
CONSISTENCY BETWEEN STRATEGIC COMPONENTS	**Consistent**	INTENTIONAL FIT	EMERGENT FIT
	Inconsistent	STRETCH	MISFIT

The relationships among strategic components can be distinguished by their degrees of consistency (consistent versus inconsistent) and intentionality of the composition (intended versus unintended). These two dimensions result in four types of consistency, i.e. four alternatives with respect to fit between strategic components. Intentional fit refers to intended consistency, a fit that has been purposely designed to be consistent. Stretch means intended tension — or inconsistency — among strategic components (or between their current and future states). Emergent fit indicates consistent fit that has emerged in an unintended way. Misfit refers to unintended, inconsistent fit, to a mismatch of strategic components (Table 3.1).

These four alternatives characterize different ways of organizing strategic components and thereby different ways to manage the underlying dynamics of organizations.

3.4   Summary

This chapter identified several themes that can be summarized as follows:

- Many organizations tend to favor exploitation over exploration. Similarly, earlier management research has focused primarily on control, fit, consistency, efficiency, and performance, and less on autonomy, self-organization, emergence, creativity, learning, renewal, and creating the infrastructure that could facilitate the emergence of new solutions.
- *Self-organization* is a property of complex adaptive systems and refers to the capability of a system to create order from chaos; for example, when pushed to the state that is 'far from equilibrium'.
- *Emergence* means that coherent new patterns, structures, and behaviors emerge from prior ones.
- Self-organization and complexity are based on theoretical definitions that differ fundamentally from the definition of chaos.
- Managers and management researchers have developed several ways to manage the dilemmas of achieving simultaneous control and creativity. Examples of them are sequential differentiation, organizational differentiation, simultaneous strategies, and hypercompetition.

- Several concepts, such as 'strategic architecture', 'strategic intent', 'strategic logic', 'competitive strategy framework', and 'strategic puzzle game' emphasize structural aspects of strategy. They add to our understanding of the role of underlying structures in capabilities, competences, and organizational learning. However, they are not sufficient for understanding the underlying dynamics of organizational learning and renewal.
- Intentionality and consistency among the strategic components characterize the living composition. The four types of consistency, i.e. four alternatives with respect to fit between strategic components include intentional fit, stretch, emergent fit, and misfit.

Notes

1. According to Nonaka and Takeuchi, fluctuation means an order whose pattern is hard to predict and causes a breakdown of routines, habits, or cognitive frameworks. "Chaos is generated naturally when the organization faces a real crisis, such as a rapid decline of performance due to changes in market needs or significant growth of competitors" (1995, p. 79). Chaos can also be created internally. This idea of chaos is thus in accordance with Heidegger's idea of breakdown.
2. According to Itami and Roehl, strategic fit can be seen as passive, active, or leveraged. Passive fit among strategic variables takes the variables as given. Active fit involves steering these variables into a favorable direction. Leveraged fit means that the organization has found ways to use limited environmental characteristics in ways that make its strategy more effective.

Chapter 4

Organization as a System

An organization can be regarded as a system. The purpose of this chapter is to clarify the idea of components and their relationships in different kinds of organizational-system approaches, and, in light of this system view, to review the implications of three approaches to understanding organizational learning and renewal. This chapter briefly introduces selected system and complexity theories relevant to organizations and analyzes how they help to explain organizational learning, renewal, and evolution. We start by highlighting open system and contingency models, the system dynamics model, and the network model. We then consider theories about complexity and chaos, and introduce a hierarchy of complexity in system theories. This classification is then used as a basis for the analysis and interpretation of living, self-organizing systems in the rest of the book. The implications of various system models and theories, including autopoiesis theory, are summarized in Chapter 5.

4.1 Open System, Contingency Theory, System Dynamics, and Network Approaches

Open system, system dynamics, and network models have been used for some time to explain the structure and behavior of various kinds of systemic phenomena. These approaches have evolved recently as our knowledge about the nature of phenomena has improved. This section starts by first discussing organization as a system. Then it introduces briefly the three approaches and analyzes their implications for organizational learning and renewal. (The system characteristics of openness and closure will also be discussed in the context of sensing and memory in Chapter 8.)

4.1.1 Organization as a System

Abstract system theory (Mesarovic & Takahara, 1989) defines a system as a set of interrelated objects that is 'more than the sum of its parts'. In general, system theory does not define the content of objects. They can be people, things, and ideas — employees, machines, software modules, or capital. There are many different approaches to understanding a system, and which one of them should be applied depends on the phenomenon to be studied.

Sanchez and Heene (2004) define a system as a collection of interacting, interdependent elements. This means that the 'state' or condition of one system element affects and may be affected by the state or condition of one or the other system elements. Morgan (1986) suggests that a system cannot be understood as a network of separate parts, but has to be understood as a whole, and as possessing a logic of its own.

The origins of *general system theories* are largely in biology, where the objective of applying systems approaches was to quantify the behavior of organisms.[1] General system theories have also influenced social science and strategy research, and have been used to explain firms' behavior in general (Kast & Rosenzweig, 1981; Scott, 1992). In the systems perspective, an organization is a unitary whole composed of two or more interdependent parts, components, or subsystems and delineated by identifiable boundaries from its environmental suprasystem (Kast & Rosenzweig, 1981). While orthodox system models represent organizations as independent of individual members, some recent system models represent organizations as continually changing products of human processes in which an organization's 'reality' is socially constructed by its participants (Checkland, 1995). Other versions of system theory focus on an organization's interactions with its environment. They characterize organizations as embedded systemically in a wider environmental context (Bailey, 1994; Whittington, 1993; Sanchez & Heene, 2004). Other system theories also help to understand various kinds of processes such as maintenance, incremental development, radical innovation, the nature of dynamic capabilities and dynamic intellectual capital, and the sources of organizational renewal capability (Pöyhönen, 2004).

4.1.2   Open System Theory

4.1.2.1   Open system   According to Sanchez and Heene (2004), organization can be viewed as a goal-seeking open system that aims to create and distribute value. An organization is an open system of resource stocks and flows — a system in which resources flow into and out of the organization, and where a 'strategic logic' acts as 'the operative rationale for achieving an organization's goals through coordinated deployments of resources'. Moreover, an organization is an open system that is embedded in larger systems (e.g. markets), which are in turn embedded in several levels of still larger systems, such as industries, national economies, and the global economy. This definition highlights two aspects of the definition of open systems in an organizational context: the internal organization of a system, and its embeddedness in and interactions with larger systems. Inherent in the concept of organization as a system of interacting resources is, according to Sanchez and Heene, the notion of a boundary that separates those resources that are internal to an organization from those that are not. As an open system, however, an organization has important interactions across its boundaries between the resources within the organization and those in its environment.

The term 'open system' implies the existence of an opposite, a 'closed system'. Theoretically, it can be difficult to differentiate clearly between open and closed systems. The two kinds of systems are often regarded as polar and mutually exclusive, but a system can also be regarded as relatively open or relatively closed (Kast & Rosenzweig, 1981). The *degree of being open or closed* varies to the extent that a system is responsive to and/or can access a relatively wide or narrow range of inputs from the environment (Morgan, 1986).

In an organizational context, such as management theory and organization theory, outputs are assumed to influence inputs. In effect, an organization takes into account or is influenced by its own influence on the environment. According to Sanchez and Heene

(1996), the interactions between an organization as a system and its environment as its surrounding macro-system are also systemic in nature. If a system's inputs and outputs are systemically interrelated as integral parts of the environment, then any system that is sensitive to variations in its inputs and is aware of its systemic structure should also be sensitive to variations in its outputs, because those variations in outputs will have at least some effects on its inputs.

The open system model has been extended to recognize three kinds of open systems in organizations: rational, natural, and open (Scott, 1992). *A rational organization* pursues relatively specific goals through formalized social structures. *A natural organization* is a collective whose participants share a common interest in survival and engage in informally structured activities to secure this end. *An open organization* consists of interdependent activities that link shifting coalitions of participants. All three kinds of organizations are characterized as embedded in the environment, maintaining continuous exchange relationships with it.

Some studies have mistakenly suggested that an open system may have the capacity for self-maintenance *in spite* of its need to process inputs into outputs and, therefore, that a system (such as an organization) could and should be buffered against environmental influences. However, an open system maintains its capacity for self-maintenance *because of* its inputs from and outputs to an environment, not in spite of them. In an open system, the *law of limited variety*[2] operates. A system will exhibit only the variety of behaviors required to respond to the variety of inputs to which it is exposed in its environment. Therefore, exposure to a flow of heterogeneous inputs that must be transformed into outputs builds and maintains the differentiated internal structures of an open system (Pondy & Mitroff, 1979).

The open system model has also been used in the context of engineering control (e.g. Forrester, 1980), and information systems design to define control structures and design information flows and processing. Control-oriented open systems, such as technical subsystems, are often defined as 'input–process–output' transformation processes. They are often described as 'black boxes' that can potentially be divided into further subprocesses. Such mechanistic systems are characterized by dynamic, predetermined changes and processes (Mingers, 1997; according to Boulding, 1956).

4.1.2.2 Contingency theory   At a fundamental level, contingency theory is an application of open systems theory to organizations that draws attention to the role of the environment in organizations. A contingency view facilitates situational diagnosis and managerial action that is appropriate in specific circumstances (Chandler, 1962; Lawrence & Lorsch, 1969; Kast & Rosenzweig, 1981). The basic idea of contingency theory is that the environmental variable is dominant and the organization's other strategic variables must adapt to it. Improving 'fit' between the environment and the internal structure of an organization therefore increases effectiveness and performance in transforming inputs to outputs. External contingencies from the marketplace should therefore influence an organization's internal structure, capabilities, administrative mechanisms, and other variables (Galbraith & Kazanjian, 1986; Martinez & Jarillo, 1989; Egelhoff, 1991, 1993).

According to Ashby's (1956) *law of requisite variety*, a system's internal diversity must match the variety and complexity of the environment in order to deal with challenges posed by the environment. This law implies growing challenges for organizations as their operating environments become increasingly global, complex, and turbulent.

Contingency theory assumes that there is no one 'universal' best way to organize, but also that all ways of organizing are not equally effective because situational context influences the effectiveness of an approach to organizing. Contingency theory has also been criticized as being based on deterministic and unidirectional causal assumptions that ignore strategic choice, and on a static perspective in which the time dimension is missing (Miller, 1981). However, three approaches to contingency theory counter this argument. *The natural selection approach* holds that fit (congruence) between context, structure, and process results from an evolutionary process of adaptation that ensures the survival of only the best-performing organizations (the effective adapters). *The interaction approach* holds that performance depends on the interplay between environmental context and organizational structure. *The systems approach* emphasizes the need for internal consistency of multiple contingencies, structural and performance criteria, contextual factors, and structural variables. It is based on systems theory, pattern analysis, and the possibility of equifinality in competitive environments — i.e. of multiple, equally effective alternatives (Van de Ven & Drazin, 1985; Drazin & Van de Ven, 1985). The systems approach to organizations thus posits the possibility of multiple, viable simultaneous and holistic patterns of interlinkages between organizations and their environments — i.e. of multiple 'fits' (Govindarajan, 1988).

According to Sanchez and Heene (2004), all perspectives on strategy are essentially contingency theories, because they hold that achieving competitive success is contingent on achieving the best possible alignment or 'fit' of the capabilities of an organization with the demands of its environment.

4.1.2.3 Learning and renewal in the open systems approach
New approaches to contingency theory go beyond simple determinism to models that include simultaneity, holism, complexity, flexibility, and the need for strategic choices. These new approaches presume evolving conflicts between external contingencies and internal consistency. These new developments can be seen as a move toward a more detailed elaboration and application of the open system model, or as a move toward conceptualizing the firm as an evolving 'dynamic system' (Doz & Prahalad, 1993). When an organization can make cause-and-effect connections between variations in its inputs, resulting variations in its essential outputs, and further impacts on inputs, it learns and can be regarded as an adaptive open system in the sense outlined by Sanchez and Heene (1996). When an organization cannot make these learning connections, it functions like a one-dimensional open system that may respond to input variations but does not produce output variations.

The open system view also implies that new knowledge flows into an organization through hiring new people, training, and other resource acquisitions. Knowledge may also be produced internally through research, invention, and culture building, and may flow out through personnel departures, imitated routines, and spinning off of resources. Among these possibilities, organizational learning is most often stimulated by personnel changes (Starbuck, 1992).

Control-oriented approaches to open systems have faced criticism in the organizational context. Such criticism is largely inspired by efforts to apply overly simplistic input–process–output models to organizational situations that require more sophisticated theories and models. Therefore, it is necessary to emphasize the development of the open system concept in the organizational context and its differences from early interpretations. The early approach of contingency theory emphasized unidirectional adaptation to contingencies (inputs), and fit between the environment and internal components. It assumed that the organization is, in effect, instructed by its environment. In this view, an organization is subordinate to environmental changes, and some deep static, linear, deterministic, simplistic, and unidirectional causal assumptions ignore the possibilities of complexity and strategic choice (Schoonhoven, 1981; Miller, 1981). Earlier approaches were also regarded as formalistic, neglecting the values and intentions inherent in an organization, which leads to oversimplification. Earlier models did not try to explain social 'reality' and how people experience it, and they sometimes tended to explain the behavior of individuals in a deterministic way. Conventional systems theory is often positivistic and functionalistic, and focuses on measurable attributes and controllable functions (Anttiroiko, 1993; Kallio, 1993; Hirschheim, Klein, & Lyytinen, 1995). It produces rational explanations, utilizes practical information, and is often problem-oriented. However, social systems are not constrained by the simple cause-and-effect relationships often used in economic-technical models (Kast & Rosenzweig, 1981).

Compared to the earlier idea of open systems as control mechanisms, the new approaches to open systems have adopted new content appropriate to the context of organizations, such as embeddedness and ways in which outputs can affect inputs. This evolution in open systems approaches to representing organizations is reflected in our analysis of the concepts of openness and closure in the context of living systems. They will be discussed in depth in Chapter 8 and Appendix 4.

4.1.3 System Dynamics

System dynamics is a branch of general systems theory that emphasizes the role of feedback in dynamic and complex systems. System dynamics models depict organizations as engaged in continuous, feedback-oriented processes of change — patterns of behavior that usually recur again and again but not in exactly the same way. Thus, a system dynamics model can be regarded as a dynamic model of an entity whose behavior changes along time. A systems dynamics model is driven by differential equations relating the changes in variables that represent a system's internal functioning and are the source of its autonomous behavior.

In system dynamics models, chains of influence and causality may be simultaneously open and closed. Dynamic systems are *open* to environmental influences and limiting factors, and are *closed* in the sense that they are driven by closed feedback loops. *Gaps* describe the difference between the desired state of a given system and its perceived state. Without responses to perceived gaps, an organization would reach a static equilibrium. Sanchez and Heene (2004) use the term 'strategic gap' in representing organizations as open systems to refer to the perceptions by strategic managers of differences between the current state and desired state of the system elements in the organization as a value-creation system.

According to the system dynamics approach, influences are embedded in reinforcing (positive) and balancing (negative) feedback loops and normally involves time delays.

Every *influence* may be a cause, an effect, or both. In a *positive feedback loop*, a change in the state of one system element influences a second system element to change in a way that then influences the first element to change further in the same direction, which may be either an increase or decrease. Positive feedback thus often drives a system to behave like a spiraling 'virtuous cycle' or 'vicious cycle'. Positive feedback, unless moderated by the stabilizing effects of negative feedback loops, lead to uncontrolled expansion or contraction of a system. *Negative feedback* creates a stabilizing effect. Negative feedback loops lead a system to a 'regression to the mean', a return of a system to a prior state, and thus have a stabilizing effect on the overall system. In the negative feedback loop, a change in the state of one system element influences a second system element to change in a way that then influences the first element to change in the opposite direction from the original change. The succession of changes in the states of a system as it seeks to return to a prior state (mean) causes fluctuations in the system.[3] *Limiting factors*, which may be internal or external, constrain a system's behavior. *System closure* in organizations is facilitated when a system is influenced primarily by internal feedback and repeats similar sequential cycles of activities.

The competence-based view of organizations uses the term *control loops* to refer to organizational feedback (Sanchez & Heene, 2004). *Control loops* are flows of data about an organization's product markets, product offers, operations, and tangible and intangible assets that managers use to evaluate the state of an organization's system elements and its environment, and to look for strategic gaps that require managerial interventions to close. *Lower-order control loops* gather data (typically through the standard financial accounting systems) on tangible assets, current operations, and product markets. *Higher-order control loops* gather data about the organization's intangible assets, management processes, and strategic logic. Strategic management as a field is concerned today with developing better methods to gather, measure, and interpret data that is gathered in higher-order control loops.

4.1.3.1 Learning and renewal in the system dynamics approach
The ideas of the system dynamics perspective have been developed further under the banner of *systems thinking* to facilitate organizational learning (Senge, 1990). Also, many conventional models of learning reflect the basic ideas of system dynamics and a cyclic learning process that may lead to accumulating knowledge and competence.

The organizational learning literature that discusses the role of errors (gap detection and response) in learning is largely based on system dynamics principles (Argyris & Schön, 1996). The strategic gap that starts a learning process may consist of a perceived error, situation, or some other aspect of an organization that motivates an individual or an organization to learn and change. However, much of this literature focuses on correcting past errors and does not address other possibilities for creativity in learning about new issues. Nevertheless, system dynamics models incorporate both organizational performance and change (exploitation and experimentation) within their framework. Organizations can increase performance by improving dynamic fit in relationships among components and between the system and its environment. The strategic gaps between desired and perceived states of the system, as well as perceived misfit between an organization and its environment, may stimulate systemic learning and renewal (Sanchez & Heene, 2004).

4.1.4 Organizational Networks

4.1.4.1 Networks   The network model provides conceptual tools for understanding the role of interorganizational and interpersonal connections in knowledge creation and diffusion. Organizational behavior and knowledge flows may be represented as occurring through interconnected networks; for example among multinational firms (Ghoshal & Bartlett, 1988; Hagström, 1992). This essentially connectionist view holds that units and individuals that are richly connected can create complex patterns of action (von Krogh & Roos, 1995). Networks may be considered a source of competitiveness and development in 'heterarchic' models of organizations. Heterarchic models refer to non-hierarchical organizations with many centers or 'nodes' of different kinds. A heterarchic organization uses patterns of coordination that are more mixed and flexible than in a hierarchical or matrix organization. Internal processes link different elements of a multidimensional system, and conflicts tend to be resolved laterally, not vertically (White & Poynter, 1990; Hedlund, 1986).

Organizations can also participate in value networks. A value network combines information, people, and machines, and aims at creating value for each node in the network. In her conceptual analysis of clusters, value networks, and business ecosystems, Peltoniemi (2004) concludes that a value network can be both global and local. In a value network, value creation occurs in a cooperative structure, whereas in a cluster it occurs through competition. A business ecosystem induces both competition and co-operation among the organizations.

4.1.4.2 Learning and renewal in network approaches   The concept of network brings new features to explaining organizational learning and creativity. It provides conceptual tools for analyzing the actors, connections, structures, functioning, efficiency, and creativity of organizations. It helps to analyze how knowledge diffuses within and among organizations. The quantity and types of units, connections, and their control influence an organization's behavior and its opportunities for knowledge diffusion. Positions in dense networks with other organizations increase possibilities for learning.

Peltoniemi (2004) observes that fierce rivalry in a cluster limits willingness to share knowledge and create it cooperatively. However, a cluster may create local 'buzz' — opportunities to monitor changes in the environment and opportunities to respond to them. In a business ecosystem, a sense of shared fate may also motivate organizations to share knowledge.

4.2   Theories about Complexity and Chaos

Complexity and *chaos* are terms that we often use metaphorically in everyday language. However, these terms also have specific theoretical definitions and characteristics, and their correct differentiation is especially important in the context of social systems, such as organizations. This section analyzes some important characteristics of theories of complexity and chaos.

4.2.1 Complexity Theories

The concept of 'complexity' has become increasingly central in organizational research. The word 'complex' is derived from the Latin 'plexus' meaning braided or entwined, and 'complexus' means braided together, being interconnected, and intertwined internally.

Theories of complexity can be characterized and classified in several ways. According to Sanchez (1997), two theoretical perspectives, systems theory and complexity theory, provide convergent insights into the composition, interrelationships, and dynamics of complex systems. *Systems theory* focuses on understanding how entities linked by interdependencies and feedback mechanisms compose systems that even in simple form may have the capability to generate complex behaviors and to maintain 'quasi-stable' internal conditions while adapting to changing environmental conditions. Examples of such robust (adaptable) systems include cells, organs, humans, groups of people, organizations, societies, and 'supranational' systems. Systems theorists build system models based on deterministic variables that are nevertheless capable of exhibiting complex patterns of behavior that range from chaotic to adaptive. Growing interest in organizational learning as adaptive behavior has revived interest in systems thinking in strategic management studies. *Complexity theory*, by contrast, starts with complex phenomena that exhibit 'chaotic' behaviors and explores ways in which system elements have interactions that can generate chaotic patterns of behavior.[4] In the midst of chaotic phenomena, 'quasi-stable' patterns of behavior may emerge. Complexity theorists tend to use advanced mathematical techniques to analyze the complex phenomena and to infer underlying relationships between system elements that are capable of exhibiting 'quasi-stable' behaviors.

Strategic management can be regarded as a process of designing organizations as adaptive systems for sustainable value creation and distribution (Sanchez & Heene, 2004). Explicitly incorporating systems and complexity concepts in strategic management theory may therefore help to sharpen and expand the theoretical base of strategic management. For example, at least some complex systems have the potential for 'self-organizing' processes that can create 'quasi-stable', 'near order' periods in the midst of chaotic phenomena. The counterpart of such processes in a management context would be self-managing organizational processes that enable better interpretation of an unpredictable and dynamic environment and faster response to it (Sanchez, 1997). Sanchez also suggests that management can reduce the impact of environmental complexity and uncertainty on organizations by devising sets of relatively simple rules that have the capability to order organizational processes, maintain quasi-stability, and facilitate adaptation to a dynamic environment in a self-organizing way.

Complexity can be defined and measured in several ways, depending on the field of research. According to Mitleton-Kelly (2003), theories of complexity provide a conceptual framework, a way of thinking, and a way of seeing the world, but there is no single unified theory of complexity. Instead, there are several versions of complexity that arise from various natural sciences such as biology, chemistry, and physics. Mitleton-Kelly advocates that 'complex social (human) systems' be studied in their own right because natural and social domains may have fundamental differences, including the capability of humans to reflect and to make deliberate choices and decisions. A theory of complex social systems is needed to explain phenomena of self-organization (the capability to create order), emergence, and adaptation in human systems.

According to Senge (1990), there are two kinds of complexity. *Detail complexity* refers to the large number of variables that must be managed so that they do not overwhelm an organization and render it dysfunctional. *Dynamic complexity* refers to the way the essential elements of an organization and its environment are evolving. Conventional forecasting, planning, and analysis methods that are often oriented toward detail complexity are not well equipped to analyze dynamic complexity. In addition, increasing the level of detail complexity in models of organizational structures and processes does not help us to understand the processes of learning and renewal that are essential in managing dynamic complexity.

In general, systems can be classified according to their *complexity of relationships between components*, as shown in Table 4.1. Each new level of complexity brings new relationships and capabilities into a system, but may also simultaneously involve previous levels. Levels 1 to 3 include conventional system models: static structures and frameworks, predetermined mechanistic systems, and cybernetic systems that include error-controlled feedback. Levels 4 to 8 include models that explain *living (self-producing, autopoietic) systems* (such as cells), multicellular systems, organisms with nervous systems, observing systems, and social systems. Living systems are complex systems capable of self-production. According to Pondy and Mitroff (1979), conventional models and explanations of organizational phenomena do not match the complexity of actual organizations, and our prevailing explanations continue to lag behind the actual complexity of the phenomena that they try to describe. Complex systems, however, are characterized by rich interconnections, iteration, holism, and dynamic fluctuations. Complexity arises from the high levels of interaction and connectivity in such systems.

Mitleton-Kelly (2003) identifies five main areas in the field of complexity research under the umbrella of complex evolving systems (CES):

- Dissipative structures in chemistry and physics — e.g. the work of Ilya Prigogine
- Complex adaptive systems (CAS) in evolutionary biology — e.g. Stuart Kauffman
- Autopoiesis (self-generation, self-production) in biological systems — e.g. Humberto Maturana
- Chaos theory
- Increasing returns in economics — e.g. Brian Arthur.

The following describes CAS and the broader concept of CES. Chaos theory will be used to differentiate chaotic systems from complex systems. A preliminary introduction to self-production (autopoiesis) will also be presented.

4.2.2 CAS and CES

CAS are complex systems that have the capacity to create order from chaos and to generate new emergent properties in an accumulative manner (Kauffman, 1993; Holland, 1995, 1998). Such capabilities have been described as self-organizing and self-structuring decentralized processes (Doz & Prahalad, 1993), self-renewal (Nonaka, 1988, Chakravarthy & Doz, 1992), and emergent internal closure (Spender, 1996). Achieving self-organization and emergence in human complex adaptive systems, however, requires reduced levels of centralized control. Although certain basic approaches have been identified as facilitating

Table 4.1: The hierarchy of complexity (Mingers, 1997, based on Boulding, 1956).

Level	Description	Characteristic	Type of relations	Example
1	Structures and frameworks	Static, spatial patterns	Topology (where)	Bridge, mountain, table, crystal
2	Single mechanistic systems	Dynamic, predetermined changes, processes	Order (when)	Solar system, clock, tune, computer
3	Control mechanisms, cybernetic systems	Error-controlled feed-back, information	Specification (what)	Thermostat, body temperature system, autocatalytic system
4	Living systems	Continuous self-production	Autopoietic relations (first-order autopoiesis)	Cell, amoeba, single-celled bacteria
5	Multicellular system	Functional differentiation	Structural coupling between cells (second-order autopoiesis)	Plants, fungi, moulds, algae
6	Organisms with nervous systems	Interaction with relations	Symbolic, abstract relations	Most animals (except, e.g. sponges)
7	Observing systems	Language, self-consciousness	Recursive, self-referential relations	Humans
8	Social systems	Rules, meanings, norms, power	Structural coupling between organisms (third-order autopoiesis)	Families, organizations
9	Transcendental systems			

self-organization (Holland, 1995), they do not fully address the interconnectedness that impacts on an organization's capability to evolve and to create and utilize knowledge.

A broader concept 'CES' has been introduced to cover five main areas in complexity research that include both adaptation and evolution, as well as several principles that go beyond complex adaptive systems. According to Mitleton-Kelly (2003), organizations are, by their very nature, complex evolving systems and need to be considered as such for two reasons. First, the characteristics of complexity cannot be mapped directly from other scientific domains into the social domain because humans have volition that generates behaviors that differ from the predictable behaviors of other objects of scientific research. Second, using the principles of complexity from physical sciences only as metaphors or analogies in studying human systems would be too limiting.

Complex evolving systems are characterized by 10 generic principles: connectivity, interdependence, feedback, emergence, co-evolution, far from equilibrium, historicity and time, space of possibilities, path dependence, and self-organization (Mitleton-Kelly, 2003). In general, these aspects of complexity enable the *creation of new order*.

Connectivity refers to inter-relatedness and resulting *interdependence* among system elements. Complex evolving systems may create new order by changing the rules that govern interactions between system elements.

Co-evolution means that the evolution of one domain or entity depends at least in part on the evolution of other domains or entities (Kauffman, 1993). There is thus a difference between adaptation to an environment and co-evolution with the environment. The first expression emphasizes the dichotomy between the system and its environment and reflects the contingency theory basis for much of the management theory, whereas the latter expression reflects an assumption of interaction between a system and its environment and the idea that co-evolution takes place within an ecosystem.

A *far from equilibrium* state — also called the *edge of chaos* — is one in which established patterns have been disrupted and new forms of organization may emerge.

Historicity and *path dependence* reflect the importance of investigating an organization's *space of possibilities* in exploration, decision-making, and flexibility. Mitleton-Kelly (2003) comments that "there seems to be a balance between [an organization's rate of] discovery and what the ecosystem can effectively sustain". Excessive rates of discovery and change may be dysfunctional for an organization.

Feedback mechanisms (or in the social context, *feedback processes*) are in complex systems and far-from-equilibrium conditions more subtler than in conventional systems theory. In human systems, such as organizations, positive and negative feedback loops are intertwined and interacting on several levels (micro and macro), and their outcomes may be difficult to predict.

Self-organization refers to a phase transition, to the emergence of a spontaneous order that is internally coherent. *Emergence* is a process that creates irreversible (dissipative) structures or reversible (conservative) new order together with self-organization. Self-organization may occur as a result of being pushed into a state of far-from-equilibrium, but the self-organization to produce new order does not necessarily happen: a system may also simply run down. In an organizational context, the concept of self-organization may take the form of 'self-organizing teams' but may also include management in which empowered individuals make decisions. Self-organization can include increasing connectivity, sharing of knowledge, and creation of new ideas and structures.

CES theories may lead to ideas about *enabling environments* and *enabling infrastructures* — socio-cultural and technical conditions that facilitate learning and the sharing of knowledge that supports self-organization.

4.2.3 Chaos Theory and 'Chaos'

Chaos theory emphasizes processes of iteration and recursiveness driven by simple rules that generate complex structures such as fractals, weather systems, and economic systems. Chaotic systems may exhibit stability, instability, or bounded instability. Bounded instability refers to a state between stability and instability, a transition phase, the 'edge of chaos'. However, the term 'chaos' is often used loosely in an organizational context, without any grounding in formal theoretical definition, to refer to a state of organization in which objectives are not clear and there is lack of control. For example, it is in this loose use of the term that Nonaka and Takeuchi recommend that periodic 'chaos' can be created to facilitate knowledge creation (1995).

Chaos theory is not identical with complexity theory. Chaos theory describes phenomena that exhibit non-linear dynamics that arise from a stable set of simple rules. By contrast, complex systems may be capable of adapting and evolving their rules of interaction. Especially in social contexts, applying chaos theory may not always be appropriate, because humans have cognitive capabilities that enable them to change their rules of interaction.

4.2.4 Self-Production (autopoiesis)

The theory of self-production (autopoiesis), which is the main focus of this book has sometimes been erroneously characterized as CAS theory, but is correctly classified as CES theory. The theory of self-production can help managers to understand alternative approaches to organizing components in a structured way that enhances the potential for self-organization. Continual production of new components and interconnections among components enable an organization to function as a living entity.

4.3 Summary

To avoid confusion and misinterpretation, it is important to distinguish clearly between different kinds of systems and to specify their characteristics carefully. The system models described in this chapter classify several kinds of system approaches. We have also described open systems, system dynamics, and network approaches as alternative ways to analyze an organization's interactions with its environment and to characterize the ways organizations become embedded systemically in a wider environmental context.

Complexity and chaos are often used metaphorically in everyday conversation. However, they also have specific theoretical definitions and characteristics that must be understood in analyzing system phenomena. Correct differentiation is especially important in the context of social systems, such as organizations.

A new concept of 'CES' has been introduced to cover five main areas in complexity research: dissipative structures, CAS, autopoiesis (self-production, self-generation), chaos theory, and increasing economic returns. In the rest of this book, the main focus will be on autopoiesis theory — the theory of living (self-producing) systems.

Notes

1. Norbert Wiener, Claude Shannon, Talcott Parsons, Herbert Simon, and James D. Thompson belong to the general systems approach, and developed the pioneering work of Ludwig von Bertalanffy further.
2. The law of limited variety supplements the law of requisite variety. Source: Ashby, W. R. (1956). The Effect of Experience on a determinant system. *Behavioral Science, 1,* 35–42.
3. This definition of fluctuation differs from the conceptual definition of the same term by Nonaka and Takeuchi, who use 'fluctuation' to refer to breakdown of routines, habits, or cognitive frameworks.
4. Chaotic behaviors are not random (and thus not purely unpredictable), but arise from complex interactions among elements in a system whose inherent properties constrain the behaviors of a system to occur with certain upper and lower limits.

PART II

THE LIVING COMPOSITION MODEL

Organizations can be regarded as living systems that continually renew themselves by producing their components and boundaries and by co-evolving with their environment. This second part of the book will develop this view, the living composition model, step by step from the assumptions of autopoiesis theory, i.e. the theory of self-producing, living systems. Part II will first investigate how to apply the principles of self-production to organizations (Chapter 5). Then, it formulates the living composition model (Chapter 6) and specifies strategic components of a living organization (Chapter 7), two major knowledge flows — sensing and memory (Chapter 8), and four parallel knowledge processes (Chapter 9).

Chapter 5

How to Apply the Principles of Self-Production to Organizations

Because the theory of living systems was originally developed in the context of biology, this chapter will analyze the opportunities and constraints that concern the theory in an organizational context. The chapter attempts to show that organizations can be regarded as truly self-producing, autopoietic systems, not just in a metaphorical sense. Therefore, this chapter starts with the presentation of the characteristics of autopoiesis theory that could be relevant to organizations. Thereafter, it will discuss the assumptions of reality and knowledge in the theory, because these aspects are relevant for understanding how an organization may cognize itself and its environment. These assumptions will be compared to conventional philosophical paradigms. The purpose is to clarify the specific nature of autopoiesis theory, the scope and limits of its explanatory power, and its implications for organizational knowledge and learning capability. The chapter will then introduce know-ledge-related concepts as they have been presented in recent literature about autopoiesis. Finally, the chapter analyzes various specific aspects of applying the theory of self-production to organizations.

5.1 Organization as a Living (Self-Producing, Autopoietic) System

The principles and criteria of self-production as defined in autopoiesis theory are quite well defined and will be presented in the beginning of this section. The core of these principles has been crystallized in a six-point key for identifying living systems (Varela, Maturana, & Uribe, 1974, in Mingers, 1995). Self-producing systems belong to the category of self-referential systems. Because of considerable differences in systemic behavior and organizational implications, it is necessary to differentiate autopoietic systems from other kinds of self-referential systems. Self-production has many implications for organizational learning. The comparison to other system models will be presented at the end of this chapter.

5.1.1 Principles of Self-Production (Autopoiesis)

Autopoiesis theory — the theory of living, self-producing systems — is based on the research of Humberto Maturana and Francisco Varela within the fields of neurobiology and biological phenomenology (1974 (with Uribe), 1980, 1987). The term 'autopoiesis' origi-nates from the Greek words 'auto' (self) and 'poiesis'/'poein' (production). Autopoiesis theory was originally developed to explain the lives of biological organisms and their phys-ical reproduction. It explains the nature of living entities as opposed to non-living ones. Autopoiesis as a field of study is concerned with the processes of self-production of components that constitute a system. It claims that a living system undergoes a continual process of internal self-production, which means that it produces itself continually by producing its own components. In contrast, non-living (allopoietic) systems produce something other than their own self-components (Mingers, 1997).

The theory of self-production is used, for example, to explain the biological basis of cognition, self-consciousness, social interaction, and language that allow human beings to coordinate their actions. It provides a powerful perspective on organizational behavior, evolution, and knowledge by explaining how living systems produce and renew themselves continually.

According to Maturana, the organization of a living system can be described as a closed network of productions of components.[1] The theory does not specify what is to be produced in their self-production process, i.e. how the components should be selected and defined. *Non-physical* autopoietic systems include human organizations, societies, and systems of laws or ideas that belong to abstract systems (Mingers, 1995, 1997). Because organizations are regarded as non-physical autopoietic entities, it is necessary also to define the non-physical components and boundaries of an organization. The production of material boundaries and components — such as buildings, products, and human beings — does not belong to the domain of *organizational autopoietic production.*

Autopoiesis theory is a relational theory. The focus and level of observation determine whether a system, such as an organization, must be regarded as *autonomous or controlled.* The control and autonomy approaches complement each other. A given system may be seen as an autonomous whole, while simultaneously its components may be seen as input–process–output systems from the control perspective (Varela, 1979). Thus, it is possible for an organization to be regarded simultaneously as an autonomous, autopoietic system capable of self-production and as a controlled system.

Certain organizational phenomena, such as learning, may imply that the organization is regarded as autonomous and capable of self-production. Thus, when we focus on the organization's learning and renewal processes, the autonomy perspective may be appropriate. Seen from this angle, the organization is controlled by its internal structure. An autonomy perspective is applicable when a system's internal structure directs the system's functioning and the system thereby controls its own behavior. Environmental influences, including externally defined purposes, ends, goals, schemes, and plans become perturbations (triggers) rather than inputs. The system has properties, internal laws that are not controlled from the outside, although the system can modify its objectives internally as part of its autonomous operation. The autonomy approach helps to understand learning and renewal processes that are motivated for example, by an organization's 'strategic choices'.

Some other phenomena, such as the transformation of raw materials into products, means that the outputs are determined by the inputs and the organization operates as a controlled system. Thus, when we describe an organization's production process, the control approach can be used. The control approach reduces a system to input–output behavior in which the environment largely determines its functioning.

Autopoietic systems are a subset of autonomous systems. Autonomy is a necessary but not sufficient characteristic for self-production. Autopoiesis is a special case of autonomy (organizational closure), in that autopoietic systems also produce their own components and boundaries (Varela, 1979). In essence, an autopoietic system produces itself. It continually transforms itself by re-creating its own components.

Autopoietic systems, as autonomous systems, are *organizationally closed* (Varela, 1979). This means that all possible states of activity must lead to or generate further activity within the autonomous system itself. Organizational (internal) closure implies that the system does not sense environmental inputs and respond to them directly. Instead, the system undergoes internal structural changes in response to the signals it detects in its environment (Mingers, 1995). Organizational (internal) closure means that environmental perturbations of an autopoietic system are not treated as inputs. Instead, the changes in its environment only trigger compensations in the system in the form of internal reorganization and restructuring (von Krogh & Roos, 1995). One consequence of organizational (internal) closure is that an autopoietic system can be said to have *identity*. Identity means that an autopoietic system is able to maintain the integrity of its internal structure.[2] Self-production refers to the system's continuous ability to renew itself in a way that maintains the integrity of its 'structure.'

Simultaneously, an autopoietic system is *open to its environment* in a specific way. The environment does not control an autonomous system. Instead the system, such as an organization, may be sensitive to *triggers* — signals from its environment that it perceives as perturbations. Perturbations can only stimulate (but not instruct or control) processes in the system. The system always follows its self-defined rules (von Krogh & Roos, 1995). This may lead to *compensations* in the internal 'structure' of a system in response to perturbations in its environment.

According to Maturana and Varela (1987), *structural coupling* refers to a system's reciprocal interactions with its environment. For example, emerging market trends may influence an organization, and the organization's innovations may influence the market simultaneously. An autopoietic system "pulls itself up by its own bootstraps and becomes distinct from its environments through its own dynamics, in such a way that both things are inseparable" (p. 46). *Social coupling* is a form of structural coupling enacted through communication based on language.

Living systems can be classified into three types according to the kind of autopoiesis they incorporate. The idea of first-, second-, and third-order autopoiesis is based on the emergence of increasingly complex and abstract structures such as societies and social organizations (Mingers, 1997). *First-order autopoiesis* explains the principles of a self-producing, living system. *Second-order autopoiesis* explains structural coupling between living systems. *Third-order autopoiesis* explains structural coupling between organisms. This level includes social systems, such as human societies that involve multiple organisms.

An autopoietic system produces new *knowledge* by creating distinctions in its internal components and structures. Distinctions are made as compensations for perturbations (Maturana & Varela, 1987[3]). In this sense, the human mind as an autopoietic system cannot represent the external world. Instead, under the stimulus of perturbations, it forms distinctions that are inseparable from the structure of its own cognitive system (von Krogh & Roos, 1995). Analogously, an organization creates new knowledge by creating increasingly refined distinctions. The capability of an organization to create new knowledge is constrained by its existing interpretation structure derived from its prior knowledge.

Self-referentiality is a key characteristic of an autopoietic system and a feature of organizational closure. Self-referential systems refer to or 'impact' themselves (Mingers, 1997). In the cognitive domain, self-referentiality means that a system creates and maintains meanings internally, and these meanings influence the system's interpretation of new signals. In other words, earlier accumulated knowledge affects the system's acquisition of new data, interpretation of signals, and creation of new knowledge. For example, managers may use their knowledge to determine what they see, and they use what they already know to choose what to look for in their environment (von Krogh, Roos, and Slocum, 1996a). According to Luhmann and Varela, a system may be self-referential not only in relation to the past, but also in relation to the future (von Krogh et al., 1996a). For example, a firm's plans may be based on self-referential interpretations about potential future alternatives (von Krogh & Vicari, 1993). Thus, although an autopoietic system operates in an *environment*, its relations with its environment are internally determined. Self-referentiality in other kinds of systems will be discussed in Section 5.1.3.

The basic characteristics of an autopoietic system are summarized in Table 5.1. The key definitions are also presented in the glossary (Appendix 1).

5.1.2   Six-Point Key for Identifying Living Systems

When applying the principles of autopoiesis theory, it is necessary to define the *components* and *boundaries* carefully. A six-point key has been developed by Varela, Maturana and Uribe to differentiate between self-producing and other kinds of systems (1974, in Mingers, 1995). The first three criteria are general, and the last three specify the core autopoietic ideas (Mingers, 1995). The criteria are

1. The system is a unity with identifiable boundaries.
2. The system can be decomposed into components in order to be analyzable as a 'whole'.
3. The component properties are capable of satisfying certain relations that determine in the system the interactions and transformations of these components.
4. The system is contained within and produces a boundary.
5. The system is maintained by the interactions of its components.
6. The system's modus operandi is a dynamic network of interacting processes of autopoietic 'production'.

The six-point key requires that an autopoietic system has identifiable components and boundaries that are continually produced by the system itself. The interpretation of components and boundaries in the context of organizations will be discussed in Chapters 7 and 15.

5.1.3   Other Self-Referential Systems

Self-referential systems[4] refer to or directly impact themselves. All self-referential systems have one or more major structural relations among components that are circular. Self-referential systems include self-managing, self-referring, self-influencing, self-regulating, self-sustaining, self-producing (autopoietic), self-recognizing, self-organizing, self-replicating, self-cognizing, and self-conscious systems. However, many systems that start with the prefix 'self' do not meet the requirements of autopoiesis, such as the continual production of components and boundaries (Mingers, 1995, 1997).

Table 5.1: Basic characteristics of a self-producing (autopoietic) system.

Characteristic	Definition (Note: the term 'system' has been replaced by 'organization')
Autopoiesis (self-production)	An organization produces its own components and boundaries, and renews itself in a way that allows the continuous maintenance of its integrity
Identity	1. Being composed of components and their relationships 2. Being distinguishable from other unities (e.g. from other organizations)
Components	Non-physical parts of the system that are continually produced by the organization
Boundaries	Non-physical parts of the system that connect the system to its environment through reciprocal interaction. Here: Boundary elements. (roles and functions)
Triggers	Signals that are treated as perturbations, not as an input to the organization
Structural coupling	Reciprocal interaction (mutual relationship or correspondence) with the environment History of recurrent interactions leading to the structural congruence
Interactive openness	The organization interacts with the environment and compensates the perturbations by improving knowledge (distinctions) and changing its 'structure'
'Organizational closure' ('Operational closure')	Any change in the organization is a structural change The product of the transformation is the very organization itself
Self-referentiality	1. Accumulated knowledge affects the structure and operation of the organization 2. The organization affects the (creation of) new knowledge
Social coupling	Reciprocal interaction (communication) by using language

Source: Based on Maturana and Varela (1980, 1987), Mingers (1995, 1997), von Krogh and Roos (1995), and von Krogh et al. (1996a).

Sanchez and Heene (2004) define *self-managing processes* as value-creation processes in which each participant understands how an organization is trying to create value and what their role is in the organization's value-creation process. Therefore, the participants can effectively manage their own activities for contributing to the performance of the organization in value creation.

Self-organization, in particular, has received increasing attention (e.g. Holland, 1995, 1998; Kelly, 1994). Self-organization builds order out of chaos. According to Mitleton-Kelly (1997), self-organization may lead to the emergence of complex system forms, processes that 'simply happen,' and the spontaneous organization of the system's elements into coherent new patterns, structures, and behaviors. It has become a popular concept in business literature and among managers, for example, in the context of team-based organization to mean relaxing control and increasing autonomy and empowerment among employees. Although in everyday language managers and researchers may use the term *self-organizing system* without specifying the concept exactly, self-organizing systems are more than simple assemblages of components and must include rules relating the components that are capable of producing a rich variety of organizational behavior (Wheatley, 1994; Wheatley & Kellner-Rogers, 1996).

Self-organization is sometimes mistakenly used as an equivalent for autopoiesis. As Luhmann notes, "Autopoietic systems, then, are not only self-organizing systems, they not only produce and eventually change their own structures; their self-reference applies to the production of other components as well. This is the decisive conceptual innovation. It adds a turbocharger to the already powerful engine of self-referential machines" (1990, p. 3).

5.1.4   Earlier Interpretations of Self-Production in an Organizational Context

The theory of living, self-producing systems has been applied increasingly to organizations and social systems (von Krogh et al., 1996a; Ståhle, 1998; Tuomi, 1999; Maula, 1999, 2000a). Many of the interpretations focus, however, on interaction among people, the social autopoiesis.

Luhmann differentiates three kinds of autopoietic systems: *living, psychic, and social systems*. Living systems, such as cells, brains, and organisms use life processes as the basic mode of reproduction, whereas psychic systems use consciousness, and social systems (such as societies and organizations) use communication as the mode of reproduction. Social systems function according to their own laws. Individuals contribute to the autopoietic process of the social system through communication. Thus they do not belong to the social system itself but to its environment. Social systems are autopoietic because they construct their own reality and are self-producing systems of meaning that produce their own components (Luhmann, 1990; Luhmann in von Krogh & Roos, 1995). Based on Luhmann's assumption that social systems in general are autopoietic, von Krogh and Vicari (1993) conclude that firms are also autopoietic production networks that produce their own components, such as distinctions in a recurrent way through interaction.

Many researchers claim that *human societies and organizations are autopoietic systems* (Beer, 1994; Luhmann, 1990; Vicari, 1991; von Krogh & Vicari, 1993; Maula, 1999, 2000a). Any social institution is likely to be an autopoietic system, because it may change its entire appearance and its apparent purpose in the process of surviving (Beer, 1994). According to Nonaka and Takeuchi (1995), a knowledge-creating organization with autonomy may also be depicted as an autopoietic system. Autopoiesis theory provides a useful theoretical basis for approaching the management of knowledge and for elaborating 'corporate epistemology' that explains how and why organizations know (von Krogh & Roos, 1995, 1996a).

Another view is that autopoiesis theory can be regarded as a fruitful metaphor for understanding organizations (Morgan, 1986, 1994; Tsoukas, 1993). Morgan, for example, uses the metaphor of 'flux'. Flux provides a concept for identifying, cataloging, and describing discrete events of change in an organization. Flux also helps to explain how events are generated by a logic enfolded in an organization's process of change itself. It reveals the underlying structure of an organization's 'reality,' and helps us to understand the world as the manifestation of a deeper generative process. Flux has concrete implications for organizations. Many social and organizational problems are unlikely to be solved in a piecemeal way, but rather only by restructuring the internal logic of a society or organization. This approach is also based on the idea that explicate (unfolded) reality realizes and expresses the potentialities that exist in the implicate (enfolded) order of a system (Bohm & Peat, 1987).

Some interpretations explain organizational autopoiesis by the recursive reproduction of *one system component only*. Examples of such explanations and components are

- *Communication* and *money* (Luhmann, 1990, 1983). For example, communications produce new communications.
- *Dialogues* and *conversations* (Varela, 1979; von Krogh & Roos, 1995). Language games and scales of socialized and individualized knowledge are essential features for understanding knowledge in globalizing firms (von Krogh Roos & Yip, 1996b).
- *Values* (Vicari, 1991). Values produce new values.
- *Mind-sets* and *conversations* in which meanings emerge (Robb in Mingers, 1995).

Other models of organizational autopoiesis include *several variables*. Beer[5] diagnosed organizations in his biologically based work as organisms and compared organizational functions to the heart, brain, and nervous system of humans. He regarded autopoiesis theory as supplementary to his Viable System Model. Organizations have also been described as networks of values, norms, and precepts that should be designed to be autopoietic (Zeleny & Pierre in Mingers, 1995). A business enterprise has been described as a replicative network that produces its own components and sub-components and embodies various replicative sub-networks (Pantzar & Csányi, 1990). This interpretation also includes the replication/renewal of people and artifacts. According to Mingers (1995), some interpretations apply autopoiesis theory 'naively' to the social domain without explaining the essential role of boundaries and the production of components.

Vicari (1991) characterizes autopoietic organizations as 'living.' However, some other models of organizations that include the term 'living' are not based on the principles of autopoiesis. For example, 'The Living Company' model (de Geus, 1997a, 1997b) is based on four characteristics: sensitivity to the environment, cohesion and identity, tolerance, and decentralization. According to de Geus, it probably does not matter much whether a company is actually alive in a strict biological sense, or whether the 'living company' is simply a useful metaphor.

A *communications view of organizational memory* is compatible with autopoiesis theory and structuration theory (Tuomi, 1996). It is based on communicative social interactions and contrasts with the view that organizational memory consists mainly of finding and storing representations of organizational episodes and knowledge. This approach brings into the discussion new areas of communication that relate to reproduction of organizational structures. It implies that an organization's collective memory is predominantly about communication and not about repositories.

5.1.5   Self-Production, Learning, and Renewal

Many earlier concepts of organizational learning have been based on the old idea of open (input–process–output) systems (von Krogh & Vicari, 1993). Those concepts regard learning as an instructed action in which a system 'takes in' or receives input from its environment, and changes its own behavior accordingly. Also, many models of learning are based on the ideas of system dynamics, such as errors and other 'gaps' that facilitate the circular learning process.

Autopoiesis theory did not originally deal specifically with learning processes, but with structural coupling and structural drift. Maturana and Varela (1987) claim that from the perspective of autopoiesis, learning is an expression of structural coupling in which the intention is to maintain compatibility between the operation of the system and its environment. However, von Krogh and Vicari propose that autopoiesis theory does provide insights into the strategic learning of organizations. The autopoietic approach to the management of knowledge emphasizes the importance of both error correction and experimentation as impetus for change and knowledge development. In order to increase the ability to make distinctions and to learn, it is necessary to experiment and detect errors. The only way a firm can stimulate the self-reproductive process is to create new distinctions using the errors provided by experiments and by selecting new data from an environment. According to Vicari, von Krogh, Roos, and Mahnke (1996), spontaneous experiments have significant learning value for an organization compared to planned ones. They have the greatest potential for creating new distinctions, if the survival of the company is ensured. Self-referentiality in distinctions and norms may limit perception and capability to interpret new data and detect errors. Experimental learning may be a means to overcome this difficulty of adaptive rational learning. Experimental learning may produce knowledge about the organization's knowledge and thereby increase its variety. An autopoietic organization attempts to maintain a degree of congruence between itself and its environment. This does not, however, guarantee the organization's viability and survival. An autopoietic system can make errors that lead to differences between desired and undesired states of the system (von Krogh & Vicari, 1993).

The principles of autopoiesis help to re-interpret organizational processes in a broad evolutionary context. They provide new insight into an organization as a holistic learning and evolving system in its own right. In particular, autopoiesis theory helps to explain the interconnection between closure that maintains the system's autopoietic functioning, and interactive openness that helps to coordinate its functioning within its environment (Luhmann, 1983). The autopoietic principle of self-production helps also to explain the impact of human cognition, social interaction, communication, and language on organizational survival.

5.1.6   Summary of Different System Approaches

This section will compare the characteristics of living (autopoietic, self-producing) systems and the system theories presented in Chapter 4. Table 5.2 will summarize their abilities to explain organizational learning and evolution.

The models and theories being compared share several characteristics. They are hierarchical or scalable. They are holistic, which means that they provide explanations about the relationship between the whole and its parts. They also help to describe complex structures and relationships. However, as the table shows, these models and theories also clearly differ from each other. Conventional approaches explain detail complexity, whereas the newer views describe dynamic complexity.

The comparison also reveals relevant differences between the system alternatives. In an open system, consistency improves performance, whereas inconsistency should be avoided. Learning is largely facilitated by the environment. In a dynamic system, the objective is to create a dynamic fit between internal and external components, and a static structure is to be avoided. Learning and renewal are facilitated by gaps, such as stretch and misfit between components or their current and desired states. In network structures, connectivity among internal and external components contributes productivity, whereas uniformity and static structure may create problems. Learning and renewal are facilitated by the number and variety of the components and connections between them. In autopoietic systems, structural coupling and compensations in internal 'structure' should be favored, whereas inefficient boundaries and internal rigidity should be avoided. Learning and renewal are enabled by co-evolution with the environment, and by self-production of components and functioning of boundary elements. Co-evolution is facilitated by structural coupling with the environment, compensating for perturbations (triggers), and by experiments. They improve the organization's distinctions, i.e. the ability to discriminate and select data.

5.2   Reality and Knowledge in Organizations

Self-referential system theories provide new understanding about knowing processes and a system's opportunities to understand itself and its surrounding world. They also provide new kinds of assumptions about reality and knowledge. On an individual level, autopoiesis theory includes *assumptions about reality and knowledge*:

- What an individual can assume about the existence of the world, about reality (ontological assumptions)?
- What an individual can know about that reality, and how (epistemological assumptions)?
- Because the purpose of this book is to understand how *organizations* co-evolve with their environment and create knowledge about it, it is necessary to clarify *organizational reality and knowledge in the light of autopoiesis*:
- What an organization can assume about the existence of its surrounding world and business environment?
- What an organization can know about that environment, and how?

Table 5.2: Implications of alternative system theories and models for learning and renewal.

	Open system and contingency theory	**System dynamics**	**Networks**	**Autopoiesis theory (self-production)**
Characterization	*Organization theory:* Output and input connected *Engineering control theory:* 'Black box,' open boundaries, no feedback-loop	Continuous, circular processes of change Positive and negative feedback loops Gap(s) between current and desired state(s)	Dense connections, interaction, connectivity Simple rules Emergent properties	*Interactive openness:* The organization compensates for the triggers (perturbations) by changing internally *Self-referentiality* (a characteristic of organizational closure). Earlier knowledge influences new knowledge
Implications for performance	Consistency (fit) between the environment and strategy improves performance THUS: Inconsistency is an error and should be avoided	Dynamic fit between internal and external components improves performance THUS: A static structure should be avoided	Connectivity among internal and external components improves performance THUS: Uniformity and static structure should be avoided	Structural coupling and compensations in internal 'structure' maintain congruence with the environment. Non-viable systems disappear THUS: Inefficient boundaries and internal rigidity should be avoided

| **Implications for learning and renewal** | Facilitated by the environment | Facilitated by a stretch or misfit between the components or their current and desired states | Facilitated by the number and variety of components | Co-evolution is enabled by:
• self-production of the components
• functioning of boundary elements
1. structural coupling with the environment
2. compensating for perturbations (triggers)
3. Experiments. They improve distinctions, i.e. the ability to discriminate and select data |

The purpose of this section is to clarify the specific nature of autopoiesis theory, the scope and limits of its explanatory power, and its implications for organizational knowledge and cognizing. To clarify these issues, this section will compare autopoiesis theory with conventional philosophical paradigms. The comparison results in the conclusion that it is not possible to associate autopoiesis theory unanimously to any of the paradigms by using available knowledge. The analysis defines a general domain, where conclusions about organizational reality and knowledge can be made relatively safely. This means a domain where the assumptions about knowledge and reality are approximately the same for all compared paradigms. Based on that result it can be assumed that autopoiesis theory can be used relatively safely within the limits of the domain. This solution also attempts to ensure that the conclusions about organizational reality and knowing are coherent with the basic assumptions of autopoiesis theory.

5.2.1   The Comparison of Autopoiesis Theory to Two Conventional Philosophical Paradigms

Autopoiesis theory will first be compared to empiricism, realism, and idealism. A further analysis then compares it to critical realism and radical constructivism.

5.2.1.1   Positioning among empiricism, realism, and idealism   *Autopoiesis theory*, as Maturana has defined it, emphasizes the dependence of the observer. Therefore, it does not belong to the *empiricist tradition*, which claims that experiences are independent of the observer (Mingers, 1995).

Instead, autopoiesis theory has been associated with both realism and idealism. *Realism* claims the independence of thought and being, and *naive realism* assumes that there is an objective, independent world that we can experience directly. *Idealism* emphasizes ideas and thought. Autopoiesis theory has parallelisms to Heidegger's phenomenology of the everyday world, particularly through the concepts of 'thrownness' and 'breakdowns' (Mingers, 1995; Winograd & Flores, 1986). This situation is called the Occam's razor problem, the difficulty of choosing between objectivism (representationism/representationalism, realism) and solipsism (idealism). More precisely, it means the dilemma between two contradicting assumptions:

- assuming that the nervous system operates with *representations* of the 'real' world (representationism, objectivism, realism)
- assuming that everything is possible (solipsism, idealism) and *denying the environment.*

According to Maturana and Varela (1987), autopoiesis theory proposes that the choice can be avoided by re-framing it and relying on *logical accounting*. The contradiction can be solved by moving away from it and embracing it in a broader context. Therefore, it is necessary to differentiate between the *ontological reality (possibly existing reality)* and an observer's *experiential reality*. In other words, "... if we presuppose the existence of an objective world, independent of us as observers and accessible to our knowledge through our nervous system, we cannot understand how our nervous system functions in its structural dynamics and still produces a representation of this independent world. But if we do *not* presuppose an objective world independent of us as observers, it seems we are accepting that everything is relative and anything is possible in the denial of lawfulness". Autopoiesis theory implies that for an autopoietic unit — such as a human being or an organization — there is no fixed point of reference because "everything said is said by someone". We cannot say that there is no real world. Instead, we can say that we do not know it.

Logical accounting implies that:

1. it is neither necessary nor possible to associate autopoiesis theory exclusively with realism or idealism
2. autopoiesis theory cannot be regarded as a compromise between realism and idealism (phenomenology).

5.2.1.2 Positioning among critical realism and radical constructivism In order to draw more precise conclusions, autopoiesis theory will be compared to critical realism and radical constructivism because it has been associated with these contradicting branches of philosophy.

Critical realism relaxes the assumptions about knowledge of the realist paradigm. It claims that observations depend on theories, and we cannot have pure access to an independently existing world. There is a parallel in autopoiesis theory in the assumption that external reality may exist but we do not have access to it (Maturana & Varela, 1987). Many different and equally valid domains of reality define our cognitive domains. We realize our existence in the physical domain. Autopoiesis theory can be successfully reconstructed in the light of critical realism (Mingers, 1995).

Radical constructivism claims that we construct our theories and experiences of the world. As our theories change, so does the world that we experience. There are similarities between Maturana's thinking about autopoiesis and von Glasersfeld's radical constructivist thinking. Maturana's interpretation of autopoiesis can be associated with constructivism, pragmatism, phenomenalism, and phenomenological biologism (Mingers, 1995).

5.2.1.3 The alternative positions of autopoiesis theory As a result of the previous analysis, autopoiesis theory can be positioned in several ways:

1. It is regarded *as a realist theory* within the paradigm of *critical realism* (Mingers, 1995).
2. It is associated with *phenomenological constructivism*, which means that an individual brings forth his/her world as a result of his/her unique features and history (McGee, 1997).
3. It is regarded as an *independent and separate philosophical paradigm* (such as 'bring-forthism').
4. It is regarded as a *neutral meta-philosophy*, as a paradigm that can reframe the conventional philosophical paradigms and their ontological and epistemological juxtapositions.
5. The positioning of autopoiesis theory relative to self-referential theories, i.e. the class of theories that include themselves in their domain, *is left open to wait for* (1) *improved understanding* about the nature and dynamics of self-referential theories, and (2) the *generalization of the concept of truth* so that at least certain kinds of contradictions can be accommodated (Bøgh Andersen, 1995).

The comparison indicates that it is neither necessary nor possible to decide which philosophical tradition autopoiesis theory belongs to. The precondition for this is that radical constructivism does not include any assumptions of the existence of external reality. As a result, it is not possible to position autopoiesis theory unambiguously. Therefore the next section takes a new approach to the question.

5.2.2   The Common Domain of Reality and Knowledge

Because it is not possible to position autopoiesis theory, the next task is to define *an ontological (reality) and epistemological (knowledge) domain* where the assumptions about knowledge and reality are the same for autopoiesis theory, critical realism, and radical constructivism. The purpose is to define the limits of a field where it is possible to draw conclusions by using autopoiesis in the context of organizations without associating it with critical realism or radical constructivism. The assumption is that within this domain autopoiesis theory can be used quite safely because it does not violate either of the paradigms, and the conclusions about the existence (ontology) and knowing (epistemology) of organizations are consistent with the basic assumptions of the theory itself. Hence, this section explores to what extent three relevant characteristics — the assumptions about the existence and nature of external reality, access to that reality, and the nature of knowledge — are similar in all three paradigms (see Table 5.3).

The *ontological (reality) and epistemological (knowledge) domain* that is common to all three paradigms is characterized by the following limits. We may assume that empirical reality exists and we have access to it through our experiences, but we cannot know whether real reality (in critical realism) or external reality (in autopoiesis and radical constructivism) exists or not. While we cannot deny the possible existence of the real/external reality, we do not have direct access to it whether it exists or not. Because we do not have access to the potential real/external reality, we cannot verify whether our knowledge really represents it, and we cannot know whether knowledge is objective or not. Therefore, knowledge is evolving, temporary, and relative, as opposed to being final and absolute. It is measured by its explanatory power and by its capability to allow us to operate adequately, for example by viable procedures. These limits define what we can assume about reality and about knowledge concerning that reality when using autopoiesis theory.

Assuming that an organization is a cognizing and self-referential unit, the domain also helps us to understand analogously how *organizations* perceive their reality and surrounding world, and what they can know. An organization, when regarded as a self-producing, autopoietic entity, has access to empirical reality through its experiences, but it cannot know whether the real/external reality exists or not. While an organization cannot deny the possible existence of the real/external reality, it does not have direct access to it whether it exists or not. Therefore, the organization cannot verify whether its knowledge really represents the potential real/external reality or not. Organizational knowledge cannot be regarded as objective. Instead it is evolving, temporary, and relative. It is measured by the organization's capability to operate adequately, for example by viable procedures.

The conclusions about the *existence* of an organization's external reality (ontology) and about an organization's *possibility to know* about that reality (epistemology) can be made relatively safely within this common domain. The domain is consistent with the basic

Table 5.3: The assumptions regarding reality and knowledge in critical realism, autopoiesis theory, and radical constructivism.

	Critical realism realism in economic theories	Autopoiesis theory	Radical constructivism
1. The existence and nature of external reality (ontological assumption)	Three domains of reality: Real, actual, and empirical reality (Bhaskar) Independent, external, and objective existence (Mäki)	'We do not know' 'We cannot speak about it' Logical accounting differentiates between ontological reality and experiential reality	No assumption 'We do not know'
2. Access to external reality	No. Access only to the empirical domain	No point of reference	No
3. Knowledge (epistemological assumption)	Serves our purposes Truth in the sense of being explanatory 'Probably true'	Operating adequately in an individual or cooperative situation	Viable procedures

Source: Based on Bhaskar (1989), Mäki (1989, 1992), Mingers (1995), Steier (1991a, 1991b), and von Glasersfeld (1991).

assumptions of autopoiesis theory, and the characteristics of the domain do not violate the two philosophical paradigms of critical realism and radical constructivism.

5.3   Knowledge-Related Concepts in Organizational Autopoiesis

Knowledge and knowing have a central role in the autopoietic explanation of a system's functioning and evolution. Therefore, this section will discuss some selected knowledge-related concepts. The purpose is to emphasize specific characteristics of autopoiesis that help to further develop the model of living organizations. This section will first analyze the differences between representatonist, cognitivist, and connectionist notions of knowledge. Thereafter, the autopoietic notions of knowledge will be described. The section will conclude by comparing cognitivist, connectionist, and autopoietic notions of knowledge.

5.3.1   Representationist, Cognitivist, and Connectionist Notions of Knowledge

Organizational knowledge can be analyzed from cognitivist, connectionist, and autopoietic viewpoints (von Krogh & Roos, 1995; Roos & Oliver, 1997). The cognitivist and connectionist notions share two assumptions. First, an organization is directed to effectively resolve a required or pre-formulated task. In order to adapt successfully in the world, an organization functioning as a cognitive system must be able to identify and represent these tasks. Second, information processing is the basic activity of an organization. Acting analogously to the brain, information is taken in from the environment through the senses and activates various components in the network of components that compose an organization (von Krogh & Roos, 1995). Both cognitivist and connectionist approaches include the assumption of representations, and therefore this section will first present a critique of representationism.

5.3.1.1   The critique of representationism   There is an assumption in Western philosophy that knowledge is true only if it is a representation of the world that exists 'in itself,' prior to and independent of the knower's experience of it. The idea of representation leads to the Cartesian split, which refers to a distinction between subject and object, and between mind and body. It is related to the Occam's razor dilemma, the choice between representationism (objectivism) and solipsism (idealism). The representationist view implies that knowledge is abstract, task-specific, and oriented toward problem solving (von Krogh & Roos, 1995; von Krogh et al., 1996a). It is universal, objective, and transferable. It represents a pre-given world, results from information processing, and enables problem solving. Information (representations) can be acquired, gathered, processed, stored, and retrieved (Aadne, von Krogh, & Roos, 1996).

The representationist approach has been criticized in the context of knowledge, knowing, managing knowledge, cognition, and computers. The 20th century has challenged the Cartesian split by emphasizing the importance of some form of interaction between the self and the outside world in seeking knowledge. This can be seen in modern and contemporary discussions on how the Cartesian dualism between subject and object or body and mind can be transcended (Nonaka & Takeuchi, 1995).

Also, the common domain that was defined in the previous section holds that we cannot know whether the external reality exists or not. Hence, we do not know whether our knowledge represents external reality or not. Western philosophy has generally defined scientific knowledge as 'justified true belief.' The common domain defined in the previous section suggests that relevance and viability are important characteristics of organizational knowledge.

5.3.1.2 The cognitivist notion of knowledge The cognitive sciences have their roots in research on brains and human cognition. They have provided new understanding of managers' and organizations' cognition (Daft & Weick, 1984; Barr, Stimpert, & Huff, 1992). An organization is a collection of brains, or 'a cognizing brain.' The cognitivist approach to knowledge holds that the mind can represent (correspond) the outer world, its objects, events, and states. Learning in the cognitivist perspective means that the individual more accurately obtains representations of the world through assimilating new experiences (von Krogh & Vicari, 1993; von Krogh et al., 1996a).

The cognitivist notion assumes that perception occurs by 'taking in' information from outside and comparing it to mental images (categories, knowledge structures). The images are stored in memory and they help to classify objects. The human brain acts as a machine of logic and deduction. Cognition is regarded as information processing and rule-based manipulation of symbols. This notion also assumes that the human brain has some competence at probability judgments and heuristics (von Krogh & Roos, 1995).

Cognitivist epistemology assumes that representations can be retrieved in organization-wide knowledge structures that are based on experiences. These structures provide the organizational members with a shared view of the world. The ability to process information is a basic activity of the brain. Organizations have competence at logic and probability judgments and act as non-trivial machines or computers. This is reflected in the language used to characterize organizations (von Krogh & Roos, 1995). "The organization is seen as an input–output device where information is picked up, processed, and finally stored and retrieved in organization-wide knowledge structures" (von Krogh & Roos in Aadne et al., 1996, p. 24).

These assumptions can be traced to studies of organization and management. For example, information systems have been built on the cognitivist assumption that information represents an objective reality.

5.3.1.3 The connectionist notion of knowledge The connectionist view implies that if simple units are richly connected, they can create complex patterns (von Krogh & Roos, 1995). The connectionist notion of knowledge is based on the network approach to interorganizational co-operation and research on brains and computers (Varela, Thompson, & Rosch, 1993; Mingers, 1995; von Krogh & Roos, 1995). These developments were a response to criticism of the cognitivist approach, especially the cognitivist assumptions of serial and localized information processing. The research revealed that brains do not function serially but in a parallel and distributed way, and they utilize dynamic global properties in a network of simple components. The components operate in their local environment and are connected to each other by rules that play a critical role in connectionist epistemology. The connected structure results, without any central control or programing, in spontaneous behavior such as self-organization, emergent properties, global properties, network dynamics, synergetics, and collective mind. The concepts 'complex systems,' 'dynamic systems,' and 'chaos' may also refer to the connectionist approach (Varela et al., 1993; Mingers, 1995). The connectionist interpretation emphasizes the emergent and historical nature of knowledge.

In an organizational context, it is not clear whether the connectionist approach should be applied only to individual members, or to the organizational system where individuals are regarded as components (von Krogh & Roos, 1995). The literature suggests that individual organizational members are regarded as the components of the networked organization. The connections among individuals are partly but effectively facilitated by information technology (Sproull & Kiesler in von Krogh & Roos, 1995). This idea is shared by Tsoukas (1996) who argues that the collective mind is a distributed system. Especially in multinational companies, organizational units and individuals are often regarded as components of a networked organization.

According to von Krogh and Roos (1995), connectionist epistemology is based on the idea of representation. Each member of an organization knows what needs to be done in relation to the others. Collective mind will not emerge unless the organizational member adequately represents the world in which he interacts. The collective mind is based on individual brains that act as mechanisms of representation in the network of activities.

5.3.1.4 Comparison of cognitivist and connectionist notions
The cognitivist and connectionist notions share two assumptions. First, an organization or brain is directed to effectively resolve a required or pre-formulated task. In order to adapt successfully in the world, an organization has to identify and represent these tasks as inner creations of the cognitive system. Second, information processing is the basic activity of an organization or brain. For a brain, information is taken in from the environment through senses and will activate various components in the network of components that compose the brain (von Krogh & Roos, 1995).

Connectionist and cognitivist approaches also differ. While cognitivists assume that information processing depends only on stimuli from the environment, connectionists claim that it may also arise from within the system itself. The two approaches also assume that organizations acquire representations in different ways. Cognitivists regard learning as a process of creating increasingly accurate representations of the external world. Connectionists understand representation as resulting from global states in a history-dependent system (von Krogh & Roos, 1995). The network as a whole learns from perceived patterns in its environment (Mingers, 1995).

5.3.2 Autopoiesis and Knowledge

In autopoiesis, an organization can be regarded as a stream of knowledge in which distinctions are changing, new ones are being created, and old ones are being abandoned. Knowledge is scalable, shared among organizational members, and connected to the organization's history (von Krogh & Roos, 1995; von Krogh et al., 1996a). Distinctions form the basis for 'knowledge landscapes' (Roos & Oliver, 1997).

Autopoiesis theory, as Maturana has defined it, emphasizes the dependence of the observer. As it was mentioned earlier, autopoiesis theory proposes that the choice between objectivism (representationism/representationalism, realism) and solipsism (idealism), the so-called Occam's razor problem, can be avoided by re-framing it and relying on logical accounting, by differentiating between the 'possibly existing' reality (ontological reality) and an observer's experiential reality (Maturana & Varela, 1987).

5.3.2.1 Three approaches to knowledge in autopoiesis theory Knowledge is often divided into personal (individual) and organizational knowledge (e.g. Nonaka Takeuchi, 1995). In the following discussion, three approaches to knowledge are differentiated personal (individual) knowledge/knowing, social autopoiesis (communication among individuals), and organizational autopoiesis. In this book the third alternative, organizational autopoiesis, is the main focus of interest. Individual knowing and the social communication among individuals are seen as a part of a larger entity, the evolving organization.

1. Personal (individual) knowledge and knowing in autopoiesis. According to Heidegger, 'being-in-the-world' is the basis for understanding cognition. "The essence of our Being is the pre-reflective experience of being *thrown* in a situation of acting, without the opportunity or need to disengage and function as detached observers. Reflection and abstraction are important phenomena, but are not the basis for everyday action" (in Winograd & Flores, 1986).

Knowledge is identified by viable behavior. Maturana and Varela (1987) write "We admit knowledge whenever we observe an effective (or adequate) behavior in a given context ...." In autopoiesis, *knowing* means operating efficiently in the domain of existence. "All doing is knowing and all knowing is doing." "This circularity, this connection between action and experience, this inseparability between a particular way of being and how the world appears to us, tells us that every act of knowing brings forth the world" (pp. 26–27). von Krogh and Roos (1995) suggest that knowledge is created through actions, perception, and sensory and motor processes. Individual processes are unique and events can never be exactly the same.

Knowledge is intimately connected to observation, which helps to make distinctions and establish norms (Goguen & Varela, 1979; Roos, 1996). In autopoiesis 'knowledge' and 'observation' are closely related, since observing systems are autopoietic systems. Individuals create knowledge in an autonomous manner. It is based on earlier knowledge, and it is created in co-evolution with the environment. It is unique and not transferable as such to other humans (von Krogh & Roos, 1995; von Krogh et al., 1996a).

Individuals' knowledge depends on their interaction in the organization. The organization functions as a specific domain of structural coupling that allows the individual organizational member to reproduce cognitive processes (von Krogh & Roos, 1995).

Distinctions and norms are two categories in autopoiesis theory (Luhmann & Varela in von Krogh et al., 1996a). Instead of representing the external world, the human mind creates knowledge by making distinctions. Through distinction-making, a unity becomes distinguished from its background, like a tree from the forest. Existing knowledge helps managers to make new distinctions in their observations. Based on their norms, they determine what they see and develop new knowledge and finer distinctions (von Krogh & Roos, 1995).

Autopoiesis theory implies that the world is not pre-given and cannot be represented (von Krogh & Roos, 1995; von Krogh et al., 1996a). Knowledge is self-referential, embodied, connected to observation, and based on distinction-making in observations. Personal knowledge is a result of experiencing through a history of structural coupling.

2. Social autopoiesis and 'languaging'. Some applications of autopoiesis theory to organizations focus on the interaction among organizational members (social autopoiesis, third-order autopoiesis). Social autopoiesis is based on the idea that organizational knowledge is embodied in individuals and shared in their social relations. The individuals' organizational world and the organization's individual world are constantly pulsating, changing, and flowing (von Krogh & Roos, 1995; von Krogh et al., 1996a). Socialized organizational knowledge can reside in an individual or in the interface between the individual and the social system (Varela et al., 1993).

The autopoietic approach to knowledge emphasizes knowledge sharing as a basis for shared distinctions, understanding, and the development of knowledge. The individuals that convey messages about their observations create 'knowledge connections.' This means that knowledge at one point in time connects with new knowledge at a later point in time (connectivity).

Organizational knowledge is conveyed through language systems. It is based on socially created and maintained distinctions that emerge from conversation between organizational members. Organizational actions are coordinated mainly through language (Vicari et al., 1996). Knowledge is created by languaging, which is an essential characteristic of an autopoietic social organization. It means the process in which language is not only maintained but also constantly created (von Krogh & Roos, 1995; von Krogh et al., 1996a). Languaging refers to a domain of consensual coordinations of action and it helps us to understand the development of organizational knowledge (Mingers, 1997). Through languaging knowledge brings forth a world (Maturana & Varela, 1987).

Luhmann claims that knowledge resides either in the individual psychic system or in a social system, but not in the interface. The social system functions according to its own laws and rules of interpretation. It is supported by individuals who belong to the environment of the social system. The social system observes, communicates, and understands itself. It has its own knowledge and rules of interpretation that are distinctive from the individual rules. Because Luhmann does not define the relationship between individual and social except by saying that the individual exists in the environment of the social, it is difficult to explain the dynamics between individual and social knowledge (von Krogh & Roos, 1995).

3. Organizational knowledge in autopoiesis. An organization can be regarded as a stream of knowledge in which distinctions are changing, new ones being created, and old ones being abandoned. Autopoietic knowledge is scalable, shared among organizational members, and connected to the organization's history (von Krogh & Roos, 1995; von Krogh et al., 1996a).

Nonaka and Takeuchi (1995) suggest that information is a flow of messages, and knowledge is created by that very flow of information. Knowledge is about beliefs and commitment, action, and meaning. Information and knowledge are context-specific and relational; they depend on situations and are created dynamically in social interaction among people.

5.3.2.2 Knowledge, information, and data in autopoiesis
In autopoiesis theory, information and knowledge refer to interpreted triggers (data or signals). "According to the firm's established distinctions and norms, it finds meaningful events, signs, and stimuli in its environment. The environment consists of facts, and the firm seeks and collects data about these facts in a very selective manner. Furthermore, it creates information from this

data through applying established norms and distinctions" (von Krogh & Vicari, 1993, p. 398). Organizational (internal) closure implies that an autopoietic system does not 'take in' input from its environment 'through a pipeline.' Instead, it treats signals as perturbations and compensates for them by changing internally and by making distinctions. Meaning is created through interpretation. "Information is not a pure fact ready to be processed in information systems. Information is very much dependent on the meaning structure or cognitive domain of the originator and receiver" (Mingers, 1995, p. 189).

5.3.2.3 Communication in autopoiesis In autopoiesis theory, communication does not mean transmission of information 'in a tube.' Instead, it takes place each time there is a behavioral coordination in a realm of structural coupling. It means coordinated behavior that is mutually triggered among members of the social system (Maturana & Varela, 1987). Communication is not about what is transmitted; rather, it is about what happens to the receiver. Since information is formed in the interpretation process, it cannot be transmitted like data and signals.

Luhmann emphasizes communication as a basic element in social systems. According to Luhmann, a social system does not consist of human beings or artifacts. Instead it consists of an ongoing stream of communication. It is a system of communication that creates its own unity, structure, and elements (Thyssen, 1995). Luhmann (1983) postulates that social systems in general are autopoietic and construct their own reality. Communication is an integrated synthesis of information, communicative action (utterance), and understanding. "Social systems use communication as their particular mode of autopoietic reproduction. Their elements are communications which are recursively produced and reproduced by a network of communications and which cannot exist outside of such network" (Luhmann in Bailey, 1994, p. 310).

5.3.3 Summary of Comparison between Cognitivist, Connectionist, and Autopoietic Notions of Knowledge

It can be concluded that the knowledge of a living organization is evolving, temporary, and relative, rather than final and absolute. It is evaluated by its explanatory power, as well as by its capability to enable adequate operating (for example, by viable procedures). The following table summarizes the characteristics of the cognitivist, connectionist, and autopoietic views of knowledge (see Table 5.4).

5.4 Specific Questions about Applying Autopoiesis Theory to Organizations

Autopoiesis theory is a theory of living systems. It has been developed within the fields of neurobiology and biological phenomenology. While it has received a position as a general system theory, it is necessary to critically evaluate the opportunities to apply its concepts in the domain of organizations. Therefore, this section will discuss in detail some specific questions about applying autopoiesis theory to organizations. It will first argue why organizations — and not only the 'brains' — can be regarded as autopoietic units in their

Table 5.4: Three approaches to knowledge.

Cognitivist view	Connectionist view	Autopoietic view
Knowledge represents the pre- given world (representationism) It enables problem-solving	Knowledge represents - the pre given world (representationism) It enables problem-solving	Knowledge is created, it is not a representation. Knowledge enables problem definition
Knowledge is universal and objective	Knowledge is emergent and history-dependent	Knowledge is emergent, history-dependent, self-referential and context-sensitive. It is communicated and has meaning
Knowledge is created through 'information processing', by using categories (knowledge structures) It resides in the individual and organizational memory	Knowledge emerges by using simple rules and a few representations. It resides in the brains of individuals and in the connections (learning rules) between them	Knowledge is based on distinction making through observation and experiencing. It is embodied in individuals as well as in the internal of 'structure' and distinctions of the organization
Knowledge can be transferred	Knowledge can be transferred	Knowledge can be communicated through structural and social coupling, but not transferred

Source: Based on Varela et al. (1993) and von Krogh and Roos (1995).

own right. Then it will review some alternative interpretations of autopoiesis theory in an organizational context.

5.4.1 Organizations — Living (Autopoietic) Systems in Their Own Right

According to Varela (1979), as long as the systemic requirements are met, there should be no limitations for extending the ideas of autonomy to the social realm. In fact, the theory of living systems can be applied in several ways to organizations, according to the kind of autopoiesis they incorporate (Mingers, 1997). However, applying the principles of self-production to organizations is a delicate task and the criteria of the six-point key have to be met, and attention should be paid to the specific nature of social systems as compared to biological systems.

The basic question is whether organizations should be seen as autopoietic entities in their own right. Three complementary approaches can be identified.

1. An organization is *a living (self-producing, autopoietic) system in its own right*. This approach regards organization as an observing system.
2. *Social autopoiesis*. This approach emphasizes communication among people, conversation, and language. Organization is regarded as an activity of many people.
3. An organization is part of a *business ecosystem*. This approach emphasizes the interaction and emergent properties among a population of organizations.

1. *Organization as an autopoietic entity in its own right*. An organization can be regarded as an autopoietic cognitive entity rather than a collection of individual brains (von Krogh & Vicari, 1993). It may observe, communicate, and understand itself and use its own knowledge and rules of interpretation that differ from those of any individual. The primacy of a social system over individuals opens up a new domain of investigation. This means that an organization is a system that carries its own knowledge and must be studied as such (von Krogh & Roos, 1995). "The firm is an autopoietic cognitive system and must be regarded as autonomous with respect to knowledge, creation of information, and the application of distinctions and norms. This autonomy stems from the self-referential characteristics of the firm" (Von Krogh & Vicari, 1993, p. 399). Also, Luhmann claims that a social system obeys its own rules. People who constitute its environment can only trigger the system. This approach also emphasizes the continual production of an organization's components in co-evolution with its environment.

Autopoiesis theory is compatible with Giddens' structuration theory that explains the relationship between the structure of rules/resources, the social system, and structuration (enabling and reproducing) (Mingers, 1995). It is also compatible with Bhaskar's (1989) critical realist explanation about the relationship between an individual and society. According to the transformational model of social activity, society is an ensemble of structures, practices, and conventions that individuals reproduce or transform.

2. *Social autopoiesis*. Social (third-order) autopoiesis refers to a variety of human organizations such as societies (Luhmann, 1990), clubs, and businesses (Mingers, 1995). They can vary from a formal and constant organization to an informal, haphazard, and temporary crowd of people. They are based on communication.

Organizations can be regarded as an activity of many people. A social system is a collection of interacting people who constitute a specific type of network of interactions and relations (Maturana in Mingers, 1995). Two elements are common to all definitions of 'social': activity of groups of entities rather than single individuals, and rule-based behavior rather than physical cause and effect (Mingers, 1995). Social autopoiesis emphasizes the production of communication, conversation, and language as well as new ways of organizing their interaction (such as communities). An organization is an arena for interacting humans who are regarded as living, self-producing systems (social autopoiesis, third-order autopoiesis). The organization itself is not analyzed into components.

Human beings are employed by the organization, but they do not constitute the whole organization. However, social communication has an important role for organizational learning and renewal capability. The social autopoiesis approach is relevant, for example, when investigating how organizations facilitate communication among people to increase knowledge sharing and creativity.

3. *Business ecosystem.* This approach means that several interacting organizations constitute a system that evolves according to the principles of complex adaptive systems. The business ecosystem approach helps to explain how an organization interacts reciprocally with its environment and as a part of that broader environment.

According to Peltoniemi (2004), business ecosystems exhibit complex behavior. They are characterized by shared fate, interconnectedness, self-organization, decentralized or shared control, co-operation, and competition. Absorptive innovation strategy has great potential for business ecosystems because it enhances co-evolutionary processes.

Conclusion. This book will focus on *an organization as a living system in its own right.* It will describe organization as a self-producing unit that is composed of components and boundaries of the organizational system. Moreover, the components and boundaries are defined as something else besides biological human beings. This means that while organizations are often regarded as social systems, the primary focus and main interpretation framework will not be the social functioning of an organization. Also, the business ecosystem perspective is used only marginally in this book because the focus here is not populations of organizations but individual organizations. However, these perspectives will be used as supplementary approaches when necessary. For example, connectivity and interdependence are needed to explain some phenomena, such as communities within the company. The concept of business ecosystem may explain the evolving larger context of the organization. Assuming that an organization is an observing system that produces its own components continually, autopoiesis theory helps with understanding organizational behavior, evolution, and learning.

5.4.2   Alternative Interpretations of Autopoiesis in an Organizational Context

If an organization is self-producing, what does it produce? Although the definition of autopoiesis refers to the production of components that constitute the entity and a boundary that separates the entity from its environment, "the definition does not specify that these must be physical components, but if they are not, then what precisely is their domain of existence?" (Mingers, 1995, pp. 120, 124).

Mingers differentiates several alternative ways to apply autopoiesis theory to organizations (1995).[6] The approaches contain assumptions about the autopoietic nature of an organization.

1. Autopoiesis theory can be applied *naively* to the social domain. This means that basic characteristics such as boundaries and the production of components remain unexplained.
2. Social systems *have characteristics of autopoiesis but they are not autopoietic as such.* These *autonomous* systems are characterized by organizational (internal) closure, autonomy, and structure dependence. They are without the specification of physical processes of component production.

3. Social systems are not themselves autopoietic, but they constitute *a medium where other autopoietic systems* (such as human beings) exist and interact within the consensual domain (Maturana).
4. Autopoiesis theory can be modified or enlarged to cover *non-physical production*. This means that it is possible to conceive non-physical systems such as games or computer-based models as autopoietic (Mingers, 1995, 1997; Varela, 1979).
5. Autopoiesis acts as a *metaphor*, without the ontological commitment that social systems are autopoietic (Morgan, 1986; Tsoukas, 1993).

There are thus several ways that autopoiesis theory may be applied to organizations. The mode of application is important because claiming that an organization is truly autopoietic, and not just metaphorically so, raises significant ontological issues (Mingers, 1995). In metaphorical applications, basic characteristics of autopoietic systems such as boundaries, the production of components, organizational closure, autonomy, and structure dependence may be asserted, but do not specify the processes of component production.

Conclusion. The interpretation and model presented in this book goes beyond metaphor to propose that *an organization can be a living (self-producing, autopoietic) system in the true sense of autopoiesis.* This approach regards an organization as an observing system that co-evolves with its complex environment — its *business ecosystem.* An organization may improve its possibilities for co-evolution by creating and utilizing boundary elements.

This book will build on the assumption that autopoiesis theory also explains organizational *non-physical, autopoietic production.* This conclusion will be discussed further in Chapter 6.

5.5 Summary

Autopoiesis theory is a relational theory and it emphasizes the dependence of the observer and the focus and level of observation. When we focus on learning and renewal processes, an organization is autonomous and controlled by its internal structure. When we focus on production (transformation) processes, *the control approach* can be used where the environment (input to the organization) largely determines the system's functioning.

Living (autopoietic) systems can be identified by using the six-point key. The most important criteria for a living system, and thereby also for organizations, are the following:

- The system is contained within and produces a boundary.
- The system is maintained by the interactions of its components.
- The system's modus operandi is a dynamic network of interacting processes of autopoietic 'production.'

Autopoietic systems are a subset and a special case of autonomous systems in that autopoietic systems also produce themselves by continually producing their own components and boundaries.

Autopoietic systems, such as organizations, are *organizationally closed.* This means that all possible states of activity must lead to or generate further activity within the autonomous system itself.

A living organization (an autopoietic system) is *open to its environment* in a specific way. Perturbations (triggers) can only stimulate, but not instruct or control processes in the organization, which follows its self-defined rules. Perturbations may lead to *compensations* in the internal 'structure' of a system.

Structural coupling refers to an organization's mutual, reciprocal interactions and co-evolution with its environment.

Living systems can be classified into three types according to the kind of autopoiesis they incorporate.

- *First-order autopoiesis* explains the principles of a self-producing, living system.
- *Second-order autopoiesis* explains structural coupling between living systems.
- *Third-order autopoiesis* explains structural coupling between organisms (e.g. social systems, human societies).

Many of the earlier interpretations focus on second- and third-order autopoiesis, concentrating on interaction among people and viewing organizations as social systems. This book selects, however, a different approach and analyzes organization as a living, self-producing system in its own right.

An autopoietic system produces new *knowledge* by creating distinctions. The distinctions are 'stored' in internal components and structures.

Autopoietic systems are *self-referential*. They make reference to or directly impact themselves. *Self-organization* is sometimes mistakenly used as an equivalent for *self-production* (autopoiesis).

The objective of this book is that its theoretical approach (autopoiesis theory) and the assumptions presented about the reality and knowledge/knowing of organizations are consistent, and that the assumptions do not collide with two major philosophical paradigms. Therefore a shared domain was defined in this chapter.

Many earlier interpretations focus on one component only. It is also possible to identify non-physical components. The living composition model will be based on the idea of several different non-physical components.

Notes

1. "The organization of a living system can be described as a closed network of productions of components that through their interactions constitute the network of productions that produce them, and specify its extension by constituting its boundaries in their domain of existence" (Maturana in Mingers, 1997, p. 305).
2. In autopoiesis theory, the concepts *'organization'* and *'structure'* of a system have a specific meaning. 'Organization' refers to an idea (such as an idea of airplane or a company in general). 'Structure' refers to the actual embodiment of the idea (such as a specific airplane or a specific company). Thus, 'organization' is abstract but 'structure' is concrete (Mingers, 1997). Over time an autopoietic system may change its components and structure but maintain its 'organization.' In this case, the system sustains its identity. If a system's 'organization' changes, it loses its current identity (von Krogh & Roos, 1995).
3. "The act of indicating any being, object, thing or unity involves making an *act of distinction*, which distinguishes what has been indicated as separate from its background. Each time we refer

to anything explicitly or implicitly, we are specifying a *criterion of distinction*, which indicates what we are talking about and specifies its properties as being, unity, or object" (Maturana & Varela, 1987, p. 40).

4. See 'self-referentiality' in the glossary, Appendix 1.

5. Stafford Beer: *The Heart of Enterprise* (1979), *Brain of the Firm* (1981), and *Diagnosing the System for Organizations* (1985). Chichester: Wiley.

6. According to Mingers (1995), alternatives 2 and 3 could be promising ways to apply autopoiesis theory in the context of social organizations.

Chapter 6

The Living Composition Model

Based on the previous analysis, this chapter will formulate the living composition model, the model of living organizations that is the central idea of this book.[1] First this chapter will specify the basic principles of living composition. Then it will present the definition of the model. The model will be applied empirically to the case organizations in Chapters 10–14.

6.1 Basic Principles

This section will present the basic ideas of the living composition model. It will combine the selected approach of applying autopoiesis to organizations with the definition of strategic components and two major knowledge flows into a comprehensive, specified model of living organizations. The particular contribution of this book is the definition of ten non-physical strategic components and their positioning, of them and the idea of living composition into the center of an interpretation of organizational self-production processes. This section also introduces the concept of boundary element as a new interpretation of organizational boundaries. The ten strategic components will be defined in detail in Chapter 7. The two major knowledge flows will be analyzed oin a detailed level in Chapter 8.

6.1.1 Organization as a Living System in its Own Right

As was concluded in Chapter 5, this book will focus on an organization as a living system in its own right. It will describe organization as a self-producing unit that is composed of components and boundaries of the organizational system. Moreover, the components and boundaries are defined as something besides biological human beings.

The objective is to show that the living composition satisfies the requirements of the six-point key that defines the necessary characteristics for a living, self-producing system. Since there is no general agreement on the relationship between autopoiesis and various dimensions of 'life' (physical, abstract/non-physical, computer-generated, [2]spiritual, and other forms of life), it is sufficient to assume here that organizations can be autopoietic and in that sense 'living'. Thereby it is not necessary to take here final position on what 'life' means, and whether autopoiesis is a necessary or sufficient condition for defining 'life'.

A living organization can be defined as an organization that produces its own components and boundaries and renews itself in a way that allows the continuous maintenance of its integrity. The living composition model is an interpretation of autopoiesis theory in the context of organizations. It provides a specified model of the components and their characteristics that enable learning and renewal of an organization.

6.1.2 Non-physical Components

If an organization is self-producing, what does it produce? In general, the concept of production has been problematic when attempting to apply autopoiesis theory to organizations. Although the definition of autopoiesis mentions the production of components that constitute the entity, and a boundary that separates the entity from its environment, the definition does not specify that these must be physical components: but if they are not, then what precisely is their domain of existence? (Mingers, 1995). As was presented earlier, the components of an autopoietic system can also be non-physical components.

This book regards organizations as non-physical autopoietic entities, which implies that non-physical components and boundaries must be defined. The production of material and biological boundaries and components does not belong to the domain of organizational autopoietic production.

6.1.3 Several Components

Some earlier interpretations of autopoietic organizations emphasize only one scaled component, such as communication or money (Luhmann, 1990, 1983), value (Vicari, 1991), or conversations (von Krogh & Roos, 1996b). The view that a company produces itself as an autopoietic entity by continually producing its own components indicates that it is necessary to specify several components that differ from each other.

The richness of organizational solutions and behavior remains unexplained if only one characteristic, such as communication, is viewed as the sole component of autopoietic production. Thus, claiming that a company produces itself as a self-producing entity requires specifying the nature of the components it produces for itself. A similar view is presented by Mingers (1995).

Varela (1979) warns against defining autopoietic unities (such as a firm) as mere composites of lower-level autopoietic systems (such as human beings) without defining the relations of production of the resulting unit. Individual persons who act in organizations are not components of the organization's renewal system because they are not produced as a part of that process. Instead, they are connected indirectly to the organizational process through their boundary roles, task definitions, careers, and participation in the workflows.

6.1.4 Specification of Ten Strategic Components

This book will introduce several different components. Moreover, this book will investigate organizations as non-physical autopoietic entities, which implies that the components and boundaries are also non-physical.

The living composition model is based on the assumption that an organization evolves by producing its strategic components as simultaneous tracks in an interacting pattern. Ten strategic components have been identified as constituting the living composition of an organization. They have a central role in the evolutionary capability of an organization. Preliminary ideas of potential components included generally known key characteristics of autopoietic systems, such as identity, triggers, knowledge (distinctions), and boundaries. These basic entities were supplemented by ideas concerning consistency among a system's components. In addition, the simultaneity of openness and closure in autopoietic systems was interpreted in the organizational context as practical solutions that facilitate sensing (interactive openness) and memory (self-referentiality) of an organization. A preliminary model of living composition was tested in a pilot project at PBS (Danish Payment Systems Ltd.) in Denmark. Feedback from managers suggested that the basic idea and structure of the composition were useful but that further specification of the components was needed. An improved model was then used as a basis for interviewing managers and consultants in four case companies: Arthur Andersen (Business Consulting), Arthur D. Little (Europe), Ernst & Young (Management Consulting) and The KaosPilots and KaosManagement. The purpose of the case analysis was to test and improve the model. The interviews were taped, and the interview material as well as other company related data were analyzed by using qualitative-analysis software. Because this analysis revealed new aspects that were relevant for an organization's learning and renewal capability, some components were further subdivided and the definitions of the components were further refined (Maula, 1999).

The strategic components of the living composition model are:

1. Identity
2. Perception of the environment
3. Strategy
4. Knowledge (distinctions)
5. Boundary elements
6. Interactive processes and communication with the environment (structural and social coupling externally)
7. Triggers/perturbations (exposure to triggers)
8. Experimentation
9. Internal standards, processes, and communication (structural and social coupling internally)
10. Information and communication systems.

6.1.5   Boundaries Defined as Boundary Elements

Boundary elements include various embedded roles and functions that enable the mutual, reciprocal interaction between an organization and its environment. They may also consist of advanced socio-technical solutions.

6.1.6   Specification of Two Major Knowledge Flows

Living organizations are characterized by *interactive openness* that coordinates an organization with its environment, and by *organizational (internal) closure* that maintains an organization's functioning. These characteristics are interconnected and simultaneous. They provide the sensing capability and memory of an organization that are facilitated by interconnected information flows. Living organizations compensate for environmental perturbations by changing internally, whereby knowledge is accumulated as changes in an organization's internal structures. The strategic components are defined so that their production and interaction facilitate sensing (interactive openness) and memory (organizational/internal closure, self-referentiality) of an organization. In-depth analysis and further specification of the knowledge flows will be presented in Chapter 8.

6.2   The Definition of the Living Composition Model

Based on the principles of autopoiesis theory, this section will define the living composition model that has been created to explain the enabling structure and dynamics of a living (autopoietic, self-producing) organization. The model is a new original interpretation of autopoiesis theory. It specifies the characteristics of living organizations and aims ato explaining their evolution, learning, and renewal dynamics. The living composition model holds that organizations satisfy certain specified requirements of a living, autopoietic system, such as the continual production of an organization's components in co-evolution with its environment. These requirements can be summarized as a 'six-point key'. The model describes an organization's major components and knowledge flows. In the living composition model, organizations produce their own non-physical strategic components and boundary elements in a continuous manner. The components and their relationships constitute a composition that has emerged partly as a result of drift and partly through organizational design.

Definition of the living composition model is as follows:

> *The living composition model* specifies the essential characteristics of living organizations. A living organization is a self-producing (autopoietic) system that is composed of ten different non-physical strategic components. Boundary elements are included as one component type. The living composition model describes the 'structure' of a living organization in which the strategic components and their interrelationships determine an organization's evolutionary capability. An organization evolves by continually producing its strategic components as simultaneous tracks with a pattern of interactions. The production and interaction of the components and their relationships facilitate sensing (interactive openness) and memory (organizational/internal closure) in an organization. Sensing and memory are simultaneous and interconnected phenomena. They enable both an organization's current efficiency and its capability to learn, to renew itself, and to co-evolve with its changing environment within its larger business ecosystem.

This new, original interpretation about an organization as a self-producing, living system is based on three major ideas. First, the interpretation proposes that the *evolutionary capability of a living organization is derived from the functioning of its living composition*. It has previously been problematic determining the components that are produced in an organizational self-production process. In this book, that problem has been solved by defining the components, including the boundary elements that constitute the living composition. Second, *a successful organization is likely to have found ways to utilize the complexity phenomena of self-organization and emergence through its living composition.* For example, an organization may utilize self-organizing teams and empowerment. It may create new knowledge, increase diversity, facilitate communication and knowledge sharing, and establish processes that are less controlled, such as communities that connect people and ideas, thereby facilitating creativity. Third, *a living organization improves its chances for co-evolving with its complex environment within its business ecosystem by creating and utilizing boundary elements.* Moreover, an organization's method to evolve can be evaluated, compared to other organizations, and developed further by using *consistency/intentionality platforms and evolution models.*

Living organizations are characterized by *sensing (condition for interactive openness)* that coordinates the organization with its environment, and by memory (*a feature of organizational closure*) that maintains the organization's functioning. These characteristics are interconnected and simultaneous. They are facilitated by interconnected information flows. The boundary elements enable sensing activities. Living organizations compensate for environmental perturbations by changing internally, whereby knowledge is accumulated as changes take place in an organization's internal 'structure'. The following Figure 6.1 visualizes the living composition model by presenting the relationship between sensing, memory, and boundary elements.

The following Figure 6.2 depicts the living composition, the structured and specified model of living organizations. It summarizes the strategic components and major knowledge flows.

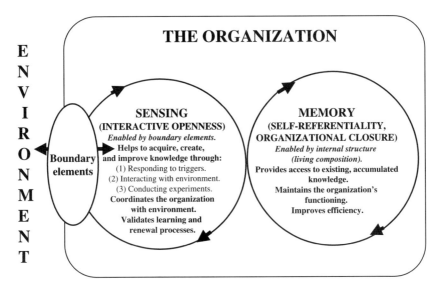

Figure 6.1: Sensing and memory — The two major knowledge flows of a living organization.

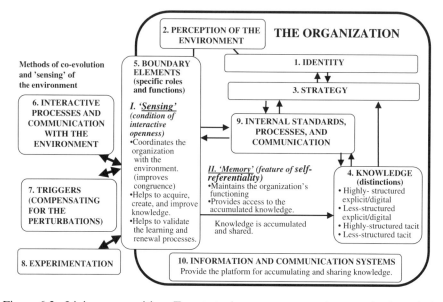

Figure 6.2: Living composition: Ten strategic components and two major knowledge flows of a living organization.

Autopoiesis theory is a neutral theory. It describes the conditions and pattern for a systemic behavior called autopoiesis that is not good or bad as such. It does not say whether longevity is good or bad, either. The living composition model is also a basically neutral model. It attempts to identify aspects that can strengthen or weaken an organization's self-production, survival, and success in its environment. The different types of consistency among strategic components — intentional fit, stretch, emergent fit, and misfit — *represent different types of living composition.*

The model of living organizations is a process model that discovers conditions for a sustainable process (creativity, learning, and evolution as a self-production process). It is not a factor model that would define a specific outcome and conditions for it.

Some aspects that are generally known to influence organizational longevity are not taken into account in the model of living organizations. Examples of them are conservatism in decision-making (de Geus, 1997a, b), financial decision-making, and the allocation of resources.

6.3 Summary

The main contribution of this book, the living composition model is defined as follows:

> The living composition model specifies the essential characteristics of living organizations. A living organization is a self-producing (autopoietic) system that is composed of ten different non-physical strategic components.

Boundary elements are included as one component type. The living composition model describes the 'structure' of a living organization in which the strategic components and their interrelationships determine an organization's evolutionary capability. An organization evolves by continually producing its strategic components as simultaneous tracks with a pattern of interactions. The production and interaction of the components and their relationships facilitate sensing (interactive openness) and memory (organizational/internal closure) in an organization. Sensing and memory are simultaneous and interconnected phenomena. They enable both an organization's current efficiency and its capability to learn, to renew itself, and to co-evolve with its changing environment within its larger business ecosystem.

The strategic components and two major knowledge flows (sensing and memory) will be described in details in the following chapters.

Notes

1. Parts of this and the previous chapters have been published earlier in Maula (1999, 2000a).
2. Varela (1979, p. 54) includes as autopoietic systems models that satisfy the criteria of topological (self-defined) boundary as well as production processes that occur in physical-like space, actual or simulated on a computer.

Chapter 7

Strategic Components of a Living Organization

Further Specification of the Strategic Components. The living composition of an organization consists of ten different non-physical strategic components. This chapter will define the strategic components in the light of previous chapters and reviews of additional literature. The properties of and relationships among these strategic components determine their interactions and transformations in the dynamic network of interacting processes of autopoietic self-production. Their interactions maintain an organization's functioning, learning, renewal, and co-evolution with its environment.

This chapter refers to the case organizations that are presented fully in Chapters 11–14. The summarizing description of the case firms' strategic components will be presented in Chapter 15. The analysis shows that while strategic components can be identified in the case firms, there is a significant variation among them. The components participate in the self-production process, and they are continually produced as a part of that process.

Drawing primarily on the general characteristics of autopoiesis theory and secondarily on the analysis of the case companies, the following ten strategic components have been identified as constituting the strategic composition of an organization:

1. *Identity* means that an organization (system) maintains the integrity of its 'structure' and can be distinguished from the background and other units (von Krogh & Roos, 1995).
2. *Perception of the environment* means that living organizations create knowledge about their environment according to their own internal rules.
3. *Strategy* helps to operationalize visions and objectives into internal standards and processes. It is based on identity, perception of the environment, and other relevant aspects.
4. *Knowledge (distinctions) facilitates and regulates* an organization's self-production process.
5. *Boundary elements* include various embedded roles and functions that enable the reciprocal interaction between an organization and its environment.[1] Boundary elements enable sensing (interactive openness) by identifying triggers, by reciprocal interaction, and by experimentation.
6. *Interactive processes (structural and social coupling externally)* include the methods used to communicate reciprocally with the environment and to influence co-evolution, for example with clients. They also include social coupling that refers to *communication among individuals externally.*
7. *Triggers (exposure to triggers, compensating for perturbations)* are perturbations that may lead to compensations in an organization's 'structure'. Triggers are not inputs to the organization *per se.* An organization can also be triggered internally.
8. *Experimentation* helps an organization to create new knowledge and learn about its environment through successes and failures. A company can shift from adaptive rational learning to experimental learning in order to facilitate learning and knowledge creation (Vicari et al., 1996; von Krogh & Roos, 1995).

9. *Internal standards, processes, and communication (structural and social coupling internally)* include various elements that influence motivation and the capability to learn, such as production processes, career structure, task definitions, and education — all of which occur in firm-specific 'packages'. They also include social coupling that refers to *communication among individuals internally.*

10. *Information and communication systems* may include a variety of more or less structured information systems.

The relationships between components enable the functioning of an organization. For example, the boundary elements, interactive processes, internal standards, processes, and communication influence each other. This can be illustrated by the metaphor of a restaurant. In the dining room, serving a dinner to a client is guided by a menu which represents the restaurant's standards. The client's choices and the schedule and process of the dinner are defined in the interactive process between the client and the waiter. The role of the waiter represents one of the restaurant's boundary elements. What happens in the kitchen has another logic that includes purchasing the raw materials, communicating between the waiter and cook, preparing and serving the dishes, and washing up. These processes represent internal coupling, internal standards, processes, and communication. In a good restaurant these two processes, interaction with the client and internal processes, are seamlessly integrated. The waiter participates in his/her boundary role simultaneously in these two processes. In a similar way, organizations co-ordinate their interaction with its environment with their internal processes through boundary roles. In the consulting industry, for example, interaction with clients has become increasingly important because process-oriented approaches have largely replaced the fact-based, directive consulting modes (Kubr, 1996). The internal processes have also become increasingly important because of global competition and the need to improve knowledge, competence, and efficiency.

7.1   Identity

The identity of a living system means that a system maintains the integrity of its 'structure' and can be distinguished from the background and other units (von Krogh & Roos, 1995). Living systems have an identity because they are composite systems, characterized by an organizational closure. Such a system subordinates all perturbations and changes, including the controlling inputs from its environment, to the maintenance of its identity (Varela, 1979). Here identity refers also to the way the organization defines itself, its history, mission, and essential characterizing features.

The image, company culture, and other qualitative characteristics have an impact on an organization's evolutionary path. While the case companies have *maintained their identity as a composition* of a specific living organization, they have purposely *altered their image* through transformations in order to improve their competitiveness.

7.2   Perception of the Environment

Perception of the environment in this context means that living organizations respond to triggers (perturbations) and create distinctions (knowledge) about their environment according to their own internal rules.

It is not possible to describe an organization's environment objectively. Instead, it is relevant to investigate the *organization's perception of its environment*, for example through strategies, reports, brochures, and employees' perceptions. This approach is faithful to the theory of autopoiesis, which says that living systems interpret triggers and create knowledge according to their own internal rules. It supplements earlier studies about perceiving the environment (Pfeffer & Salancik, 1978; Daft & Weick, 1994). Moreover, it is also in line with the common domain defined in Chapter 5, which says that we cannot verify whether our knowledge really represents reality because we do not have direct access to that reality. The perception of the environment has implications for:

1. What is necessary to learn and change for an organization and an individual
2. What is possible to learn and change
3. How to organize learning and renewal.

Perceiving the world as rapidly changing may lead to two different and complementary reactions. An organization can respond to the changes by improving its knowledge about its environment (interactive openness) and/or by changing itself (structural change). In both cases, the perception of the environment becomes continually reproduced as a component of the self-production process. However, it cannot be guaranteed that the perception is correct or even relevant.

7.3 Strategy

Strategy is a pattern or plan that integrates an organization's major goals, policies, and action sequences into a cohesive whole (Quinn, 1996). The objective of a strategy is to help operationalize visions and objectives into internal standards and processes. It is based on identity, perception of the environment, and other relevant aspects.

Mintzberg (1996) characterizes strategy as five Ps: strategy is a plan, a ploy, a pattern, a position, and a perspective. He also differentiates between intended, deliberate, unrealized, emergent, and realized strategies. An intended strategy refers to a plan or a specific ploy. However, only some of the intentions may become realized (deliberate strategy) and some others may go unrealized (unrealized strategy), while a pattern in a stream of actions may emerge without preconception (emergent strategy). Deliberate and emergent strategies constitute the realized strategy.

According to Sanchez and Heene (2004), *strategic management* is the process that defines an organization's goals for value creation and distribution and designs the way an organization will be composed, structured, and co-ordinated in pursuing these goals.

7.4 Knowledge and Knowledge Management

As Chapter 5 revealed, the concept of *knowledge* is central to living organizations. This section will further discuss the role of knowledge and knowledge management for organizations.

A learning organization is skilled at creating, acquiring, and transferring knowledge, and at modifying its behavior to reflect new knowledge and insights (Garvin, 1993). According to Sanchez (1997), there are three different components of organizational knowledge. 'State-knowledge' (know-how) is practical understanding that enables producing and refining activities. 'Process-knowledge (know-why) is theoretical understanding that enables adaptation and development. 'Purpose-knowledge' (know-what) is strategic understanding that enables imagining activities.

Knowledge can be defined as a capacity for making distinctions that enable an effective or adequate behavior in a given context (Maturana & Varela, 1987). New distinctions made, in turn, enable the development of knowledge (von Krogh & Roos, 1995). In this way, knowledge (the ability to make useful distinctions) facilitates and regulates the autopoietic self-production process.

Firms as living organizations are autopoietic cognitive systems that are autonomous with respect to knowledge, creation of information, and application of distinctions and norms (Vicari, 1991; von Krogh & Vicari, 1993). Instead of being a mere end result of a knowledge creation process, knowledge is a component of the autopoietic process (Maturana & Varela, 1987) and an essential component in a continuous organization-wide learning and renewal process that aims at survival and evolution. In this sense, an organization can be regarded as a stream of knowledge that drives a continuous re-creation of knowledge (von Krogh et al., 1996b). Autopoiesis therefore requires theories of knowing rather than theories of knowledge, and concepts of a system of knowing activity rather than notions of applications of abstract knowledge (Blackler, 1995; Spender & Grant, 1996).

Knowledge is created in response to stimulation or disturbance from the environment or by endogenous structural change. It is embodied in the organization's internal 'structure' in the form of improved distinctions, in changes in its ten components, and in their relationships. Organizational knowledge depends largely on the experiences of individual people, and it is formed through actions, perceptions, and sensory and motor processes (von Krogh & Roos, 1995). Exposure and sensitivity to the environment, boundary elements, and work processes influence the availability of new experiences for individuals. Knowledge flows commonly extend beyond geographic, temporal, hierarchical, functional, and organizational boundaries. Networking among employees at all levels of the organization is more relevant for the global accumulation and sharing of knowledge than conventional formal communication, such as vertical and horizontal knowledge flows among subsidiaries and headquarters. In the organizations studied as cases here, knowledge flows among employees, teams, and global knowledge bases rather than between organizational units.

Several earlier studies emphasize language and conversations between organizational members (von Krogh & Roos, 1995; Vicari et al., 1996). Interpretation has an increasing role in organizations (Mingers & Stowell, 1997), and language can be used to manage knowledge (von Krogh et al., 1996a). As to information systems, self-referentiality, communication, and action have an increasingly important role (Hirschheim et al., 1995).

7.4.1   The Management of Knowledge

Knowledge is a strategic factor of production and it supplements the traditional factors of labor, land, and capital. *Knowledge management* therefore increasingly draws attention. However, it is not a clear concept, due to the different origins of offered solutions.

According to Essers and Schreinemakers (1996), it is not possible to differentiate between knowledge management and information management by differentiating between knowledge and information. Instead, they can be differentiated by their objectives. *Information management* is historically a part of the control-inspired managerial ideology that aims to decrease freedom of choice (uncertainty) by providing an answer to a question or a solution to a problem. *Knowledge management* attempts to increase alternatives. It attempts to manage "... the incommensurability and difference between rivaling mental models that are operative within and between organizations [which] is of paramount importance to their creativity and ability to learn" (p. 103). This means that while information management reduces the freedom of choice, knowledge management increases it.

'*Managing knowledge*' can be differentiated from knowledge management. 'Managing knowledge' includes, for example, the methods to create favorable conditions for communication and the creation of knowledge (von Krogh & Roos, 1996a). A firm's method of managing its knowledge has implications for its organizational structure. Effective knowledge management takes into account various characteristics, such as employment systems, career patterns, and organization structure (Hedlund, 1994). Because knowledge flows depend on several aspects such as an organization's identity and perception of the environment, the nature of services, workflows and tasks, boundary elements, and ICT systems, the management of knowledge is related to *managing the living composition*.

This book identifies *two major knowledge flows* that enable the sensing and memory of an organization. The management of knowledge includes the creation and maintenance of the solutions and other conditions that enable these knowledge flows. The two major knowledge flows will be presented in more detail in Chapter 8.

This book also differentiates *four parallel knowledge processes*. The management of knowledge in this case refers to the identification of different knowledge types in an organization, and the creation and maintenance of the solutions and other conditions that enable these knowledge processes. The four parallel knowledge processes will be discussed in Chapter 9.

7.5   Boundary Elements

It is a common understanding that in the business environment, which is characterized by cross-border communication and networking, organizational boundaries are disappearing or at least becoming lower or blurred. On the other hand, increasing pressure to outsource activities has forced firms to reconsider and specify the boundaries of the firm, and consider also the formal, contractual basis that defines ownership and various kinds of responsibilities. In the theory of living systems, boundary has a slightly different meaning since it is related to the identity, self-production processes, and co-evolution of the living system.

To be considered a living system requires that an organization has identifiable *boundaries* and that it is capable of continually producing a boundary, but does not require an explicit definition of the boundary or require specific boundary elements. For example, Mingers (1995) simply suggests that the components involved must create a boundary defining the entity as a unity — that is, a whole interacting with its environment. Luhmann (1990) defines social systems as recursively closed systems with respect to communications, and boundaries are identified by the limits of the interactions of people. Boundary can also be defined as the fundamental distinction between the system and its environment, although the nature of the distinction can vary with time and location. For example, in organizations as systems, "the boundary is created by individuals' knowledge pertaining to the organization–environment criterion. Each individual will form his or her own boundaries of the organization and recreate these dynamically as a part of their individual knowledge base" (von Krogh & Roos, 1995, p. 57). In this sense, the autopoietic notion of boundary differs fundamentally from various atomistic notions of boundaries in the theories of firm.

A living (autopoietic) system is a unity contained within and producing an identifiable boundary. The living composition model holds that in the context of organizations the boundary consists of non-physical *boundary elements* that connect the organization with its environment and enable interaction with it. They enable and maintain the reciprocal interaction and co-evolution between the organization and its environment.[2] They enable sensing of the environment.

The living composition model holds that an organization's learning and renewal is enabled by boundary elements that are defined as various *roles and functions*. They can be embedded in employees and other persons, groups, units, or information and communication systems. They may also consist of other kinds of advanced socio-technical solutions embodied in roles and functions. For example, a project manager role can be embedded in various persons within an organization. Project managers interact with clients, acquire experiences, and accumulate new knowledge about projects into a global knowledge base. Such roles (but not the physical persons themselves) are continually produced by the self-producing, autopoietic organization.

An organization can be connected to its environment in various ways, and therefore the term 'boundary element' includes many ways to constitute boundaries. For example, roles and functions can be permanent or temporary, and they can be embedded in various ways. In contrast, 'boundary spanner', a familiar concept in organizational research, has an established meaning that is not directly related to self-production (e.g. Scott, 1992), because 'boundary spanner' is associated primarily with individuals and not with roles, functions, or information systems.

Therefore 'boundary' here does not refer to the separation of the organization and its resources from its environment. Instead the living composition model emphasizes the active interaction of boundary elements — roles and functions — with the environment, leading to an organization's capability to absorb and create new knowledge. Boundary elements act like connecting absorption surfaces between an organization and its environment (Sivula, van den Bosch, & Elfring, 1997; Maula, 2000a). This potential has not been thoroughly investigated in earlier interpretations of autopoiesis theory, because many of them have focused on isolation (organizational closure) rather than connection and absorption. The findings of this study support the conclusions that the ability to manage the interface between internal and external networks becomes increasingly important for multinational service companies (Campbell & Verbeke, 1996). While the network approach to organizations implies that boundaries are disappearing, the self-production approach indicates that their importance as absorbing and proactive boundaries is increasing, because they enable and facilitate co-evolution and acquisition of new knowledge for the organization.

7.6   Interactive Processes and Communication

Interactive processes (structural and social coupling externally) include the methods used to communicate reciprocally and co-evolve with the environment, for example with clients. They also include social coupling that refers to communication with individuals in the external environment of the organization.

Knowledge flows and knowledge flow patterns connect a firm's units and employees and facilitate interaction internally and with its environment (Gupta & Govindarajan, 1993; Hedlund, 1993). The processes must satisfy both internal and external requirements simultaneously.

7.7   Triggers (Exposure to Triggers)

A living organization accepts *triggers* only as perturbations that may lead to compensations in its 'structure'. It does not treat them as input to the organization. An organization can also be triggered internally.

Living organizations treat all triggers in relation to their own identity, survival, and evolution. They interpret all signals and other inputs from the environment as perturbations that potentially lead to compensations in their own system.

Triggers facilitate changes. The triggers themselves are not reproduced by the system, but exposure to the triggers and the capability to respond to them is. Organizations can increase the utilization of perturbations, for example, through interaction and communication with the environment, by improving exposure and sensitivity to triggers, and by experimenting. The case firms continually reproduce their potential to be perturbed and to respond to triggers. For example, Arthur Andersen multiplies the 'disturbing' impact of triggers by accumulating and sharing them globally through the Global Best Practices and by facilitating changes in the organization.

7.8   Experimentation

Experimentation is a strategic component that helps an organization to create new knowledge and learn about its environment through successes and failures. A company can shift from adaptive rational learning to experimental learning in order to facilitate learning and knowledge creation (Vicari et al., 1996; von Krogh & Roos, 1995).

7.9   Internal Standards, Processes, and Communication

Internal standards, processes, and communication (structural and social coupling internally) may include various elements that influence the motivation and capability to learn, such as production processes, career structure, task definitions, internal communication, and education. They constitute firm-specific packages.

As the earlier restaurant example indicated, internal standards, processes, and communication constitute a multifaceted strategic component that is integrated with the methods to interact with the environment.

7.10   Information and Communication Systems

Information and communication systems may include a variety of more or less structured digital information systems. The analysis of the case companies indicates that these systems may have a central role in enabling the integrated sensing and memory of an organization.

According to Hirschheim et al. (1995), the debate about information systems development has recently taken a new turn. It emphasizes communication among people. "For self-referential (-) systems, either communication or action are the fundamental building blocks and this differs from the 'elements' and sub-systems as typically defined in engineering and natural sciences. Recent systems theory makes clear ontological distinctions between machines, organisms, social and psychic systems" (p. 236). The social autopoiesis interpretation is compatible with a language/action approach to information systems that is based on conversations and commitment (Lyytinen & Klein, 1985). A study of the information systems' discipline concludes that the importance of organizational behavior and culture has been recently recognized, and there is a move toward interpretivism (Mingers & Stowell, 1997). Autopoiesis theory has contributed to the ideas and development of sophisticated technical solutions such as enabling network systems.

7.11   Summary

The living composition is composed of ten strategic components that are produced as simultaneous tracks in an interacting pattern. They are:

1. Identity
2. Perception of the environment
3. Strategy
4. Knowledge (distinctions)
5. Boundary elements
6. Interactive processes and communication with the environment (structural and social coupling externally)
7. Triggers/perturbations (exposure to triggers)
8. Experimentation
9. Internal standards, processes, and communication (structural and social coupling internally)
10. Information and communication systems.

The strategic components and relationships among them enable the two major knowledge flows in the functioning of an organization.

Notes

1. Boundary elements are regarded as special kinds of components. They are continually reproduced in the autopoietic process.
2. Boundary elements are included as components because they are continually reproduced in the autopoietic process.

Chapter 8

Two Major Knowledge Flows — 'Sensing' and 'Memory'

Knowledge flows have a crucial role in the reproduction of organizational structures (Tuomi, 1996). However, it is not clear how knowledge flows should be defined. This chapter will elaborate the idea that maintaining a living organization requires processes of *sensing* (a condition for interactive openness) and *memory* (a feature of self-referentiality, internal closure), each of which constitutes a major knowledge flow. Sensing and memory are likely to be a simultaneous and interconnected phenomena. Sensing helps to coordinate the functioning of an organization within its environment, while memory maintains an organization's capacity for autopoietic functioning and facilitates efficiency.

First, this chapter analyzes the concepts of openness and closure. The emphasis will not be on organizations as open systems or closed systems, but rather on the variables that describe openness and closure in general. Then this chapter will introduce the two major knowledge flows, sensing and memory, that are part of the original interpretation of autopoiesis theory in this book. This chapter also emphasizes the importance of interconnecting sensing and memory. Some specific questions about openness and closure are also addressed in Appendix 4.

8.1 Openness and Closure

This section will focus on two variables, openness and closure, that are generally regarded as characteristics of a system. The purpose here is to analyze the nature of these variables and their combinations in order to understand the nature of closure and openness in autopoietic systems. Moreover, the purpose is to understand the theoretical basis of the functioning of living systems and the major knowledge flows. The assumption here is that openness is not the same as open system, and closure is not the same as closed system. The primary purpose is therefore not to analyze the nature of open or closed systems, or the nature of an organization as an open system, but to prepare the reader for understanding the specific nature of simultaneous interactive openness and internal closure in the context of self-producing systems, such as firms. It is important to note that openness and closure are *neutral and analytical system concepts* that explain certain characteristics of a system's behavior and should not be associated with any value judgments.

Openness and closure can be described by two dimensions, boundary and feedback.[1] In a very simplistic interpretation they could have the following values:

1. *Boundary* of the system is closed (closure) or open (openness).
2. *Feedback* exists (closed feedback) or is missing (the system is open).

Table 8.1:   Boundary and feedback and four resulting system alternatives.

		FEEDBACK	
		Internal closure self-referentiality	**Feedback loop via the external environment 'open feedback'**
	Open boundary through input or interaction (interactive openness, co-evolution)	1. *Connected system (open and closed)* Open (open boundary) Closed (internal closure)	2. *Open system (double open)* Open (open boundary) Open ('open feedback' via the environment)
BOUNDARY	**Closed boundary, no input, no interaction**	3. *Isolated system (double closed)* Closed (closed boundary) Closed (internal closure)	4. *Passive system (closed and open)* Closed (closed boundary) Open ('open feedback' via the environment (but no effect))

It can also be assumed that boundary and feedback may represent degrees of openness and closure. Openness does not only mean receiving input but also proactive interaction and co-evolution with the environment. Moreover, it can be assumed that feedback exists always in one way or another, in a shorter or longer period, directly or indirectly even if it may be difficult to identify. Therefore the characterization above will be redefined as follows:

1. *Boundary.* The boundary is closed (closure; no input or interaction) or open (interactive openness through open interaction and co-evolution with the environment).
2. *Feedback.* The system is characterized by self-referentiality and internal closure (internal closure) or by feedback loops via the external environment ('open feedback' through external closure).[2]

The combinations of the two variables and their values result in four theoretical alternatives that are presented in Table 8.1.

1. *A connected system* (open boundary; internal closure) co-evolves with its environment through reciprocal interaction with it. It is simultaneously characterized by an open boundary through input or interaction (interactive openness, co-evolution) and internal closure (e.g. self-referentiality). This kind of organization is capable of acquiring new knowledge and it has access to its earlier accumulated knowledge.
2. *A double-open system* (open boundary; 'open feedback' via environment) is connected to its environment via an open boundary (interactive openness, co-evolution) and has an 'open feedback-loop' from the external environment. This kind of organization is very open to external input, but learning does not accumulate or the organization does not have access to its earlier accumulated knowledge through self-referentiality and internal closure.

3. *An isolated, double-closed system* (closed boundary, internal closure) is not connected to its environment but is instead based on internal closure. This kind of organization does not react to signals from its environment and does not interact and co-evolve with it. However, it has access to its earlier accumulated knowledge. Because of the lack of new input there is a danger that the existing knowledge becomes outdated and irrelevant.

4. *A passive, closed and open system* (closed boundary, 'open feedback' via environment) does not react to signals from its environment and does not interact with its environment. Moreover, learning does not accumulate or the system does not have access to its earlier accumulated knowledge. This kind of passive organization is not connected to the environment and has access neither to new knowledge nor to its own earlier knowledge.

The analysis of openness and closure provides a more diversified characterization of systems than the mere division into 'open system' and 'closed system'. The analysis shows that openness and closure are not mutually exclusive features. Rather, a system can be simultaneously open and closed according to the variables of boundary and feedback.

It is especially interesting to compare the first alternative above, a connected system, to the self-producing (autopoietic, living) system model. A 'connected system' is linked to its environment via an open boundary and interaction, and simultaneously to its accumulated knowledge via internal closure and self-referentiality. This alternative has parallels to autopoiesis theory, but there are also differences. First, an autopoietic system is open to the environment but in a specific way. It does not accept *input* as such. Instead it compensates for perturbations and creates new knowledge in the co-evolutionary process with its environment through its boundary (boundary elements). This feature is called 'interactive openness' in this book. Second, *'internal closure'* and *'self-referentiality'* are characteristics of autopoietic systems. They can be regarded as specific forms of feedback. Self-referentiality may provide the system with the capability to 'understand' itself, to create a memory, and to utilize its existing knowledge in its evolutionary process. However, to be identified as autopoietic, a system must also have the capability to continually produce its own components and boundaries. Interactive openness and internal closure alone are not sufficient characteristics for defining organization as 'living'.

8.2 'Sensing' — Interactive Openness

In order to survive, adapt, learn, and renew itself, a living organization needs a capability to co-evolve reciprocally with its environment. The boundary elements influence an organization's learning and renewal capability by enabling three kinds of sensing activities:

1. Exposure or awareness of the organization to triggers — perturbations in its environment that elicit compensating reactions.
2. Interactive processes and communication with clients, suppliers, and other entities.
3. Experimentation through new forms of exposure to and interactions with its environment.

These activities enable an organization to maintain openness. In this way, autopoietic boundary elements function as connecting and absorbing elements, rather than as separating elements.

Sensing (a condition of interactive openness) means here that an organization interacts with its environment by being aware of and compensating for perturbations, by improving its knowledge (distinctions), and by changing internally. As an organization is exposed to its environment, its boundary elements and components are engaged in a process of mutual co-evolution (structural coupling) with the environment. An organization conducts experiments, interacts reciprocally with its environment, and compensates for triggers by making specific compensations in its living composition (internal structure). Some degree of interactive openness is thus necessary in creating and accumulating new knowledge that helps an organization to sense and respond to its evolving environment.

8.3 'Memory' and Self-Referentiality

Von Krogh and Roos (1995) describe *organizational closure* as the condition that exists when environmental perturbations are not treated as inputs but trigger compensations in an organization in the form of internal reorganization and restructuring. Organizational closure therefore does not deal with outputs and feedback in the traditional sense. Instead it deals with structural changes and an organization's self-referential capability to understand itself, to get access to own knowledge, and to utilize that knowledge.

In this sense, living organizations have the property of being organizationally closed. They construct their reality in relation to their past and future. This *self-referential capability* that is based on organizational closure gives an organization *memory*, without which an organization would depend only on external impulses without an ability to steer its own functioning. Self-referentiality therefore implies that an organization has a capacity for organizational closure.

While organizations navigate the turbulence in their environments and co-evolve with them, memory maintains an organization's capacity for daily functioning by providing access to earlier knowledge and experiences. *Organizational memory* thus does not refer here only to accumulated data, but to the fundamental capability to access and interpret experiences that are stored in an organization's whole internal 'structure,' in all its strategic components, and in its living composition.

Memory (self-referentiality) in this context means that:

1. The organization has access to its existing knowledge.
2. Old accumulated knowledge affects the organization's 'structure' and operation.
3. The organization's 'structure' and operation affect the acquisition of new information and the creation of new knowledge. This can occur, for example, through an organization's use of accumulated knowledge to interpret new signals in its environment. Self-referentiality facilitates access to and learning from earlier experience and knowledge. Here self-referentiality is also used to refer to organizational memory.

In other words, memory means that *an organization has access to its accumulated knowledge and this knowledge affects its functioning and learning.* In the case examples, the availability of globally accumulated knowledge enables the firms' daily functioning and facilitates their learning and evolution. Having memory also means that *an organization's functioning affects its acquisition and creation of new knowledge,* because its ways of interpreting and the methods it uses to accumulate knowledge influence its acquisition of new knowledge. In the case studies, companies have developed screening mechanisms to identify new knowledge for their knowledge base.

8.4 Linkage between 'Sensing' and 'Memory'

An empirical analysis suggests that the case companies utilize two processes, one that provides new knowledge for the organization and coordinates it with the environment (sensing), and another that provides access to existing knowledge and increases effectiveness (memory). Moreover, in the case companies these processes are interconnected, for example through global information and communication systems. This means a continual coordination of these flows so that the new knowledge becomes a part of the existing knowledge base, and the existing knowledge base helps to find, create, and evaluate new knowledge both locally and globally. The description of the sensing and memory of the case companies is presented in Chapter 15.

8.5 Summary

The boundary elements influence an organization's learning and renewal capability by enabling three kinds of sensing activities:

1. Exposure or awareness of an organization to triggers — perturbations in its environment that elicit compensating reactions.
2. Interactive processes and communication with clients, suppliers, and other entities.
3. Experimentation through new forms of exposure to and interactions with the environment.

Openness and closure can be described by two variables, boundary and feedback, and it is possible that a system is simultaneously open and closed:

1. *Boundary.* The boundary is closed (closure; no input or interaction) or open (interactive openness through open interaction and co-evolution with the environment).
2. *Feedback.* The system is characterized by self-referentiality and internal closure (internal closure) or by feedback loops via the external environment ('open feedback' through external closure).

Autopoietic systems are simultaneously open and closed. Organizations, as autopoietic systems, are therefore open and closed (interactive openness and internal closure/ self-referentiality). The maintenance of a living organization is based on *sensing and memory*, each of which constitutes a major knowledge flow and is part of the core of the dynamic process of the living organization. Sensing and memory are likely to be simultaneous and interconnected phenomena. Figures 6.1 and 6.2, presented earlier, illustrate the content and simultaneity of sensing and memory of organizations.

Sensing (a condition of interactive openness) means here that an organization interacts with its environment by being aware of and compensating for perturbations, by improving its knowledge (distinctions), and by changing internally. As an organization is exposed to its environment, its boundary elements and components are engaged in a process of mutual co-evolution (structural coupling) with its environment. An organization conducts experiments, interacts reciprocally with its environment, and compensates for triggers by making specific compensations in its living composition (internal structure). Some degree of interactive openness is thus necessary in creating and accumulating new knowledge that helps an organization sense and respond to its evolving environment.

Memory (self-referentiality) means that:

1. The organization has access to its existing knowledge.
2. Old accumulated knowledge affects the organization's 'structure' and operation.
3. The organization's 'structure' and operation affect the acquisition of new information and the creation of new knowledge. This can occur, for example, through an organization's use of accumulated knowledge to interpret new signals in its environment. Self-referentiality facilitates access to and learning from earlier experience and knowledge. Here self-referentiality is also used to refer to organizational memory.

Linkage between sensing and memory (interactive openness and self-referentiality) means that they are simultaneous and interconnected phenomena in a living organization. Sensing helps to coordinate the functioning of an organization within the environment, while memory maintains the organization's efficient functioning.

Notes

1. This analysis is based on Maula (2000a).
2. In a strict sense, self-referentiality is not an expression of 'feedback' that necessitates some kind of 'output'. The only product (output) of an internally closed self-producing system is the system itself, and traditional output and feedback do not exist. Therefore 'feedback' may be understood metaphorically to describe the system's capability to refer to itself and change itself structurally.

Chapter 9

Four Parallel Knowledge Processes[1]

In order to understand how knowledge is flowing in practice in organizations, it is necessary to further analyze the concept of 'knowledge' and to review the processes that are used to process and share information and knowledge in organizations. For this purpose this chapter first critically discusses the concepts of tacit and explicit knowledge that are generally used in the context of knowledge management. However, this conventional division between tacit and explicit knowledge is no longer sufficient as digitalization has considerably changed the opportunities to save, modify, and distribute information. Therefore this chapter presents four parallel knowledge processes to address this situation.

9.1 The Conventional Division between Tacit and Explicit Knowledge

The theory of knowledge creation based on Polanyi's and Bateson's idea that individuals are the origin of all knowledge, divides knowledge into two classes, tacit and explicit knowledge (Nonaka & Takeuchi, 1995):

1. *Tacit (subjective) knowledge*

   (a) Knowledge of experience (body)
   (b) Simultaneous knowledge (here and now)
   (c) Analog knowledge (practice).

2. *Explicit (objective) knowledge*

   (a) Knowledge of rationality (mind)
   (b) Sequential knowledge (there and then)
   (c) Digital knowledge (theory).

The theory of knowledge creation assumes that knowledge is created (or rather converted) by a spiral-like process. It consists of four steps of interaction between tacit and explicit knowledge: socialization, externalization, combination, and internalization (SECI model). According to Hedlund (1993), the many references to Polanyi's tacit knowledge in economics and organization theory do not adequately stress that Polanyi focused on personal knowledge, and that the analysis of tacitness becomes more complex if it is seen at the social level. There are also other reasons to reevaluate the definitions of tacit and explicit knowledge.

First, transforming tacit knowledge into explicit form does not make it objective. For example, transforming a subjective or false statement into a digital form does not make it more objective or true. Instead, digital technology and mass media enable the creation and distribution of misleading knowledge or purposely created illusions.

Second, it is not possible to reliably know whether knowledge is objective or not. The division between subjective and objective is based on representationism. It assumes that explicit knowledge is objective and represents external reality exactly. However, knowledge is influenced by our senses and previous knowledge, and we do not have direct, pure access to reality. Therefore, we cannot be sure whether knowledge — whether tacit or explicit — represents reality. Our knowledge may only approximate the potentially existing reality. Thus, the theory of knowledge creation perpetuates the Cartesian split between mind and body (Crossan, 1996).

Third, the definitions of tacit and explicit knowledge are not logical and consistent. For example, experience can be located in the body as well as in the mind. In addition, the mind can be associated with rationality as well as with irrationality.

Fourth, the definition also assumes that explicit knowledge is created through the rational functioning of the mind. However, explicit knowledge can be created in informal and even irrational processes, such as chatting on the Internet, or through an interaction with intelligent software. While the resulting digital knowledge cannot necessarily be regarded as objective or rational, it can, however, be an invaluable source of innovative ideas. On the other hand, software that is created by human beings can also be regarded as a functioning of the mind. Therefore, the results of automated systems could be regarded under certain conditions as 'knowledge of rationality'.

Fifth, tacit knowledge is not only about 'here and now'. As the case of Arthur D. Little (Europe) will illustrate, tacit expert knowledge can also consist of specialism that has been accumulated during a long period 'there and then'. On the other hand, new technologies enable creating explicit knowledge 'here and now', for example when talking on a digital phone, taking a digital photo, or using e-business services. Explicit knowledge is an increasingly integrated part and enabler of our everyday activities.

Sixth, digitalization of knowledge does not transform it into a theory. Bateson's term 'digital knowledge' originates from 1973. Since then, digital technology has become pervasive in society, and in many cases separate transformation processes are not needed because the information, such as speech, pictures, etc., is digital from the very beginning.

In addition to the aforementioned weaknesses in the definition of knowledge, the theory of the firm in terms of knowledge creation remains unexplained. Nonaka and Takeuchi's theory "... is precisely focused on the transformation and communication of what is already known by employees, i.e. on the way other employees learn what an individual has discovered, rather than on Nelson and Winter's notion on the firm itself learning by acquiring better routines. For Nonaka and Takeuchi (1995, pp. 62, 239), organizational knowledge is the knowledge shared by the individuals, albeit transformed and amplified, and the four dimensions of knowledge conversion are the means of communicating the two modes of knowing around the firm. Their theory of the firm, in the sense of explaining (a) how individuals generate tacit knowledge, and (b) how the obvious agency problems are resolved, remains unexplained" (Spender, 1996, pp. 50, 51).

The theory of knowledge creation is also characterized by a relative lack of interest in information technology and ICT solutions. But as the analysis of the case firms in this book indicates, information and communication technology have an important role in knowledge and information management, and new technologies have challenged the division between tacit and explicit knowledge.

Moreover, the theory is based on Japanese culture and the practices of large firms that emphasize the role of people in knowledge management. However, many knowledge-generating firms are small start-ups and they work by rules and practices that differ considerably from the established Japanese firms.

The theory of knowledge creation suggests periodical fluctuations or even purposely created crises to facilitate knowledge creation. However, the case companies that apply structured methodologies and standards do not favor fluctuations or crises. Instead they facilitate self-organizing networks and communities, as well as tools and methods that help them to navigate in the environment and to co-evolve with it.

Nonaka and Takeuchi's theory assumes that knowledge is created through four sequential modes of conversion between tacit and explicit knowledge: socialization, externalization, combination, and internalization. However, the case companies also create, share, and utilize knowledge without converting it into explicit form. For example, Arthur D. Little (Europe) creates and accumulates expert knowledge in tacit form by managing the careers of specialists and by supporting communication among people. The KaosPilots and KaosManagement function in an action-oriented way in the tacit sphere of consulting.

The theory of knowledge creation focuses on creating new knowledge that facilitates product development and thereby competitiveness. While the concepts of tacit and explicit knowledge depict global knowledge sharing and the connecting of individual and organizational knowledge processes in management consulting firms, they do not deal with the larger strategic question that concerns an organization's co-evolution, survival, and success in its turbulent environment, and the methods to organize a firm's strategic components accordingly. While the theory recognizes interaction with the environment as a source of knowledge creation, it does not explain the roles of environment and boundaries, or the proactive changing of the environment through interaction. Moreover, it does not explain how co-evolution with the environment occurs.

To conclude, the theory of knowledge creation does not sufficiently explain firms' knowledge processes from their strategic survival and success perspective in a turbulent socio-technical environment. In contrast, these aspects are central in the model of living, autopoietic systems.

9.2   Four Parallel Knowledge Processes

Traditionally, information systems have aimed for the systematic and highly structured processing of information. New information and communication technologies, such as the Internet and telecommunication technology, and their convergence with media, provide increasing opportunities to present knowledge in explicit digital form, such as digital photographs, video, music, phone calls, faxes, 'chatting' on the Internet, discussions in professional communities, electronic mail, and other less structured content. Moreover, new knowledge can be created directly in digital form without transforming it from tacit to explicit form. For example, an interactive, intelligent software may suggest the form of presentation and even a draft of the content.

Polanyi's division of tacit and explicit knowledge was developed at a time when personal computers, mobile devices, digital multimedia, Internet, and intelligent, interactive software did not exist. Today, there is a need for a classification of knowledge that is more operational and consistent and that takes into account the impact of information and communication technology on society. Evidence from the case firms reveals that information and communication technology helps to express subjective, unstructured, uncodified, and informal knowledge in explicit, digital form. This digital, less-structured knowledge may have an increasingly important role in the management of knowledge.

Empirical study of knowledge-intensive organizations shows that it is helpful to classify knowledge along two dimensions:

1. *Highly structured knowledge and less/non-structured knowledge.* The degree of structure depends on the formalization of knowledge and the possibilities to systematically process that knowledge. However, it can be emphasized that less and non-structured knowledge can also be processed by modern tools (such as data mining), which increases the value of this kind of knowledge, for example for identifying weak signals and for knowledge creation.
2. *Explicit/digital knowledge and tacit knowledge.* The differentiation here is only related to the form of presentation, and not with any value judgments concerning the truthfulness, objectivity, time-relatedness, or theory/experience-relatedness of the knowledge in question.

This leads to the following four types of knowledge:

1. Highly structured, explicit/digital knowledge
2. Less-structured, explicit/digital knowledge.
3. Highly structured, tacit knowledge.
4. Less-structured, tacit knowledge.

The distinctions between these types are not always clear, but they indicate the basic differences between the types concerning the creation and sharing of knowledge.

Highly structured explicit/digital knowledge refers to explicit, often digital or printed, formal, classified, processed knowledge. It is processed in a pre-defined manner and by pre-defined rules. Conventional information systems belong to this class.

Less-structured explicit/digital knowledge refers to explicit, digital, informal, unclassified, and often personal knowledge. Examples are digital pictures and images, digital audio and video material, games, virtual reality in general, communication by electronic mail, and discussions in the Intranet. It may be created in man–machine interaction or through communication in electronic networks without transforming tacit knowledge separately into an explicit form. Less-structured explicit/digital knowledge may contain unstructured personal elements, such as electronic mail messages. Less-structured explicit/digital communication and production of knowledge may be an important integration as a part of an organization's normal *modus operandi* and knowledge management practices, because they bring an element of surprise to the organization. For example, the case companies have established knowledge processes that benefit from these new technologies. In order to identify innovative ideas, they organize networks, communities, groups, and teams and monitor their knowledge flows. The firms facilitate these processes by ICT solutions that help to express subjective, unstructured, uncodified, and informal knowledge quickly and easily in an explicit digital form. This knowledge may include 'knowledge nuggets', and is therefore important for organizational creativity.

Highly structured tacit knowledge includes tacit, often professional, personal, or organizational knowledge, such as medical expertise. This kind of knowledge is often gained from education. The case firms develop tacit specialist knowledge (Arthur D. Little), as well as competences and intuition (The KaosPilots/KaosManagement). Tacit knowledge can also be organizational. It may include team skills, methods, or cultural aspects that are embedded in the internal 'structure' of the organization.

Less-structured tacit knowledge refers to tacit personal or organizational knowledge. It may include pre-understanding or knowledge that combines many kinds of knowledge, intuition, skills, capabilities, and competences that are difficult to describe and explain.

The four types of knowledge constitute the basis for *four parallel knowledge processes* that are depicted in Figure 9.1. The classification helps to better clarify the nature of knowledge processes and the role of information and communication technology in those processes.

The four parallel knowledge processes complement each other. For example, all case organizations have established traditional highly structured information systems, and all face an increasing need to transform at least selected knowledge into an explicit and structured form. However, only part of the knowledge of professional service organizations can be codified.

Two trends could be identified in the case firms.

First, *the organizations that are oriented toward innovation, unique solutions, and expertise* (Arthur D. Little, Europe), and *an action-based exploration* (The KaosPilots and KaosManagement) accumulate their knowledge largely in a tacit form. Their need to convert knowledge into an explicit form is relatively small. Instead they facilitate communication among colleagues and other parties in the networks.

Second, *methodologically oriented organizations*, such as Arthur Andersen and Ernst & Young (management consulting), accumulate their knowledge largely in an explicit form

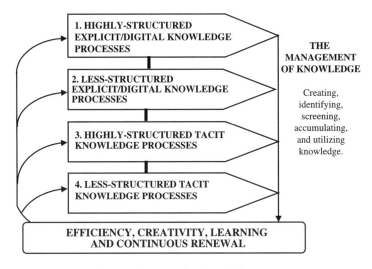

Figure 9.1: Four parallel knowledge processes.

into global knowledge bases in order to reuse and share it globally among themselves and increasingly with clients via 'cyberspace'. In addition to that, they facilitate a continuous 'productive chaos' in the form of 'communities' and self-organizing networks.

Transforming knowledge into an explicit form increases the value of knowledge capital. This is indicated for example in the cases of Arthur Andersen, Ernst & Young (management consulting), and increasingly by Arthur D. Little (Europe). This conclusion may contrast with earlier studies, which conclude that codification decreases the value of knowledge, for example because competitors then have an easier access to it (Kogut & Zander, 1993). Transforming knowledge into an explicit and codified form may become increasingly difficult, because clients' businesses continually become more complex and sophisticated.

Organizations can also develop and share tacit knowledge and skills, such as The KaosPilots' teamwork and 'navigation' skills, in tacit ways without transforming them into an explicit form. This possibility has received less attention than the tendency to transform knowledge into an explicit knowledge.

9.3 Implications of Four Parallel Knowledge Processes

The classification of four knowledge processes has several practical implications. It identifies and differentiates the role of information and communication technology and modern digital media for the knowledge processes. The classification also helps in understanding the value and nature of tacit knowledge in relation to other knowledge types and the need for personal, interpersonal, and organizational activities for increasing human capital. The classification also recognizes the difference between professional, structured tacit knowledge and less-structured tacit knowledge. Moreover, the classification accepts the idea that tacit knowledge also can reside in an organization and not only in individuals. Finally, the classification is neutral toward any value judgments concerning knowledge.

All four knowledge types and knowledge processes are part of the living composition of an organization. The objective is that the classification helps managers to identify relevant knowledge processes and to understand their differences, complementarity, and role in the living composition. Thereby the classification may help to clarify the role of different knowledge types and processes for the survival and success of an organization, and the methods of developing them accordingly.

Highly structured explicit/digital knowledge processes require clear principles and rules, codes, taxonomies, search mechanisms, and efficient information systems with user-friendly interfaces. This knowledge can be accumulated in knowledge bases. Information and communication systems that enable the integration and functioning of sensing and memory, and thereby the learning and renewal of the organizational system, are an essential part of an organization's knowledge management and living composition.

Less-structured, explicit/digital knowledge processes are built around new technologies, such as the World Wide Web or digital multimedia. Their role for the living composition and major knowledge flows may be easily undervalued since they represent new explicit forms of presentation. However, they facilitate creativity individually and organizationally, and there is a need for promoting, accessing, protecting, and utilizing this knowledge, which may be partially organizational and partially personal and private.

Highly structured tacit knowledge processes can be supported, for example, by education and research at individual and organizational levels. This kind of knowledge has high value in professional organizations.

Less-structured tacit knowledge processes can be facilitated by an organizational culture that supports creativity, intuition, multidisciplinarity, innovation, and teamwork, encourages risk-taking, and rewards for successes and learning from failures. Tacit knowledge is accumulated in individuals and in an organization's strategic, living composition.

The classification of four knowledge processes provides a relevant and consistent basis for analyzing and evaluating knowledge, expertise, and intellectual capital in general. It takes the contemporary socio-technical and operational context into account. Thereby it also helps to develop knowledge processes and related business processes and knowledge flows, and to structure the objectives and procedures of knowledge management. It helps to establish proper management principles for each knowledge process and to link them together by knowledge flows and necessary principles and rules, such as screening, monitoring, and incentive systems. Moreover, it provides a basis for measuring knowledge processes and prioritizing them.

The increasing opportunities to access informal, digital knowledge also raises some ethical questions. They concern, for example, privacy in networks and ownership of ideas and digital material. In order to guarantee successful knowledge management and sustainable composition, organizations should create clear rules about these issues.

9.4 Summary

The conventional definitions of tacit and explicit knowledge suffer from several weaknesses. This chapter elaborated on the concepts further, with the purpose of defining them so that they better correspond with the current socio-technical organizational environment. As a result, four parallel knowledge types and corresponding knowledge processes were defined:

1. Highly structured explicit/digital knowledge
2. Less-structured explicit/digital knowledge
3. Highly structured tacit knowledge
4. Less-structured tacit knowledge.

Notes

1. The topic of this chapter has been published in a modified form in Maula (2000b).

PART III

THE CASES: HOW TO APPLY THE LIVING COMPOSITION MODEL IN PRACTICE

This third part of the book will present the empirical cases. Chapter 10 provides an introduction to the case analyses. The cases will be presented in alphabetical order:

- Arthur Andersen (Business Consulting) (Chapter 11)
- Arthur D. Little (Europe) (Chapter 12)
- Ernst & Young (Management Consulting) (Chapter 13)
- The KaosPilots and KaosManagement (Chapter 14).

Chapter 15 summarizes the findings concerning how to analyze case organizations with the living composition model. In the case companies, the model was used only for analysis, but the model can also be used for implementing changes. The six steps for improving a living composition are presented in Section 16.4.

The key concepts and definitions can be found in the Glossary in Appendix 1. The research objective, method, and main conclusions of the study are presented in Appendix 3. Additional details about the case firms can be found in Appendices 5–8.

Chapter 10

Introduction to the Cases

This chapter will discuss the purpose of the case analyses. A brief overview of the characteristics of management consulting will also be presented, highlighting the aspects that are relevant for organizational learning and renewal in a complex, globalizing environment. This chapter will also present the criteria for selecting the case companies for the analysis.

10.1 The Purpose of the Cases

In the previous chapters, the living composition model was developed and its components and features were explained. In the following discussion, we will show how the living composition model helps in understanding how different kinds of organizations learn and evolve. This kind of systematic approach helps managers and researchers to understand the interconnectedness of organizational variables and their impact on learning and renewal capability. The case analyses have also proven to be useful for teaching purposes, as they provide students with a method to quickly understand the variations of internal logic among the firms and their organizational solutions.

All descriptions follow the same structured method. The purpose is to illustrate the capability of the living composition model to depict the enabling structure in different kinds of organizations. The first part of each case presents strategic components, and the second part analyzes the firm's learning and renewal dynamics.

10.2 Management Consulting Industry

Management consulting is a relatively young industry.[1] The pioneer stage started in 1886 and lasted until the 1950s. It was based on technical knowledge, engineering skills, and scientific management. During the development stage (1960s–1970s), new marketing related services were developed. The growth stage (1980s) was characterized by an explosive growth, diversification of services, and an extension into the areas of business science and behavioral science (Kyrö, 1996).

In the management consulting industry, a few large, global firms dominate and benefit from scale and scope advantages. The vast majority of firms are, however, very small, employing 1–4 persons. The barriers to entry are low for newcomers to the industry.

Most large, global management consulting firms have their base in the USA. The need for a global network of offices is partly influenced by the needs of globally operating clients. Recent growth in the industry results from outsourcing, and as a consequence, the demand for talent exceeds the supply. Professional service firms compete fiercely in two markets. They aim at recruiting and keeping the best professionals and winning the most interesting clients and projects (Løwendahl, 2000).

Management consulting firms are characterized by producing knowledge as their main product. Continuous learning and renewal are important for management consulting firms, and many of them therefore invest in developing learning, knowledge, and communication.

10.2.1   Knowledge as the Main Product

Knowledge in some form is the main product of management consulting firms. The International Council of Management Consulting Institutes (ICMCI) defines management consulting as the rendering of independent advice and assistance about the process of management to clients with management responsibilities. Management consulting is an independent professional advisory service, assisting managers and organizations in achieving organizational purposes and objectives by solving management and business problems, identifying and seizing new opportunities, enhancing learning, and implementing changes. The management consulting industry has moved from fact based and directive roles toward process orientation, pragmatic problem solving, and implementation solutions. In general, the consulting marketplace consists of four areas: strategy, operations management, information technology, and human resources. In the 21st century, the main directions could be outsourcing and analytical assignments (Czerniawska, 1999).

Management consulting firms are participants in a global race where new management methods, techniques, and solutions can be regarded as modes and fashions (Abrahamson, 1996). They implement these solutions rapidly on a global scale, and there is a perception that the sector bends too much with the wind and cashes in on management fads (Murdoch, 1996).

On the other hand, management-consulting services are frequently closely linked to scientific knowledge development within the relevant area of expertise. Services are delivered by qualified individuals with higher education. They involve a high degree of customization, discretionary effort, personal and subjective judgment, and quality assessment by the experts delivering the service. They typically require substantial interaction with representatives of the client firm and are delivered within the constraints of professional norms of conduct, which includes setting client needs higher than profits and respecting the limits of professional expertise (Løwendahl, 2000). There is pressure for management consulting firms to manage their professional competence in terms of problem solving capabilities, creativity, and specialization. Consulting firms are increasingly aware of the need to improve their knowledge flows, interaction capabilities, and learning skills. Consultants' educational backgrounds consist of degrees in technical, economic (business), and behavioral sciences. As a profession, the industry is not based on any single scientific platform (Kyrö, 1996).

Professional service firms can be classified by their strategic focus into three generic groups. *Client relation-based strategy* means that the firm focuses on its unique capability to understand and help particular client groups. *Solution or output-based strategy* means that the firm develops a core portfolio of services, methods, or solutions and grows by adding new markets or client groups where similar services are needed. *Problem solving or creativity-based strategy* refers to services that involve a high degree of innovation (Løwendahl, 2000).

The typical employee profile of a consulting firm will tend toward more experienced senior consultants who are capable of understanding the manager's role, supported by the juniors (Collis, 1996). On the other hand, many management consulting companies aim to become less dependent on 'human superstars and experts' by making large investments in knowledge management (*Consultants' News*, October 1997).

10.2.2 Learning and Renewal in Management Consulting Firms

The management consulting industry acts in society as a broker and applier of scientific knowledge that is relevant for managers. The rapid cycles of this interaction can be seen especially in the area of strategic planning (Kyrö, 1996). According to Murdoch (1996), the management consulting industry utilizes the ideas of business school professors but has itself produced few new thinkers. Consultants have been slow to develop new techniques and ideas. "A key selling point has been a supply of bright, multi-talented individuals with a unique insight into industry" (p. 14).

On the other hand, they are increasingly involved in networks, or rather in business ecosystems, where many different kinds of participants collaborate, compete, and co-evolve, producing new knowledge. Gibbons et al. (1994) claim that marketability and commercialization of knowledge as well as massification of research and education have changed knowledge production in society and created two complementary modes: know-ledge production in universities (Mode 1), and knowledge production in networks (Mode 2). In Mode 1, universities produce new knowledge, and consultants and other actors apply it. In Mode 2, knowledge is created directly in the context of application in networks of multiple actors that include universities, consultancies, polytechnic institutes, industry, laboratories, and think tanks. The networks are temporary, flexible, collaborative, non-hierarchical, and heterogeneous. Problem solving skills are needed to put things together in unique ways. Brokering skills are needed to put the problem identifiers, solvers, and necessary resources together, and to facilitate the continuous, dynamic creation of knowledge, technologies, skills, and other resources in collaborative arrangements.

In order to stay competitive, management consulting firms have to learn continually. They have to develop their qualifications because their services are knowledge intensive and becoming ever more complex. The sophistication of clients and the complexity of their problems increase the need for problem solving capabilities, creativity, and specialized knowledge.

The value creation of professional service firms is based on three critical processes that constitute a learning cycle. First, the firms have to sell a credible promise. Second, they also have to deliver what has been promised. Third, they have to learn from the project and institutionalize this learning so that it improves service quality and efficiency with future clients (Løwendahl, 2000).

The international management consulting associations have formulated Codes of Conduct and Codes of Ethics that aim to regulate and provide guidelines for management consulting firms' activities. Analysis of these Codes indicates that the majority of them still tend to support unidirectional, i.e. 'directive', 'content-based' and 'transplantation based' type of consulting. Only in two cases do the Codes directly and explicitly indicate the dynamic aspect of consulting, i.e. that consulting firms should develop their skills and knowledge continually. Therefore, there are several unutilized opportunities to develop the Codes to better meet the needs of the knowledge society (Maula & Poulfelt, 2002).

10.2.3 Investments in Learning, Knowledge, and Communication

Consulting firms have to make investments to keep up with the constantly changing technology and to train and retrain people. They have a double interest in deploying technology and developing knowledge management — they aim to manage knowledge in their own business, and they also counsel clients and sell knowledge management projects to them (Reimus, 1996, 1997).

In management consulting firms that provide highly customized and context dependent solutions for clients, the problems and solutions are unique and hard to codify into explicit knowledge. The decentralized, loosely coordinated knowledge management systems have emerged 'bottom-up' from the initiatives of the firm's consultants. These systems put more emphasis on people and internal communication than on information technology. They are market-driven and self-regulatory, but on the other hand, they are also reactive. People have little incentive to spend their time on building knowledge, and the management misses the opportunity to integrate information from outside the firm and to direct resources to study new areas. The lack of oversight of the inflow of experience may lead to a superficial understanding.

Other companies offer highly standardized solutions to clients. Their knowledge is less context-specific and easier to codify. Knowledge management is built and managed from the top, and it is based on advanced information technology. The knowledge management systems provide the opportunity for visionary and proactive breakthroughs. On the other hand, these systems are very expensive, they need to be maintained, and their benefits are hard to measure. Firm-wide norms, incentives, and corporate culture must be explicitly built around them.

Knowledge management has changed the competitive landscape in the management consulting industry. Firms that implement knowledge management successfully exhibit positive feedback mechanisms and enjoy increasing returns where a small initial advantage leads to a larger advantage. People are more likely to contribute to knowledge management when they see it as a powerful resource. Knowledge management makes people's daily jobs more challenging, and helps people concentrate on problem solving and improving their human capital (Sarvary, 1999).

10.3   Introduction to the Case Companies

The four case companies are Arthur Andersen (Business Consulting), Arthur D. Little (Europe), Ernst & Young (Management Consulting), and the small network (value chain) of The KaosPilots and KaosManagement. Chapters 11–14 represent a detailed analysis of the four cases. The main focus is not on management consulting or the case companies themselves, but on the capability of the living composition model to systematically identify and present organizational characteristics that are relevant for enabling an infrastructure in any organization. This section will first present the criteria for selecting the cases, and then it will present an introduction to the four case organizations.

The original interviews were made in 1997–1998 and the major conclusions were made in 1999 and 2000. The goals of the research were to apply the living composition model to the case firms in order to determine whether the components and principles of the living composition model can be identified in practice, to understand and describe the underlying structures that enable the firms' learning and renewal, and to develop the model further. The case analyses were published with the consent of the case companies in a doctoral dissertation in 1999. Because of evolution in the management consulting industry, the firms have undergone many changes, including mergers and acquisitions, since then. Many of the interviewees have advanced in their careers or changed their jobs after the study. Therefore the cases discussed below do not necessarily depict the current situation of these organizations. The cases are, however, included in this book as illustrative examples. In quotations, the position of the interviewee in the firm is presented as it was during the interviews.

10.3.1 The Criteria for Selecting the Case Firms

The case firms were selected to represent the expected variety of living composition. Each case company serves a specific research purpose. The selected organizations vary in age, size, growth, orientation, and background, their approach to learning and renewal, and investments in knowledge and communication. Table 10.1 summarizes their key variables. Two cases (Arthur Andersen Business Consulting and Ernst & Young Management Consulting) were selected to represent intentional fit composition. The assumption was that a consistent organizational solution that is enabled by advanced technical solutions is an increasingly relevant issue theoretically and managerially. It was also assumed that there is variation among intentional fit companies. Therefore, two cases were selected to illustrate their variations.

Arthur Andersen (Business Consulting) represents a very large, multinational professional services company. It was selected to represent intentional fit composition because it had implemented learning organization principles and had invested in global knowledge management and ICT solutions. Arthur Andersen was regarded as an information technology-oriented consulting company[2] (*Consultants' News*, March 1997). The company was in the middle ground between expert-driven and methodology-driven consulting firms, but slightly more toward the methodology end (Reimus, 1996, 1997). In addition to Business Consulting, Arthur Andersen had other practices that utilized the same or similar principles and systems.

Ernst & Young (Management Consulting) (later Cap Gemini Ernst & Young after a merger) was a relatively young and very large multinational consulting company, characterized by an explosive growth. The firm was selected to represent the intentional fit composition because it had invested extensively in consistent solutions, global knowledge management, and ICT-supported knowledge sharing. It was classified as a strongly methodology-oriented company (Reimus, 1996, 1997) and an information technology-oriented consulting firm (*Consultants' News*, March 1997). Ernst & Young had other businesses in addition to Management Consulting.

Table 10.1: The characteristics of the case organizations.

	Andersen (Business Consulting)	Arthur D. Little (Europe)	Ernst & Young (Management Consulting)*	The Kaos Pilots and Kaos Management
Founded	1913. Earlier: Arthur Andersen Business Consulting	1886. Oldest consulting firm in the world	1989, Ernst & Young (through a merger). 1999, Cap Gemini Ernst & Young (consulting)	(Roots in 1982), KaosPilots, 1991, Kaos Management, 1993
Size	Large multinational	Multinational. Large among middle-sized firms	Large multinational	A small value chain.
Orientation and background	Consulting. Background in accounting. A methodology driven company	Consulting. Background in technical specialist consulting. An expert (and methodology) driven company	Consulting. Background in accounting. A methodology driven company	Consulting and education. Background in project work and media
Approach to learning and renewal	A 'learning organization'	A specialist organization. Systematizes learning capabilities through organizational transformation	A 'learning organization'	Continuous change, 'navigating in chaos'
Investments in knowledge and communication	Extensive knowledge sharing system. Explicit knowledge	A knowledge sharing system. Tacit (and explicit) knowledge	Extensive knowledge sharing system. Explicit knowledge	Experiments with knowledge sharing. Mainly tacit knowledge
Assumed strategic composition	Intentional fit	Stretch	Intentional fit	Emergent fit

*Before the merger of Ernst & Young Management Consulting with Cap Gemini.

Arthur D. Little (Europe) was a large multinational firm, characterized by an orientation toward innovation and expertise in diversified areas of specialization. The company was selected to represent stretch composition because it is known for its focus on innovation and new challenges and the company was going through a major transformation process. Arthur D. Little was regarded as an operations-oriented company (*Consultants' News*, March 1997) and positioned in the middle ground, slightly more toward the expert end than the methodology end (Reimus, 1996, 1997). Arthur D. Little had a strong technical background and the firm regarded itself as an expert-oriented firm.

The KaosPilots and KaosManagement constituted a small action-oriented and experimental value chain.[3] They were selected to represent emerging fit principles in living composition because they were very flexible and specialized in 'navigating in chaos'. It was assumed that they could provide new knowledge about learning and evolution at an early stage of a multinational organization's development. Their organization emphasized human resources, action, and experimentation.

No case company was selected to represent the misfit (unintentional inconsistency) composition, because that alternative was regarded at that time as less relevant theoretically and managerially.

Notes

1. Consulting companies can also have other businesses, such as accounting, auditing, and advisory services.
2. Consultants' News classified consulting firms into strategy, operations, IT, and human resources-oriented companies.
3. The KaosManagement is a management consulting firm. The KaosPilots is an educational institution. In this study, they are regarded as one interconnected value chain. Professional service organizations that are not organized as firms have many of the same characteristics as professional service firms (Løwendahl, 2000).

Chapter 11

Arthur Andersen (Business Consulting)

This chapter will describe how the living composition model helps in understanding Arthur Andersen Business Consulting as a living (self-producing) organization. The original case analysis was published in 1999. Here some figures have been updated to correspond with the situation in 2001. Arthur Andersen's other practices utilized the same or similar principles and systems as the Business Consulting Practice. Therefore, in the following discussion the term 'Arthur Andersen' will be used as a general term to describe the case organization. Section 11.1 describes Arthur Andersen's strategic components. Section 11.2 describes the dynamics, especially the major knowledge flows, learning, and renewal. Additional information about Arthur Andersen Business Consulting can be found in Appendix 5.

11.1 The Strategic Components of Arthur Andersen (Business Consulting)

11.1.1 Arthur Andersen's Identity

According to the principles of self-production, a firm's identity influences its learning and renewal capability. Arthur Andersen's identity is characterized by several aspects: a large, global, multidisciplinary and integrated company, a supplier of knowledge, and an entrepreneurial company. Moreover, the firm has always regarded itself as a learning organization, committed to education and training.

Arthur Andersen is *a large, global, multidisciplinary and integrated company*. It was founded in 1913 by Arthur Andersen and Clarence DeLany, and it grew to be one of the largest auditing and consulting companies. The firm, including all practices, had 85,000 employees in 390 offices in 84 countries worldwide in the year 2001. In the fiscal year that ended in August 31, 2001, its revenues were US$ 9.3 billion. Of that, US$ 1.7 billion were revenues from the consulting practice.

Arthur Andersen is a professional services firm, owned privately by international partners. It consists of separate practice entities that are organized under the laws of the country where they are based. Its integrated organization means that individual consultants communicate globally with each other in international assignments, and personal knowledge is accumulated and shared globally.

The firm has specialized units, such as the knowledge enterprises unit that develops knowledge-related issues and facilitates organizational learning. It includes the Global Best Practices® (GBP) Group and the Next Generation Research Group.

Arthur Andersen is a *supplier of knowledge* to clients. The company helps clients to improve their business performance. The firm's purpose is to acquire knowledge and to share it so that the clients can grow and profit. Knowledge comes from three sources: experience, education, and research.

> Knowledge is the only product that we do deliver. In certain cases we deliver
> it through personal services and in other cases we deliver it through know-
> ledge bases, but it's the only product that we have to sell. So, fundamental
> to our knowledge strategy is that 'we are knowledge' (Robert J. Hiebeler).

The objective of Arthur Andersen is to become 'the first place to go for business knowledge', to be the world's number one supplier of knowledge. To that end, the company has
established a knowledge strategy. According to the knowledge mission, the purpose is to
'transform the capability of Arthur Andersen, and of our clients, to create, share, apply, and
value knowledge'.

Arthur Andersen is *a learning organization. Education, training,* and the *knowledge
sharing system* are aligned with the organizational architecture and task definitions. Arthur
Andersen introduced the profession's first centralized training program that consists of
more than 400 technical, business, industry, and management development courses. The
curriculum defines what a person needs to know at each level of his or her career. Learning
plays an important role in the process of creating new organizational knowledge. A true
'learning organization' in its broadest sense is a comprehensive concept.

> (It is) ... an organization that is capable of collectively understanding itself.
> This would include the capability to reflect and learn from the experience
> of individuals. Given this definition, a true 'learning organization' is far bet-
> ter equipped to manage its organizational knowledge creation process
> effectively than a company that has not 'learned to learn' (Robert J.
> Hiebeler).

Arthur Andersen is also an *entrepreneurial company.* This means that the firm's ability to
develop new services depends on the entrepreneurial spirit of its employees.

11.1.2   Arthur Andersen's Perception of its Environment

Learning and change are motivated by changes in the environment. Arthur Andersen perceives the world as 'a place of constant and rapid change' where the volume of information is exploding. Its business environment is also characterized by increasing
sophistication of client assignments.

11.1.3   Arthur Andersen's Strategy

Arthur Andersen's *mission* is to build relationships and develop innovative solutions that help
people and organizations to create and realize value. The *strategy* is to serve the marketplace
and to grow globally. Arthur Andersen grew first from a regional into a national firm, and
during the 1980s into a global firm. After starting as an accounting firm it has evolved into a
global, multidisciplinary professional services organization. Part of its international strategy
is to establish *alliances* to provide small, fast-moving companies with the power of Arthur
Andersen's global presence.

Arthur Andersen provides information and applies knowledge to improve business performance. Robert J. Hiebeler says that Arthur Andersen understands change: "Our concept is productive chaos". This means a combination of divergent processes of exploration and convergent processes of creating a shared understanding. Also, continuous improvement of all processes and the assessment of results and expectations fuel performance and learning. Client satisfaction is assessed by a specific program, which is a methodical approach for co-operation with clients.

11.1.4   Arthur Andersen's Knowledge and Knowledge Management

11.1.4.1   Personal and organizational knowledge   For Arthur Andersen, knowledge is a strategic resource, prime competition parameter, and a key future asset. Knowledge means 'information that has value'. The value for clients is created by combining personal and organizational knowledge.

> We think the playing field in the future is going to be based upon persons' individual knowledge and their capability to tap into organizational knowledge. Personal knowledge is that knowledge you gain by experiencing something, learning from that experience, and then gaining greater capability to create something yourself. Once you create something new then you learn from that new experience, and that creates an increasing value of the learning experience. When two circles of personal knowledge come together a new behavior sphere emerges: the sharing behavior. The organizational knowledge system has to take that shared knowledge, analyze it, synthesize it, apply it, value it, and play it back. It's a spiral going back to the individual, so that an individual can experience the new knowledge and then make the cycle greater. This happens along the lines of Nonaka and Takeuchi.
>
> This doesn't just automatically happen. You need to have something in the middle, which is in many ways technology, and processes that allow you to gather that individual knowledge and distribute it into the organizational systems, and allow you to have the entire organization increasing that value. And that's where the innovation happens. That's the mixture of individual creativity and the organizational systems (Robert J. Hiebeler).

Organizational knowledge processes refer to the continuous creation of 'packaged knowledge' into global knowledge bases (Figure 11.1). They enable the accumulation and sharing of knowledge globally. Organizational knowledge is also available in local knowledge bases that contain documentation about local projects in native languages. *Personal knowledge processes* refer to solving the client's business problems.

11.1.4.2   Divergent and convergent knowledge processes   Personal and organizational knowledge is created in sequential divergent and convergent processes (Figure 11.2). The *personal divergent* process means asking questions, sharing knowledge with others, and joining Communities of Practice. The *personal convergent* process means using the collected

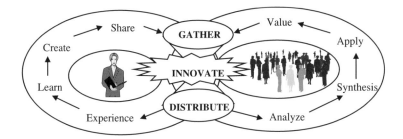

Figure 11.1: Arthur Andersen's model of creating value by connecting personal and organizational knowledge processes.

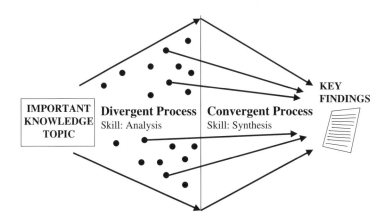

Figure 11.2: Arthur Andersen's divergent and convergent knowledge processes for creating packaged knowledge.

material and preparing the solution for a client's problem. The *organizational divergent* process means analysis of a more general problem. The *organizational convergent* process means synthesis and creation of packaged and globally shared knowledge.

The divergent and convergent processes constitute chains. Learning is in reference to what has been learned earlier.

Arthur Andersen has built two complementary ways to access knowledge (Table 11.1). The divergent AA Online acts as a discussion forum, and the convergent KnowledgeSpace^SM is a storage of accumulated knowledge.

> When someone is looking for a solution or some ideas to take out to the clients, he would first look at our convergent packaged knowledge systems to find out if there are any packaged solutions that are 'on the shelf'. If the solutions are not on the shelf it provides an opportunity to go into AA Online and to pose the question to all the people in the community that can answer that question (Robert J. Hiebeler).

Table 11.1: Arthur Andersen's organizational and personal knowledge processes.

	Divergent process	**Convergent process**
	AA online	KnowledgeSpace^{SM}
Personal level. Solving the client's business problem	Asking questions. Sharing knowledge with others. Joining the Communities of Practice	Preparing the solution for the client's business problem
Organizational level. Creating packaged knowledge	Analysis. Identifying knowledge nuggets	Synthesis. Packaging

11.1.4.3 Divergent knowledge process and system — AA online   The divergent process analyzes a specific issue. It involves selecting an important knowledge topic and enhancing knowledge about that topic. The divergent knowledge process is supported by the AA Online information system. It allows people to join communities and ask questions. In AA Online, about fifty Communities of Practice around the world converse with each other, sharing knowledge and new ideas. Each community has a knowledge manager who monitors the traffic and what's going on in that community, and identifies the information that has value. Once they identify valuable information, they send it to the refining process to be put into the packaged knowledge systems (Robert J. Hiebeler).

11.1.4.4 Convergent knowledge system — KnowledgeSpace^{SM}   The divergent process provides material for the convergent knowledge process. After the divergent process, know-ledge is filtered and structured ('packaged') in a convergent packaging process before it is accepted as a part of organizational knowledge. This means that Arthur Andersen has developed methods to find meaning and understanding in the information and to converge it down into some key findings. Knowledge is then stored in the global know-ledge bases that can be accessed via KnowledgeSpace^{SM}, Arthur Andersen's Intranet on the World Wide Web. It also contains knowledge about clients, consulting methodologies, and tools and techniques.

The Global Best Practices® knowledge base transcends service lines and industry categories. It contains knowledge about more than 200 generic business processes that are collected from global sources. The processes can be applied in principle to any firm in any industry. It combines more than 4000 documents and 20,000 pages of best practices information with more than 140 benchmarking tools. GBP also contains knowledge about 'Best Companies' that have been identified by Arthur Andersen's experts as leading examples of best practices. Moreover, it contains evaluated and rated articles about specific topics and customizable presentation material. GBP can be accessed via the network and CD-ROM.

All business processes are organized by the Universal Process Classification Scheme, a universal language for the firm's professionals. It contains 13 process categories, over 200 business processes, and nine categories of information for each process.

11.1.4.5   Knowledge management   Arthur Andersen regards knowledge as an asset and has created a conceptual system for knowledge management. It is based on the principles of personal and organizational knowledge. Knowledge sharing includes four key areas: people, process, leadership, and technology. The employees' contribution to knowledge sharing is measured as a part of their performance evaluation. The measurement is linked to organizational values.

> You don't really get anything by keeping the information and knowledge to yourself. You are recognized for giving it out to other people.   I am measured on how good I am at working in teams. That's how good I am in knowledge sharing ... but also how good am I at getting the knowledge that other people created (Sanne Prestegaard).

Arthur Andersen's knowledge management organization consists of specialized units and roles. The Andersen Knowledge Enterprises unit develops electronic commerce and interactive media business opportunities. The Global Best Practices® Group and the Next Generation Research Group structure knowledge and develop knowledge management solutions. The writers and editors at the Global Best Practices® Group update the packaged knowledge bases continually. They go through the knowledge about 2–3 times a year and update all packaged knowledge (Robert J. Hiebeler).

Communities of Practice are about 50 groups of people that communicate and share ideas, expertise, and advice about specific topics via AA Online. Each community has a knowledge manager who captures and synthesizes new knowledge. They monitor global communication and knowledge traffic in the communities, and search for information that could have value. The ability to create 'knowledge nuggets', to extract information, is their core skill.

Several competence centers, such as the Arthur Andersen Business Consulting competence center, function as knowledge management centers. Each of these centers has a knowledge manager.

All employees, including the project groups, are expected to document and evaluate their knowledge at the end of the project. Capturing knowledge is often difficult because after the project the consultants have a great feeling of accomplishment and are looking forward to new challenges.

11.1.5   Arthur Andersen's Boundary Elements

Arthur Andersen interacts with its environment via several roles and functions that act as boundary elements (Table 11.2). They help the firm to identify, capture, and convey knowledge and convert it into an explicit form. They structure, pack, and store knowledge and influence the environment. The boundary elements include technical solutions that act as information bridges and 'cyberspace', facilitate communication, and provide an access to internal and external sources of information. Moreover, they help to acquire relevant knowledge that facilitates the firm's learning and change.

Table 11.2: The boundary elements of Arthur Andersen (Business Consulting).

Boundary elements/Andersen	Purpose of role/function Arthur
Global partners	Convey knowledge about the environment to the strategic decision-making process
Alliances with 'block-buster' firms **Employees, project teams**	Provide new knowledge and opportunities Create and capture tacit knowledge from interaction with clients. Convert it into an explicit form by documentation and by communicating via AA Online
Knowledge-management process **(divergent–convergent process)** **Communities of practice**	Absorbs and packs knowledge into the global knowledge bases Create knowledge and convert it into an explicit form, e.g. through electronic communication
Knowledge managers	Monitor global communication and knowledge traffic in the Communities of Practice
AA experts	Acquire knowledge about specific subjects Act as contributors and experts worldwide
Global Best Practices® group **(writers, editors)**	Selects and collects information from external sources and converts it into internal knowledge
Next Generation Research Group	Acquires knowledge by conducting research and experimentation
Arthur Andersen Knowledge Enterprises	Monitor electronic commerce and interactive media business opportunities
Competence centers	Capture knowledge that is related to their specialization
Education centers	Convey knowledge to Arthur Andersen and employees through education
User communities **Knowledge SpaceSM. Information and** **communication systems**	Interact in the KnowledgeSpace^{SM} Act as information bridges within the company and in relation to the environment. Support the accumulation of knowledge

11.1.6   Arthur Andersen's Interaction and Co-evolution with its Environment

The boundary elements enable Arthur Andersen's daily interaction with clients, and help to create value for clients and generate knowledge for Arthur Andersen. The client projects facilitate new ideas and knowledge. The experiences are captured and utilized in the organizational divergent–convergent value-creation process.

Clients require an increasing degree of sophistication to solve the challenges they confront because their businesses are becoming more complex. For this purpose, Arthur Andersen utilizes the range and depth of its expertise by establishing multidisciplinary teams and by partnering when necessary. The consulting processes are also based on methodological approaches that are supported by BC Consultant's Advisor^{SM} methods, tools, and techniques.

KnowledgeSpaceSM is a 'cyberspace' and knowledge absorption boundary that helps the firm to interact with clients. In 1997, it was launched as a service also for User Community Groups. These groups are communities of subscribers, such as Chief Financial Officers, who face similar issues in a particular industry. The KnowledgeSpaceSM offers subscribers, customized access to a bank of knowledge such as Global Best Practices® and BusinessRadarSM that is an interactive tool for obtaining personalized news and information. The services also include access to online conferences, password-protected discussions with authorized groups of people, and market research professionals in the Knowledge Enterprises Unit.

11.1.7   Arthur Andersen and Triggers

Arthur Andersen utilizes triggers from external and internal sources. KnowledgeSpace^{SM} provides access via the Internet to external sources of knowledge. The competence centers, other units, and knowledge managers absorb and accumulate new knowledge into the Global Best Practices® knowledge base. The global sharing of triggers through the knowledge base multiplies their effect within the company.

> Our system, as I see it, is always open to new things coming in, open to being disturbed. The goal of Global Best Practices® is to disturb the system. It also distributes the disturbances in a positive way within the organization. So the trigger gets very powerful and makes people more open to experiment. Disturbance dissolves current tradition, and moves us towards change. So, the Global Best Practices® is a trigger of the change (Robert J. Hiebeler).

Arthur Andersen organizes and co-sponsors events that focus on timely and critical areas. In addition, universities (such as MIT and INSEAD), external education programs, mergers, and influential organizations and individuals help to identify new knowledge.

11.1.8   Experimentation at Arthur Andersen

Arthur Andersen implements new solutions and services by experimenting with them first in a smaller environment, testing their feasibility first, and then gaining their acceptance elsewhere. The success stories are identified and forwarded by the board. Some organizational units, such as The School of the Future and the Next Generation Research Group, specialize in experimentation and research.

11.1.9 Arthur Andersen's Internal Standards, Processes, and Communication

11.1.9.1 Work Processes and Communication Global communication enables the internal work processes at Arthur Andersen. The employees share knowledge daily via AANet (Arthur Andersen's Global Area Network). They often work in multidisciplinary, cross-functional, and multinational project groups. The knowledge sharing and communication system helps them to co-operate globally across time and geographic barriers.

> It does not really matter whom you share the knowledge with or where you get the knowledge from. I mean ... you don't really notice it if it comes from the UK or Denmark ... It's just there. It's the people you talk to, and you don't think so much where they are in the world (Sanne Prestegaard).

The accumulation and sharing of knowledge helps the consultants to reuse each other's knowledge and to learn from each other. It releases a consultant's time from repetitive tasks and 'reinventing the wheel' to innovative tasks where he or she can add value to a project.

11.1.9.2 Organization and Career Structure The degree to which an organization is hierarchical or flat has implications for co-operation among employees, individual careers, and organizational learning. Arthur Andersen's organizational solution consists of standardized career steps,[1] defined tasks, curriculum, and training structure. According to Carsten Dalsgaard,

> the organizational levels are needed because a learning organization invests much in the education of people. The idea is that the company has a very specified, well-structured curriculum for all of our consultants. So, for a consultant at a given level, one can set expectations on a person according to this level, based on the education he or she has received. One of the barriers to sharing knowledge is a fear that the others are not capable of using the knowledge. But it seems that within this curriculum, since the company has this education for everybody, there is a higher trust on the others' capabilities. At the same time, there is no idea of investing a big amount of money on knowledge, especially when hiring the best people, without being sure that they remain in this firm. There is no idea of investing a big amount of money if they are not able to go up to the next level within a few years when they have received all this education.

In spite of several specified organizational levels, the qualified peers are able to make decisions among themselves because they are trained to do it. Everyone knows what everyone else knows because of the standardized education and specification of tasks.

The organization is flat in the sense that the *proportion of partners is small compared to the consultants*. This means that individuals have to learn and demonstrate progress. Moreover, this means that there are not many partner positions available.

> The main complication would be if there is no progress as expected. If you are not able to advance in this curriculum, you have to leave the company. But everybody leaving the company is successful elsewhere. There is no problem; they can easily find jobs (Carsten Dalsgaard).

The organization structure is complemented by internal networks, such as Communities of Practice.

11.1.9.3   Education   Arthur Andersen is famous for its commitment to staff training which is a central element in its knowledge management. Employees are continually educated in the international Arthur Andersen Community Learning Center in Illinois. The company also has learning sites in The Netherlands, Spain, and 10 sites in the Asia/Pacific region and Latin America. Employees receive on an average one month's teaching every year.

11.1.10   *Arthur Andersen's Information and Communication Systems*

Arthur Andersen has concluded that learning organizations use information technology as a strategic resource. Information technology facilitates knowledge sharing, accelerates the dissemination and transfer of knowledge, and reduces geographical and temporal barriers. In knowledge sharing, special priority is given to technologies such as electronic mail and groupware systems that function as information bridges. All of Arthur Andersen's employees are connected to organizational knowledge through AA Online that is based on Lotus Notes groupware, and through KnowledgeSpace^{SM} that is built on Intranet.

Each non-administrative employee has a portable computer and standard office software packages. In a number of Arthur Andersen's divisions, the offices have no assigned seats. Each seating arrangement contains a table equipped with a docking station for the mobile computer and a connection to the telephone network. The purpose is to increase flexibility of persons and project teams, facilitate knowledge sharing, and reduce costs. Local networks are connected to AANet that is a global, interconnective data network (wide area network [WAN]).

11.1.11   *Summary of Arthur Andersen's Strategic Components*

The strategic components of Arthur Andersen are summarized in Figure 11.3. Their content is firm specific, and they are interconnected. They are relevant for the firm's learning and renewal capability.

11.2   Arthur Andersen (Business Consulting) as a Living Organization

This section will focus particularly on the organizational sensing (interactive openness) and memory (self-referentiality) that enable Arthur Andersen's renewal and evolution.

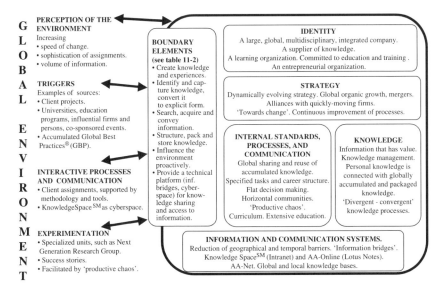

Figure 11.3: The strategic components of Arthur Andersen (Business Consulting).

11.2.1 'Sensing' and 'Memory' of Arthur Andersen

Arthur Andersen is *open* toward the rapidly changing operating environment through three sensing activities: interaction, experimentation, and response to triggers. It has invested considerably in knowledge management resources and placed experienced specialists in key positions, such as knowledge managers. The firm has organized its boundary elements to facilitate *sensing* that supports the firm's identity as a learning organization.

For Arthur Andersen, *memory* means access primarily to globally accumulated knowledge bases, and partially to local knowledge. The firm's knowledge is also stored in people and organizational structures, such as standardized career paths, task specifications, curriculum, consulting methodologies, tools and techniques, and the knowledge-management system including the Universal Process Classification Scheme. Efficient access to knowledge is important because the firm identifies itself as a supplier of knowledge to their clients.

While new knowledge affects Arthur Andersen's learning and renewal system, the system also affects the accumulation of new knowledge. For example, the methods to acquire, screen, structure, package, and accumulate knowledge influence the amount, content, and quality of new knowledge. The repositories of explicit and tacit knowledge enable the firm's daily functioning and help the firm to learn further. "The learning is always in reference to all that you have learned earlier" (Robert J. Hiebeler). This principle is embedded in the firm's cyclic model of creating value that connects personal and organizational learning processes to each other. Accumulated knowledge helps Arthur Andersen to develop its strategy, strengthen its identity, and understand itself in the historical perspective. On a larger scale, its composition, its strategy of global growth, and its identity as a supplier of knowledge facilitate the creation and utilization of new knowledge.

11.2.2   Summary of Arthur Andersen as a Living Organization

Arthur Andersen functions, from the perspective of learning and renewal, as a living (autopoietic) organization (Figure 11.4). Its composition is characterized by an intentional fit, which means that the firm has built consistency intentionally among its strategic components.

Arthur Andersen has defined its identity from the very beginning as a firm that is committed to education, and later as a supplier of knowledge and a learning organization. The firm motivates personnel to learn from the environment and from earlier experiences and each other through knowledge sharing. The motivation is strengthened by the perception of the environment as rapidly changing, increasing in sophistication and information, and by the strategic growth in objectives. At Arthur Andersen, sensing and memory complement each other. They are enabled by major knowledge flows that are supported by extensive information and communication technology solutions, organizational solutions, knowledge management systems, and ultimately the whole composition.

As to sensing, Arthur Andersen co-evolves with its multinational environment and improves knowledge by interacting in client assignments, identifying and capturing GBPs from external sources, and experimenting. The interaction occurs via a variety of boundary elements (roles and functions), such as global partners, employees, competence centers, and KnowledgeSpace[SM]. Knowledge is captured in the 'linear' process of global knowledge accumulation that consists of the divergent process of exploration and the convergent process

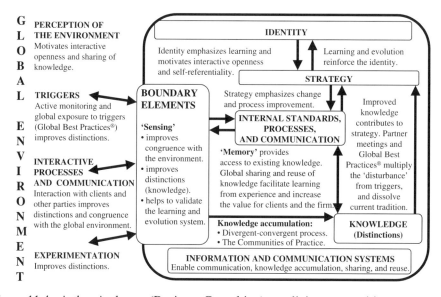

Figure 11.4: Arthur Andersen (Business Consulting) as a living composition.

of creating a shared understanding. It is supplemented by networks such as Communities of Practice where knowledge managers monitor emerging issues. Openness triggers internal changes, provides new knowledge, helps to influence the environment, and validates the learning and renewal system continually.

As to memory, the packaged knowledge is accessed and utilized globally. Employees learn from each other and from earlier experiences through sharing and reusing knowledge. Access to organizational knowledge reduces the need for preconceived notions in engagements, which is necessary for increasingly sophisticated assignments. Global access to knowledge increases its value for clients and Arthur Andersen.

Learning and renewal are made possible by the global information and communication system, which reduces geographical and temporal barriers. It provides information bridges and helps to create and accumulate knowledge. It enables memory by providing access to accumulated knowledge. KnowledgeSpace^{SM} extends these capabilities to also cover clients and external sources of information.

Sharing of knowledge, for example, in partners' meetings helps Arthur Andersen to achieve its strategic objectives and set new ones. One of the objectives is to continually improve the processes. 'Disturbing' knowledge, such as new GBPs whose impact is multiplied through their global distribution, reinforces the firm's identity as a learning organization, helps to evaluate the strategy, and influences internal standards and processes that have a further impact on new knowledge.

> Disturbance dissolves current tradition and makes us change. (-) Triggers can disturb the strategy, which then has impact on internal processes. It then acts on the knowledge, and the knowledge has, again, impact on the strategy. Through communication the new knowledge has a system dynamics impact — it's the internally generated changes on strategy that then change the company (Robert J. Hiebeler).

Organizational learning is facilitated by individual motivation to learn and the necessity to advance in one's career. Internal standards and processes, such as the hierarchical career structure, defined tasks, and extensive education, also influence an individuals' motivation. These processes are increasingly supplemented by communication in networks.

Arthur Andersen compensates for the perturbations that are caused by triggers, experimentation, and interaction with the environment by changing internally and improving knowledge, for example, by the divergent–convergent process. Also, the measurement of peers' contribution to learning helps to improve the learning system. The dynamic self-production process helps Arthur Andersen to 'learn to learn' and to 'collectively understand itself'.

Arthur Andersen, a large, methodologically oriented firm, shares and reuses knowledge (exploitation). As a result, the consultants can focus on the essential aspects of the assignments, and the whole firm learns from co-evolution with the environment (exploration). The firm represents a new solution to the classic dilemma between exploration and exploitation.

The application of the living composition model indicates that clarity and efficiency are the major strengths of Arthur Andersen's learning and renewal system. The open and self-referential knowledge flows are connected together, implemented throughout the company, and supported by considerable organizational and technical solutions. Moreover, the system has the capability to validate itself by utilizing the Global Best Practices® as a reference.

Note

1. The career steps are: Consultant, Senior Consultant, Manager (Regular — Experienced — Senior), Principal Consultant (experienced higher consultant, not owner), Partner (national partner, not owner), and Partner S.C. (owner).

Chapter 12

Arthur D. Little (Europe)

This chapter will present the second case and will show how the living composition model helps to analyze a completely different company, Arthur D. Little (Europe) (hereafter Arthur D. Little), as a living organization. The original analysis was published in 1999. Some information has been updated to reflect the situation in 2001. The first section will analyze the strategic components, and the second section will discuss the dynamics of the firm's learning and renewal. Additional information can be found in Appendix 6.

All interviews have been conducted in Europe and therefore the conclusions cannot be generalized to other regions. The analysis of Arthur D. Little's operations in North America would be very different. During the interviews, the company was going through a profound transformation process on a global scale. The strategic decisions were not fully implemented in all parts of the organization.

12.1 The Strategic Components of Arthur D. Little (Europe)

12.1.1 Arthur D. Little's Identity

Arthur D. Little has a long history. Its managers describe the firm as a globally operating consulting company based on employee ownership. The firm is a specialist organization with high diversity and shared values. It has created a reputation as an innovative and entrepreneurial company with a strong emphasis on people internally and externally. Operating side-by-side with its clients is a key characteristic of the firm.

Arthur D. Little (ADL) *is a globally operating consulting company based on employee ownership.* It is the world's oldest consulting firm and was founded in 1886 by two chemists, Arthur Dehon Little and Roger Griffin, as a contract research organization. The headquarters are located in Cambridge, Massachusetts, USA. The firm employs 3500 people in 52 offices and 30 countries worldwide, as well as more than 100 research laboratories. Until 1979, Arthur D. Little was among the largest consulting companies in the US. Today it is considered a large firm in its market segment, and a medium-sized firm when compared to the largest consulting companies. Its annual revenues are about US$600 million. Ownership is shared by the Memorial Drive Trust (the MDT), the Employee Ownership Plan (ESOP), and current individual employees. The company is structured as a corporation with a board and a CEO.

Arthur D. Little operates in one business: consulting. In 2001 it provided four services globally: Management Consulting, Technology and Innovation, Environment and Risk Consulting, and Incubator Services. However, the company is characterized by two complementary personalities: management consultants and technologists. While in Europe there is a happy co-existence, in the USA there has been internal rivalry between the two groups. As a result, the market's perception of the company has become different in the USA and Europe (Consultants News, June 1997).

Arthur D. Little has two technology centers. *Arthur D. Little School of Management* is an accredited management school. *Innovation Associates (IA)*[1] is a specialized center for learning organization development. In addition, Arthur D. Little has several other business units (Appendix 6).

Arthur D. Little is *a specialist organization with high diversity and shared values.* It is a boardroom consulting company that specializes in technology, organizational change, and innovation management. It differs from its competitors by developing technology on a broad scale, and because its roots are in research and not accounting. The firm is universally recognized for its expertise in scientific research and development (Consultants News, June 1997).

> (In the past) people came to Arthur D. Little either for the superior knowledge or creativity of its people; they came with problems wanting a solution (Kamal Saad).

Arthur D. Little is also regarded as an operations-oriented consulting firm (Consultants News, March 1997).[2] It is known for its commitment to hands-on problem solving, and for its zest in tackling knotty and 'impossible' problems. Sensitivity to market needs has resulted in diversification, which is also a result of a natural evolution over time. This evolution has its roots in the founder's belief in the motto "Scatter ye acorns that mighty oaks may grow" (Kamal Saad). Arthur D. Little has identified the need to focus its activities. Its orientation is shifting from markets to global and local industry practices (18 in Europe). Activities are organized in Europe around markets and industrial and functional practices that are collaborating and partially overlapping virtual knowledge organizations. The functional practices focus, for example, on strategy, technology, innovation, and information management. The European offices and local cultures are quite strong and different from each other (Jacques Hurkmans).

Arthur D. Little is *an innovative and entrepreneurial company with an emphasis on people internally and externally.* The firm has traditionally oriented toward innovation, creativity, and problem solving instead of repetitive work. A large proportion of the innovative action involves modifying earlier solutions. The consultants want to have the freedom to innovate.

> What we sell is innovation. Which means that we are collectively and individually extremely capable of resolving new problems or bringing new solutions to existing problems. We are lousy at implementing the same solution over and over again. That simply doesn't interest people. (-) But you have the economic imperative. If it's too chaotic, it doesn't work (Philippe Alloing).

Arthur D. Little generates new ideas in several ways. People are free to develop their own ideas or reflections from the market. They can pick ideas that are 'floating around' and work on them with their colleagues. New ideas are also generated in laboratories and specialized units. They are generated in Europe in co-operation with functional and industry leaders and market managers. Global practice leaders create worldwide programs around new ideas, taking local needs into account. Moreover, the firm has acquired new knowledge through acquisitions. 'Gurus' have been an invaluable source of new knowledge for the innovation-oriented consulting firm. However, it is not easy to maintain conditions in a consulting organization that are favorable for them.

According to Jacques Hurkmans, Arthur D. Little gives highest priority to the client, second to the employee, and third to the company. Arthur D. Little employs two kinds of people. The *specialists* possess solid 10–15 years' experience and industry knowledge and pragmatic skills to tackle clients' problems. The *young, high-achieving, and ambitious people* often have scientific backgrounds and academic sharpness, for example Ph.D. degrees.

> One of the things that makes Arthur D. Little special is that we attract people who are highly intellectual and analytical, who are independent free-thinkers, and who are self-starters. The other side of the coin, of course, is that they don't take kindly to direction when this does not fit their own ideas. (Kamal Saad).
>
> In the screening of people, we look for people that have something special. We want people that are able to stand out in the crowd (Nils Bohlin).

New consultants often join the firm through 'bonding' that occurs at an early stage. According to Nils Bohlin, the people who are attracted to the company join because they like certain things about the company as a whole, and then they 'bond' with one or two key individuals. 'Bonding' is a very important element in making the decision to join the firm.

Arthur D. Little is known for *working side-by-side with its clients*. This means interacting with clients at several levels of the organization. Serge Pegoff mentions that Arthur D. Little's management consultants have always been able to address different layers of management within the customer organization. Therefore the firm has a good capacity to adapt to a customer situation.

According to Nils Bohlin, the firm has established Key Client Teams to serve local and global key clients. Long relationships, over 5–10 years for example, fundamentally change the value-creation context. They add value for the client because the consultants know the client well, start working quickly on the client's problems, and know the impact of their services. Long relationships increase the responsibility of the client and make it possible to take risks.

12.1.2   Arthur D. Little's Perception of its Environment

Arthur D. Little believes that most changes in the environment of corporations over the last 20 years stem from a single cause: our entire society is in the early stages of a new era. Instead of the land, labor, and capital based economies, we are living today in an economy based on knowledge and learning. This breeds change at an increasing rate (see Managing in a Learning-Based Society. An Arthur D. Little Point of View).

12.1.3   Arthur D. Little's Strategy

During the 1980s, the capacity of the consulting industry increased rapidly and competition hardened when accounting firms and new companies entered the market with a generalist approach. Mergers to gain scale benefits in the industry caused dramatic polarization and pushed the industry toward an hourglass shape. The disparity between the largest consulting firms and the rest of the industry became more pronounced and weakened Arthur D. Little's position. In 1994 the firm started to reshape and respecify its strategy, policy, and procedures toward the One-Company Management Platform that focused the company on 'one business' (consulting) and on the application of best practices to the firm's seven major business processes. The One-Company Management Platform is a framework for creating a coherent, integrated, and collaborative organization. It was implemented to unify the relatively autonomous North American, European, Latin American, and Asia Pacific consulting groups by developing a shared culture and emphasizing cross-business opportunities and cross-allocation of resources among the regions. The purpose was also to clarify the firm's brand position and formulate a common strategy. At Arthur D. Little, making strategic decisions is relatively easy because of the legal structure (the Board and CEO), but implementing them is difficult because of the individualist tradition.

Arthur D. Little has grown organically and supplemented its growth with acquisitions. Growing in its current niche of innovation is not easy. According to Philippe Alloing, one of the firm's strategic challenges is that the firm is getting fairly big in its present niche, and there is a limit to its growth. It is not possible to grow at a rate of 25–30% when the market is growing at a rate of 15%.

12.1.4   Arthur D. Little's Knowledge and Knowledge Management

Personal knowledge   Arthur D. Little's consulting is based largely on individual specialists' tacit and action-oriented knowledge. Consultants are expected to have 'T-shaped' skills: a breadth of functional skills, in-depth knowledge in their own specialty, and long experience in a specific industry. Most of them have an MBA degree and many of them have been working in the industry for 10–15 years. The company's workforce has more than 100 Ph.D. degrees.[3]

The firm places great value on collaboration, team spirit, and interpersonal skills. Tackling 'impossible' problems also requires conceptual and methodological skills, initiative, and problem solving capabilities.

Organizational knowledge   Arthur D. Little defines organizational knowledge capital as the sum of experience and understanding. These two factors are embedded in the ideas and skills of employees, systems and procedures, research labs, brand equity, and the activities and aspects of culture. Part of the firm's knowledge is stored in knowledge bases, and some in the form of patents.[4] Arthur D. Little's industry knowledge "is not what can be found in management books; it is at the forefront of innovation" (Philip Alloing).

Knowledge about employees, 'Who Is Who' and 'Who knows What', is important for the specialist firm. Employees also have access to 'best practices' and information about project cases.

Prism is Arthur D. Little's quarterly point-of-view journal, a medium for presenting knowledge about emerging topics. It helps to distribute new ideas among employees and clients and increase the company's visibility in its market.

Knowledge management   For Arthur D. Little, learning, knowledge, and change constitute a self-perpetuating cycle. Learning generates knowledge, knowledge fuels change, and change accelerates learning. The objective is to facilitate organizational learning and capitalize on knowledge.

Nils Bohlin mentions that Arthur D. Little builds *tacit specialist knowledge* 'within people' by managing their careers toward specialization and focus. The firm also gives them broad opportunities for managing client projects.

> All employees, even young analysts, are given the opportunity from the very beginning to build client relationships. At ADL, analysts take part at a very early stage in all aspects of the business. However, the proportion of different tasks is dependent on an employee's status (Jacques Hurkmans).

Processes among people facilitate knowledge creation, organizational learning, and change. Examples of these processes are Jamborees, extensive co-operation among directors, office lunches, Monday morning meetings, practice meetings, and other gatherings and networks. Some gatherings are organized on a regional basis, across offices and career stages. Informal leaders facilitate creativity and innovativeness across boundaries in this diversified company.

In the beginning of the 1990s, Arthur D. Little identified seven major business processes in order to manage its business more effectively. Knowledge management was later formulated into a business process as well, and the firm decided to implement a systematic and explicit knowledge sharing culture. Knowledge management is based on four domains: content, culture, process, and (technical) environment. *Content* refers to knowledge elements and their relative importance. The purpose is to systematize the multitude of communication through shared global knowledge bases, explicit and generic knowledge, and the search for 'knowledge nuggets'. *Culture* means identifying cultural realities, such as business impact, that act as barriers or enablers for knowledge management.

Process refers to building knowledge management into the existing every-day work processes instead of separate knowledge processes. The purpose is to capture the learning from the assignments more effectively. For example, the Case Closing "is a routine that we want the case teams to do in order to crystallize, to move from tacit to explicit knowledge" (Nils Bohlin). 'Process' refers also to managing knowledge (capture, evaluate, cleanse, store, provide, and use) and to knowledge management roles (not jobs) for consultants, analysts, and information specialists. A central team, located in the US, is responsible for developing knowledge management practices and systems. The team is headed by the Global Director of Knowledge Management. The industrial and functional practices accumulate knowledge according to their own needs. Each industry practice follows trends and relevant issues. The functional practices focus on products, generic methods, tools, and techniques. A 'knowledge steward' is a full-time junior project manager whose task is to extract and abstract knowledge and make knowledge management work within a practice.

The *technical environment* refers mainly to ADL Link, the global information and communication system. "While technology is critical for effective knowledge management, it is at best only about 20% of the challenge. The company has to have rules, trained people, coding structures, and so on" (Larry Chait).

Structure and discipline   Arthur D. Little's growth and the need to capitalize on knowledge assets increase the demand for structure and discipline. According to Frederick Bock, the company is searching all over the company for examples, tools, methodologies, and so on, to lead to development of a company-wide structure.

> Now we are growing to the size where you cannot know everybody anymore. So you need some structure. But structure goes against the nature of ADL consultants. They don't like structure. They don't like to be told … they want to be independent, creative, developing their niches, and that's how we work. (Boudewijn Arts).
>   At Arthur D. Little you have a lot of space. It is not an easy environment. However, there is structure, formalization, and guidance available if you need it (Alexander de Wit).

12.1.5   Arthur D. Little's Boundary Elements

Arthur D. Little is connected to its environment via various boundary elements (roles and functions). They help to create new knowledge and experiences through interaction. They identify, select, capture, structure, accumulate, share, evaluate, and convey knowledge in tacit form as specialization and convert it into explicit form when necessary. The boundary elements also help to influence the environment and provide a technical platform that assists in communicating, finding, and sharing knowledge (Table 12.1).

12.1.6   Arthur D. Little's Interaction and Co-evolution with its Environment

Arthur D. Little regards clients as allies and aims at long-term relationships with them. The firm analyzes and solves problems side-by-side with their clients at several organizational levels, including the boardroom level. The purpose of the Key Client Teams and Key Client management is to create value for increasingly global clients.

As to information technology and information management services for its clients, Arthur D. Little focuses on the front-end activities and the most important decisions. The firm does not normally participate in detailed repetitive work and implementation at other than a project management level.

Arthur D. Little uses pragmatic methodological approaches and issue-driven cases. Several methodologies concerning strategic and organizational development are available, and new ones are developed according to the need. An 'organizational learning' approach is often included in a larger consulting project.

The firm also organizes Best of the Best colloquiums for 10–15 top CEOs from various companies. Prominent senior executives share insights, experience, and best practices about relevant topics for 3–4 days. Each year Arthur D. Little, together with external evaluators, selects 20 Best of the Best companies within the key functional practices.

Table 12.1: The boundary elements of Arthur D. Little (Europe).

Boundary elements/ Arthur D. Little	Purpose of role/function
Top managers	Scan environment and the opportunities to acquire new knowledge e.g., through acquisitions
Recruitment process	Supports hiring (1) people with solid experience, and (2) young, high achieving people with university knowledge
Employees and case teams, Key Client Teams	Create new knowledge together with clients. Capture and convey knowledge from the interaction with clients. Accumulate knowledge about local and global clients
Product management and documentation	Convert knowledge about client needs into new products
Functional/industry practices	Help to create and accumulate specialist knowledge
Gatherings, meetings, etc.	Capture, share, evaluate, and convey knowledge
Information specialists in the main offices, 'Knowledge Stewards'	Acquire information from external sources. Identify and extract knowledge from the global knowledge bases. Facilitate access to the knowledge
Specialized units, such as: • **Innovation associates** • **Research centers**	Create, accumulate, and disseminate new knowledge
Formal training	Provides a forum for sharing knowledge and experience
In USA: Arthur D. Little School of Management, executive education program	Facilitate interaction with (potential) clients and specialists from universities like Harvard University and the Massachusetts Institute of Technology (MIT)

Table 12.1: Continued.

Boundary elements/ Arthur D. Little	Purpose of role/function
Best of the Best colloquia, International conferences, Research program/ INSEAD, Prism (point-of-view journal)	Facilitate interaction and acquisition of new knowledge. Distribute relevant issues internally and externally
Information system link, collaboration tools, such as Team Rooms, Internet connections	Facilitate access to specialist knowledge, communication in teams and with clients, capture knowledge increasingly in explicit form, and find facts from external sources

Arthur D. Little cooperates with universities and research institutions, participates in international conferences, and organizes education via the Arthur D. Little School of Management. The *Prism* (Arthur D. Little's quarterly journal) and mobilizing projects (such as writing books) help to develop new ideas and gain visibility outside the firm.

12.1.7   Arthur D. Little and Triggers

Arthur D. Little is very sensitive to market needs and searches for relevant information from the Internet and other external sources. In the main offices, 2–3 specialists are specifically assigned to scout knowledge according to the office's needs. Because the firm's specialist knowledge is very diversified, this is a more cost-effective way to find knowledge than building extensive knowledge bases.

According to Philippe Alloing the firm has traditionally had strong connections to universities such as Harvard, MIT, and INSEAD. The Massachusetts Institute of Technology (MIT) held 80% of Arthur D. Little's shares for many years. Consultants who deal with 'learning organization' issues are connected to INSEAD, where Arthur D. Little is funding a research program. Individuals specialize because they want to become a focus of know-ledge creation in a specific field. Arthur D. Little's specialists often participate as speakers at conferences.

Hiring new people at the top level of organizations and building personal networks provide new knowledge and views. Clients often signal about issues that are of particular interest even if they are not related to a specific project. Moreover, the acquisitions of companies such as Cambridge Consultants and Innovation Associates have provided new knowledge and acted as triggers for Arthur D. Little.

12.1.8   Experimentation at Arthur D. Little

Arthur D. Little has an entrepreneurial culture that accepts failure. The firm tests new ideas with top CEOs at the Best of the Best colloquiums. Consultants are also keen to experiment and test new solutions to client problems. Clients differ from each other and their needs are treated as unique. However, some people feel that the firm is not sticking enough to established methodologies.

12.1.9 Arthur D. Little's Internal Standards, Processes, and Communication

Work processes and communication   At Arthur D. Little, the work in all engagements and practices is based on teamwork across borders. Project teams are relatively small. According to Boudewijn Arts, the persons on the teams have different skills, which accelerates learning. The teams are also well balanced, which means that a young person can get exposure to clients and casework early.

   Arthur D. Little has evolved from a 'tribal' culture to one of standard practices. In the process of industrialization and globalization, the firm has maintained its capability to act in an organic way. The attempt to institutionalize decisions about how things should be done has not been very successful.

> So we still see that maybe the best way to get things done in our company is to bring people together who have the necessary determination and energy. They just do it. (-) … when we try to organize things in a structured way, the result has been disappointing. So there is something special about this organic way of developing things where the interest and passion of the people drives progress. In our culture it seems to be that the moment you start to organize, too many people move away from the activity and they are not really interested any longer (Nils Bohlin).

Arthur D. Little behaves like 'a heap of sand'. Instead of creating fixed structures, the firm creates favorable conditions and gives an orientation.

> At best what you have is, say, a heap of sand. Each of the people in ADL are really like sand grains. And there are relations of proximity with the other sand grains in the neighborhood. The sand is constantly shifting by what the clients want, by economic constraints. So giving it a structure is extremely difficult. The best you can hope is to create the right conditions and give an orientation, and to hope that then the conditions will push the heap of sand in the right direction. This 'sand heap' system works because it is … I think it is coherent with the shared purpose of the whole sand grains. They are basically orientated within the same magnetic field. (Philippe Alloing).

Moreover, Arthur D. Little's way of operating can be regarded as 'friendly chaos' that provides freedom, variety, and intellectual stimulation.

> It's a friendly chaos. (-) We are living in this chaos. There is no strong structure so there is a place for all kinds of strange aberrations, let's say. (-) I cannot give you the 'typical ADL consultant' or the 'typical ADL office' or 'week' or … it's impossible. These people are so different. And that's also

very stimulating, because it makes you also adapt yourself to all these different kinds of people (Boudewijn Arts).

Work processes are increasingly based on knowledge, methodologies, and models that are shared at the country, European, and global levels. However, communication occurs mainly in the local context.

> The most important context is still typically the local one, and in any organization what is most important is what the boss says (Maurice Olivier).

Organization, cylindrical hierarchy, and alternative career paths   Arthur D. Little Europe's organizational structure is a matrix that is based on markets and practices. Each employee has responsibilities within an industrial and functional practice. The organization can be described as a cylinder instead of a pyramid (Figure 12.1). This means that there is one director for two managers and three consultants, whereas in a pyramid structure the manager is responsible for a much bigger number of subordinates. The cylinder structure is required because Arthur D. Little attempts to increase clients' performance through strategy work instead of cost reduction, and strategy work requires senior people.

The cylinder structure has implications for recruiting, careers, learning, and renewal. First, it means long-term commitment from the firm's side, provides employees with opportunities to advance in the firm, and creates the possibility of lifetime jobs.

> Most of the consulting companies recruit people and then select them on the job. They test fit when the people are in the job. That's the so-called 'up-or-out' policy. In our case it's very different. We (first) select people

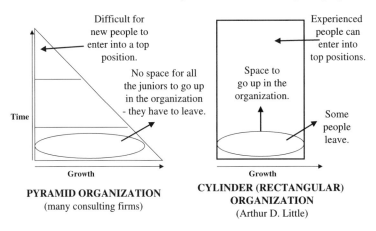

Figure 12.1: Career opportunities in pyramid and cylinder organizations (*source*: Arthur D. Little).

and then we recruit them. But once they are in, there really has to be a recruit mistake to be thrown out. And people will help a new colleague be successful (Philippe Alloing).

Because there are a high number of people from the customer working on the problem, and a very low number of people from us, all the people including the junior one are very exposed to the customer. There is no place to hide. So they must be damned good. They must be very, very good. But that's OK, because we do not have too many of them. So we can be very choosy. And because they must be so good, because of the career structure, when we hire one of those young guys, it is very clear that what we offer them is a potential lifetime job as long as they meet the economic equation (Serge Pegoff).

Second, in order to maintain the organizational structure, Arthur D. Little recruits young, high achieving, and ambitious people from universities as well as people with long experience at all organizational levels.

Third, the even distribution of people in the different age groups makes it easier to staff and manage the client projects.

If I live in a company which has a classical pyramidal structure, I am putting myself by definition in a situation where I have a lot of inexperienced people to keep busy, and this will conflict at some point with the fact that I have to solve the customer problem — not our own problem (Serge Pegoff).

Fourth, it is possible to create alternative career paths in addition to the normal career path where each step[5] takes 2–3 years. Consultants may obtain high responsibilities quickly because the progression plan is based on demonstrated capability that is evaluated every six months by a coach. However, they tend to be more interested in the cases and intellectual challenges than in day-to-day management. The employees own their destiny in the company; they are not told what to do. They are equals, independent of their professional career position. They are expected to be entrepreneurs and to sell themselves in the internal market. This also means that a successful leader has to create followership rather than leadership, to sell ideas rather than to force them on others. The firm provides opportunities to change the area of expertise if needed.

Arthur D. Little's employees have agreed to balance the human environment and intellectual challenge with fair compensation. The earlier single-dimensional incentive system was regarded as divisive and ran counter to organizational learning. Today the company applies a modified multi-dimensional incentive system.

Education   The Arthur D. Little School of Management has provided education for clients from 1964. However, the formal education of the firm's own employees is quite a new phenomenon. It is guided by Consulting Career Standards and organized (in Europe) by Acorn Professional Development in France and another education center in the US. During the first seven years of their career, consultants will have one week of formal training a year. Senior people will receive special education. Regular education facilitates networking among colleagues. Its content has changed from facts and methods toward skills and behavioral issues, the ladders of personal development.

At Arthur D. Little an employee must learn and acquire knowledge actively. The motivation for work originates from intellectual analysis and interest in solving the client's problems successfully. A case " … is what we care about. It is where we get pride, our satisfaction, our recognition" (Nils Bohlin). Philippe Alloing believes that people join consulting companies because they want to develop themselves extremely fast and far. At Arthur D. Little " … their ambitions, private ambitions, are legitimate. And we proclaim that." People may not be motivated by money or any institutional reward systems. They are 'high achievers' who are extremely ambitious and want to work in a warm and supporting environment and to get to their desired level of success.

12.1.10   Arthur D. Little's Information and Communication Systems

Arthur D. Little increasingly utilizes information and communication technology to facilitate organizational learning and change. After World War II, a lot of the MIT specialists moved next door to ADL to apply their computer skills to business. In spite of this strong historical background, information technology has not been a high priority for the firm until recently. The emphasis has been on people and communication rather than on technology. Voicemail, electronic mail, and videoconferencing are currently widely utilized.

ADL Link, the global information and communication system developed by Arthur D. Little, USA, helps to systematize communication. It is a group of applications that are based on Lotus Domino groupware. It provides interfaces to all information systems and supports knowledge sharing across the company. It provides access to shared global knowledge bases concerning employees, their availability, languages, assignments, cases, qualifications, documents, client contacts, and project management. Knowledge bases also contain structured profiles of all current customers worldwide. ADL Link provides opportunities for discussion groups, collaboration tools, Internet connections, and WEB-publishing (Larry Chait).

12.1.11   Summary of Arthur D. Little's Strategic Components

The following figure summarizes the strategic components that constitute Arthur D. Little as a living organization (Figure 12.2).

12.2   Arthur D. Little (Europe) as a Living Organization

This section will analyze the learning and renewal of Arthur D. Little, especially in terms of sensing, memory, and dynamics.

12.2.1   'Sensing' and 'Memory' of Arthur D. Little

Arthur D. Little *acquires, creates, and accumulates new knowledge* because of its identity as a global, innovative, and entrepreneurial specialist organization. Also, the

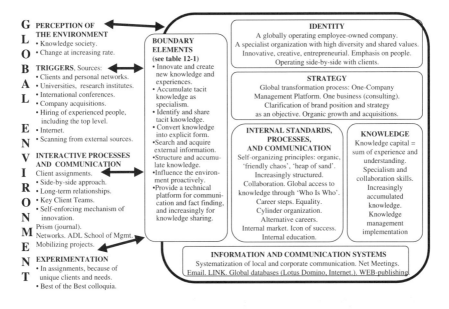

Figure 12.2: The strategic components of Arthur D. Little (Europe).

firm's strategy (transformation, organic growth, and acquisitions) emphasizes the need for new knowledge. Openness is also needed because the pace of environmental change is increasing. The firm interacts with clients in unique projects and conducts experiments. Consultants adopt new knowledge that is relevant to their own field of expertise. Various boundary elements participate in the interaction with the business environment.

Arthur D. Little needs *access to accumulated knowledge* because it is a specialist organization and aims to act as One Company. The firm facilitates communication among employees and shares knowledge that is accumulated in experts and increasingly also in global knowledge bases.

Arthur D. Little defines knowledge capital as the sum of experience and understanding and claims that accumulated knowledge is embedded in the firm's systems and procedures, research labs, brands, activities, and the aspects of culture that contribute to its success. This experience and understanding that has been accumulated during the firm's long history influences its daily functioning, acquisition of new knowledge, learning, and renewal. For example, the firm's consulting approach influences its business processes, recruitment, and methods of managing knowledge. The firm's learning and renewal are largely based on informal processes and the accumulation of tacit knowledge in experts in the cylindrical organization. The firm has been more oriented toward innovating new solutions than utilizing earlier ones. However, the knowledge management system has improved the firm's capability to accumulate and access explicit knowledge from internal and external sources, which has further impacted the firm and its evolution as a living organization.

12.2.2   Summary of Arthur D. Little as a Living Organization

Arthur D. Little constitutes an autopoietic (self-producing and not only autonomous) learning and renewal system (Figure 12.3). The firm continually produces its non-physical strategic components and maintains its identity and boundaries.

Arthur D. Little's current composition is a result of its long history. Its identity as an innovative specialist company is based on the values of the firm's founder. While the company has re-defined its identity as a result of competition in the industry, it has maintained the continuity of its evolution (autopoietic identity). Its identity influences the firm's daily functioning, facilitates individual and collective learning, and contributes to openness (sensing). Also, the perception of the environment as a changing knowledge economy, and the strategic objective of growth, motivate the firm's employees to learn from their environment and from each other.

Arthur D. Little interacts with its environment through boundary elements, such as employees, global partners, and Key Client Teams. Boundary elements facilitate learning from the environment, improve congruence with it through specialization and diversification, improve knowledge, and help to validate the learning and renewal system.

Arthur D. Little maintains interactive openness and improves knowledge and congruence with its environment through reciprocal interaction side-by-side with clients and other parties, by responding to triggers from client cases and other sources, by acquiring new knowledge via acquisitions and new experts, and by experimenting. Knowledge capital is accumulated within people by managing their careers and cases, and also increasingly in the global knowledge bases. Knowledge processes are supported by the global knowledge management organization.

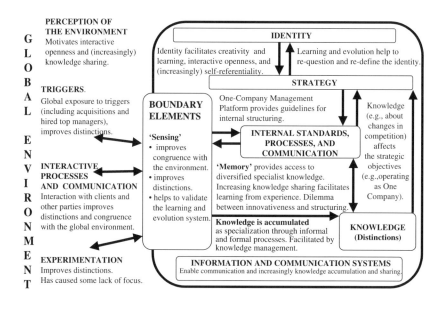

Figure 12.3: Arthur D. Little (Europe) as a living composition.

Self-referentiality (memory) refers to accumulated expertise, whether in individual specialists or global knowledge bases. Access to existing and new knowledge helps to provide innovative, unique services for clients and increases the value of knowledge for clients and the firm itself. Informal processes, such as gatherings and meetings, and formal ones, such as ADL Link, help employees to communicate and share knowledge.

The competitive situation has contributed to the strategic decision to act as One Company. The need for an innovative company to structure and standardize its chaotic, organic, and 'heap of sand' ways of functioning occurs paradoxically at the same time as the more structured and standardized competitors implement chaotic, organic, and self-organizing principles to foster creativity and inspiration among employees.

At Arthur D. Little, organizational learning depends largely on individuals. The personal motivation of autonomous self-starters arises from their ambition to solve clients' problems in expert teams, to specialize, and to obtain an image of success rather than a managerial position or other compensation. Leadership means creating followership in the internal market. The cylindrical organization and alternative career paths allow the injection of experienced new people at all levels of the firm, and encourages long-term commitment. Learning is supported by education that focuses on personal development rather than on the distribution of information.

Arthur D. Little compensates for the perturbations that are caused by triggers, experimentation, and interaction with its environment by improving knowledge through specialization and diversification, and by changing internally toward acting as One Company, which aims at maintaining congruence with its globalizing environment.

Arthur D. Little is an example of a carefully aligned intentional fit composition in a diversified specialist organization. On the other hand, the firm's composition is of the form 'stretch' (intended inconsistency between the strategic components). The purpose of the transformation process is to considerably improve internal consistency and congruence with the environment, to move proactively from the earlier intentional fit to a new, improved intentional fit composition. In the longer perspective, Arthur D. Little's evolution has occurred as a sequence of minor changes and major transformations (several 'stretches').

The application of the living composition model indicates that Arthur D. Little is capable of interacting in a close relationship side-by-side with its clients and creating new knowledge through innovation. The firm benefits from teamwork and organic principles that influence internal standards, processes, and culture in subtle ways. The firm also inspires and motivates experts through shared identity and ownership.

NOTES

1. Innovation Associates was co-founded by Peter Senge and Charles Kiefer in 1976.
2. The other categories are strategy oriented, information-technology oriented, and human-relations oriented.
3. The Ph.Ds are mostly related to technical consulting in the USA, not to management consulting and Europe.
4. The patents are related mainly to the technology and product development services.
5. The basic professional career path consists of the following steps: Research Associate (Business Analyst), Consultant, Manager, Senior Manager, Associate Director, Director.

Chapter 13

Ernst & Young (Management Consulting)

This chapter will demonstrate how the living composition model helps to systematically analyze Ernst & Young's Management Consulting practice. It describes the situation before Ernst & Young Consulting Services became a part of Cap Gemini Ernst & Young through a merger in 1999. The new company combines the resources of Gemini Consulting, Cap Gemini IT Services, and Ernst & Young Consulting Services. In the following analysis, the focus will be on Ernst & Young's Management Consulting practice even if some aspects applied to the entire Ernst & Young organization. The first section describes the strategic components and the second section describes the dynamics of the firm. Additional information is included in Appendix 7.

In 1999 Ernst & Young was growing fast and changing quickly as a global organization. Some systems and solutions that were created in the USA had not been fully implemented in the local offices yet. At the top level the visions were global and future-oriented, whereas in the local offices and in countries other than the USA, the vision was more regionally or locally oriented.

13.1 The Strategic Components of Ernst & Young (Management Consulting)

13.1.1 Ernst & Young's Identity

Ernst & Young represents *a large, globally operating consulting company composed of many local member companies.* It is a result of a merger between Ernst & Whinney and Arthur Young in 1989. It is one of the largest accounting and consulting companies in the world, operating globally in more than 130 countries and employing 84,000 professionals in 2002. In 1997, Ernst & Young's Management Consulting Practice merged with Cap Gemini, and its revenues were US$2.7 billion, growing 29% that year.

Ernst & Young defines itself as an account-centric company that creates value for the client. Moreover, Ernst & Young's managers depict the firm as an information technology and methodology oriented company and a knowledge sharing culture.

Ernst & Young's headquarters are located in New York and main development occurs in the USA. The company is composed of Ernst & Young International (EYI) and local (national) member firms that are privately owned by local partners, with some parallels to franchising. Consensus and the 'all for one and one for all' ethic underlie the firm's global culture.

In the beginning of the 1990s, Ernst & Young went through rapid growth and a profound transformation process. It adopted a new image and reorganized itself to learn and share knowledge on a worldwide basis. The firm works across borders and services multinational clients. The Centers for Business Knowledge™ (CBK) on various continents facilitate knowledge management.[1] Other centers serve as 'thought leadership' units, as centers for methodological development, and as promoters for information technology utilization.

Ernst & Young is *an 'account-centric' company.* Its purpose is to *create value for clients* by pursuing thought leadership and developing new ideas, methodologies, and solutions.

Ernst & Young's Management Consulting practice is *oriented around information technology* (Consultants News, March 1997). Services include, for example, the planning of IT strategies, customized services, and implementation of complex standardized software packages in the clients' businesses. *Structured methodologies and pragmatism* enable the consultants to 'talk the same language' with their large multinational clients.

Ernst & Young is *a knowledge sharing culture.* The firm's member companies have made a formal agreement about knowledge management and sharing. John G. Peetz, the Chief Knowledge Officer (CKO) of Ernst & Young US, assumes that at least part of the firm's increasing growth resulted from the knowledge sharing vision (3% in 1993, 8% in 1994, 16% in 1995, 21% in 1996 and 1997). One of the major benefits from the knowledge sharing initiatives is the creation of a new image for the company as a knowledge sharing culture (Emerson, 1997). According to Ralph W. Poole, the firm accelerates learning by applying its earlier problem-solving experiences to new situations. It does not copy solutions but learns from them and is able to do this globally.

13.1.2   Ernst & Young's Perception of its Environment

For Ernst & Young, its environment means global markets that are characterized by increasingly rapid changes and discontinuities. It means an arena of competition where knowledge is the most important competitive factor.

13.1.3   Ernst & Young's Strategy

Ernst & Young has grown rapidly. Most of the growth after the merger in 1989 has been organic but the company also grows by entering new markets. In 1993, four years after the merger, the company was still fragmented and loosely organized. A Vision 2000 team was established to develop a vision and strategy for the company and to lay out a knowledge strategy. The team suggested initiatives for improving five 'mega-processes': sales, service, delivery, people, and knowledge. They became the basis for further knowledge management efforts. High growth combined with the 15–20% annual turnover of people has caused challenges for the company (John G. Peetz).

The large-scale organizational transformation and rapid improvement of the mega-processes relied on an ambitious implementation plan, supported by more than 160 member firms. Moving Ernst & Young from the middle-of-the-pack to the recognized leader in the application of internal technologies and knowledge sharing was a 'formidable challenge' (Emerson, 1997). The investments, especially in knowledge management, were a strategic move to provide clients with customized higher margin services, to become more flexible and future-oriented, and to prepare for the changes and discontinuities of global markets. Balancing between standard offerings (such as the implementation of standard software packages) and new offerings (such as knowledge-management services) is one of the major challenges for Ernst & Young (Digrius, 1997).

13.1.4 Ernst & Young's Knowledge and Knowledge Management

Personal knowledge   Ernst & Young attempts to capture, share, and reuse individuals' tacit knowledge globally through the knowledge management system.

> If a person left the company ten years ago, the knowledge went with him. Today no, it is not true, because during his career we have produced documents, knowledge and so on. Normally — not everything but most of this knowledge — is stored in these databases. So we can keep part of the knowledge. And specifically, if he is a guru or an expert, the Subject Matter Expert, he produces and shares a lot (Michel Constant).

The documentation of the firm's expertise enables Ernst & Young to leverage its size, reuse its problem-solving experience, accelerate the delivery of value to the marketplace, and emphasize the importance of team learning and experience sharing (Emerson, 1997).

Organizational knowledge   For Ernst & Young, information is the raw material from which knowledge is formed. Knowledge is achieved through learning processes, and it is linked to business processes and information.

Ernst & Young's 'content imperative' in knowledge management means achieving thought leadership, injecting more content into work, and gaining world-class status in transferring knowledge. 'Knowledge content architecture' refers to unfiltered knowledge (such as discussion databases), moderately filtered knowledge (content-specific and firm-wide knowledge bases), and highly filtered, 'packaged' knowledge (PowerPacks and practice-specific knowledge bases). Stored knowledge can be accessed via EY/KnowledgeWeb (EY/KWeb), Ernst & Young's 'pathway to knowledge' that is managed by the Center for Business Knowledge™ (CBK), Cleveland. EY/KWeb is the collective, catalogued information available via a network to all professionals worldwide, 24 hours a day. It contains 470 databases, 62,000 documents, discussion databases, external reference material, news feeds and periodicals. It is used more than 200,000 times per month.

PowerPacks include Ernst & Young's 150 constantly updated and customized compilations of relevant topics. They constitute the firm's documented expertise in its core competences. The PowerPacks can be loaded via EY/KWeb or CD-ROMs onto a desktop or laptop computer. They are organized according to a standardized table of contents and they contain, for example, industry knowledge, methods, and service-related knowledge. They facilitate knowledge sharing among 'disconnected users', employees who normally spend 75% of their time outside the office traveling or working at the clients' premises.

The global knowledge bases include large document repositories, client-team knowledge bases, and administrative knowledge bases. The Leading Practices Knowledge base contains best operating practices about business functions and industries within Ernst & Young. Project managers and knowledge managers are expected to store key facts into the 'MC Quals and Value Statements' database at the end of every project. Ernst & Young's knowledge is also published and shared in the form of books, articles, conferences, surveys, and research documents.

EY/InfoLink is a standardized interface and proprietary profiling software that provides access to external knowledge, including more than 60 publications and external research databases. It monitors trends and daily events and distributes the results via electronic mail every 24 hours.

Knowledge management   The Vision 2000 initiative is aimed at creating a global knowledge strategy and infrastructure. Ernst & Young originally had a loose organization that consisted of national firms, and the information systems were based on multiple software and hardware platforms. In 1993 the member companies in various countries signed an agreement creating a shared global knowledge infrastructure and knowledge management organization. In 1997, Ernst & Young was classified as the leader in knowledge management, measured by the completeness of vision and the ability to execute (Digrius Gartner Group, 1997). Ralph W. Poole mentions that rapid success was based on central planning and building, and local commitment and implementation.

According to John G. Peetz, the objective of knowledge management is to achieve consistency, contribute to thought leadership, leverage intellectual capital, and unlock the power of size, capability, and market dominance. Ernst & Young also aims at providing background knowledge for employees so that they can improvise an approach that suits the particular client situation (Davenport, 1996).

In order to create an entirely new knowledge-sharing culture, Ernst & Young has not only focused on technologies but also addressed the content, people, and process issues. The firm has created content and processes to collect, update, store, add value to, and deploy knowledge, and it has trained people in these aspects. The global knowledge bases were created in three steps — first by persuading the firm to change the way it thinks about knowledge, then by overcoming the functional divisions, and finally by linking consultants' job evaluations to their contribution to the database (John G. Peetz). One-fourth of a person's annual performance (in the US) is based on his or her contribution to the knowledge process. Junior associates are graded by the quantity of their submissions. Contribution to a PowerPack may provide extra points (Bank, 1996).

Ernst & Young depicts knowledge management with the Knowledge Process Landscape model. According to Ralph W. Poole, the small cycle describes how the bottom-up filtering processes and networks that are dedicated to searching and packaging knowledge into PowerPacks accumulate knowledge and its value. The big cycle describes how knowledge is applied in assignments, how value is created for clients, and how the organization learns from all of that. The Knowledge Process Landscape is adopted as a mental model at all organizational levels, and it provides the basis for building the knowledge organization (Figure 13.1).

According to Ralph W. Poole, Ernst & Young has created an extensive global knowledge management organization where the professionals have a specified role in knowledge management. They are employed by the knowledge centers and involved in knowledge

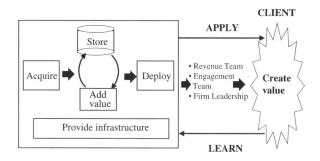

Figure 13.1: Ernst & Young's knowledge process landscape model.

networks, for example in the role of a Subject Matter Expert. They work as National Chief Knowledge Officers, as Knowledge Managers in the management consulting practice, or as Knowledge Stewards in engagements, and many of them are connected to the Knowledge Based Businesses (KBB) Practice that is a service line. Other global development centers also employ numerous specialists.

Several executive steering committees and process owners are dedicated to building, maintaining and developing the knowledge management system. Knowledge processes are owned by the US Chief Knowledge Officer (CKO) and four main knowledge centers in Cleveland, Toronto, Paris, and Sydney. The main knowledge center, The Ernst & Young Center for Business Knowledge™ (CBK) in Cleveland, employs more than 200 knowledge professionals. It provides knowledge and information to the firm's management and other professionals. It also manages the transfer of practice experience and knowledge, conducts fact-based business research, and promotes organizational learning and knowledge development. The center is globally responsible for the EY/KnowledgeWeb, repository management, acquisition of external information, and knowledge network support. It also has regional responsibility for business unit support within the US region.

SME (Subject Matter Expert) Knowledge Networks accumulate knowledge into the PowerPack databases. The nearly 100 networks consist of core groups of 12–20 nominated practice professionals called Subject Matter Experts. They collect, store, update, and advance knowledge about a specific area of business expertise. The core team is supported by a discussion database that is available to all people belonging to the industry in question. Depending on the region, the team is also supported by transnational knowledge managers, information coordinators, or facilitators from a knowledge center. According to Dick Loehr who organizes the networks, many people are involved informally in the networks and there is a lot of 'chaos'.

Local Chief Knowledge Officers (CKO) promote knowledge management in local member companies and within all practices. Knowledge Managers and Knowledge Coordinators are organized by country or industry. For example, within the management-consulting practice there are 40 knowledge managers in the Europe, Middle-East and Africa (EMEA) region alone. Other practices have their own knowledge managers, and their number varies from one practice to another.

Knowledge Stewards support specific engagements in knowledge acquisition and management. All employees are invited to utilize the knowledge management system and to contribute to it as a part of their work processes.

E&Y Knowledge Services Group (KSG) consists of 100 industry-bound knowledge professionals at the Center for Business Knowledge™ (CBK). Sixty of them are Information Professionals (IP professionals), or 'cybrarians', who collect information from external sources. They are highly skilled information and library science specialists without being librarians. They are industry specialists who find information for the professionals from external sources, databases, and the Web. They continually monitor the sources of information and answer more than 400 requests per day, each within 2 hours. They also teach other employees how to use the EY/KnowledgeWeb.

The global Knowledge Based Businesses (KBBs) Practice sells knowledge management services to clients and helps them capitalize on business opportunities by developing their knowledge. The practice employs 70 KBB advisors around the world.

Ernst & Young measures knowledge management through business processes by following the contribution to knowledge, the access to knowledge, and the reuse of knowledge. Knowledge Survey is a monthly measurement that covers the usage and awareness of the various services. It also assesses the value for the client, which is the most difficult aspect to measure.

13.1.5 Ernst & Young's Boundary Elements

As a result of the strategic decision to establish a new culture, Ernst & Young interacts with its environment through a broad range of boundary elements, including knowledge management roles and functions that have been created to increase the firm's sensitivity and impact. They search, acquire, and convey information to the company systematically and efficiently from internal and external sources. They identify and capture knowledge from client projects and convert it into explicit form. They structure, pack, and store knowledge. They also influence the environment proactively. The boundary elements include technical solutions that provide new opportunities for interaction and accessing internal and external sources of information (Table 13.1).

13.1.6 Ernst & Young's Interaction and Coevolution with its Environment

Client projects occupy a central position in the interaction between Ernst & Young and its environment. The knowledge application process (the bigger cycle in the Knowledge Process Landscape model) helps the firm to create value for clients and learn from the projects. Because clients have become increasingly global, Ernst & Young has created Global Client Consulting (GCC) units in Europe, Asia Pacific, and Latin America. They manage global assignments and absorb knowledge from them.

Client connectivity is a strategic issue for Ernst & Young. Ernie℠ is an Internet-based knowledge service that supplements traditional consulting methods and connects Ernst & Young and its small- and medium-sized client firms. Ernie℠ is 'Ernst & Young's On-line

Table 13.1: The boundary elements of Ernst & Young (management consulting).

Boundary elements/Ernst & Young	Purpose of role/function
Local and global partners	Convey (e.g. local) knowledge to strategic decision-making (consensus)
Employees, project teams	Capture tacit knowledge from the interaction with clients by documenting it
Global client consulting groups (GCC), account managers	Accumulate knowledge about global clients (GCC) and local clients (account managers)
Knowledge management org., Center for Business Knowledge™	Capture and structure knowledge. Pack and store it into PowerPacks and global-knowledge bases
Global centers like Center for Business Innovation™ (CBI)	Acquire information about business environment. Create knowledge through research, and distribute it in the form of books, articles, conferences, surveys, and reports
Knowledge based businesses practice, KBB advisors	Capture tacit knowledge from the reciprocal interaction with clients
E&Y Knowledge services group	Trace knowledge, for example, by using Knowledge navigation tools
Information professionals (IP professionals), 'cybrarians'	Search and collect information from external sources
Subject matter experts SME knowledge networks	Filter, structure, pack, and store knowledge to PowerPacks Are supported by information coordinators and facilitators.
Local chief knowledge officers, knowledge managers, knowledge coordinators	Filter relevant internal knowledge and convey it further
Knowledge stewards	Provide knowledge for specific engagements
Education centers	Convey new knowledge to the firm through education
Technical solutions like • **EY/KnowledgeWeb** • **EY/Infolink**	Support capturing knowledge from internal and external sources. Support accumulating knowledge into global knowledge bases
Electronic services (Ernie™, EYT Storefront)	Act as platforms for direct interaction with clients. Help to capture and accumulateknowledge about client needs

Business Consultant' that has '1000 years of experience and over 150 professional degrees'. It is a subscription-based, password-protected, private website that helps clients to use the firm's professional services over the Internet. Clients ask questions and the answer is provided within 24 hours. Ernie[SM] provides access to SuperTools such as Ernie Business Analysis and Web Store Front. It helps Ernst & Young interact with entrepreneurial companies independent of their location, and to reuse and accumulate knowledge included in the questions and answers.

> We can reuse the contents that enter to us. (-) Ernie[SM] means that we need not reinvent the wheel all the time. (Michel Constant)

13.1.7   Ernst & Young and Triggers

Ernst & Young's decision-making aims at consensus among local member companies that are globally dispersed and subject to a variety of cultures and business practices. The process of creating consensus conveys local and regional information as triggers to the global decision-making process.

The client assignments serve Ernst & Young's own learning. The knowledge management organization monitors knowledge about industries, competitors, trends, and learning resources from external databases, articles, publications, research reports, and other sources. EY/KWeb provides customized access to external knowledge.

The Ernst & Young Center of Business Innovation™ (CBI), the thought leadership unit, studies emerging management trends, problems, and solutions. It is a link between Ernst & Young, academics, and persons in the U.S.-based client organizations. It publishes new knowledge, for example, in the form of research reports.

13.1.8   Experimentation at Ernst & Young

Ernst & Young regards continuous experimentation as a basic component of organizational learning. Management must promote experimentation at all levels. The working methods may, however, decrease the need for experimentation because they tell what an employee is expected to do in each situation. Also, developments in certain industries and the availability of global knowledge bases decrease the need for experimentation and innovation. For example, the health care industry "doesn't just want really bright people anymore. They want people who know three-quarters of the answer the minute they walk in the door, and that is not possible without a knowledge base". (Bank, 1996, referring to John G. Peetz).

Experimentation and the development of new approaches, methodologies, and technical solutions are delegated largely to knowledge centers and development centers in the USA. However, experiments can also be made by SME networks, local units, and groups of people working on a specific engagement or service line. In some countries, employees can spend some of their time developing and experimenting with new methods, techniques, and tools (Michel Constant).

13.1.9   Ernst & Young's Internal Standards, Processes, and Communication

Work processes and communication   Consulting work is a combination of a methodology, skills to acquire knowledge about industries and processes, and the capability to link it to the client's own expertise. Ernst & Young's standardized methodology provides guidelines and instructions for projects and supports their documentation. Shared instructions are possible because Ernst & Young's management consulting services are similar everywhere. However, the needs vary depending on the country and the client.

Ernst & Young's consultants are guided by methodologies that are documented in the PowerPacks. They start searching for knowledge in the knowledge bases. If necessary, they contact knowledge managers or utilize Knowledge Navigation services via knowledge centers.

Organization and career structure   Ernst & Young recruits at leading MBA and undergraduate programs from a broad range of educational backgrounds. The company employs junior and more experienced people, depending on the task.

Ernst & Young claims to be a meritocracy. The organizational hierarchy consists of specified steps.[2]

> You know exactly where you are and what you have to do. (Michel Constant)

The firm has also implemented new kinds of organizational forms, such as SME (Subject Matter Expert) Knowledge Networks that are supported by discussion databases.

Education   The steps in training and development are defined by a general curriculum and by specific curriculums for specialist needs. Training in the education centers is based on actual situations and real knowledge bases.

13.1.10   Ernst & Young's Information and Communication Systems

Consultants are empowered by PowerPacks that can be loaded onto their laptop computers. While connected to the EY/KnowledgeWeb, they have global access to electronic teams, shared-knowledge bases, and external databases. By using and sharing accumulated knowledge bases, consultants learn and benefit from each other's experiences and knowledge.

According to Ralph W. Poole, Ernst & Young spends about 6% of its annual revenues on knowledge and information technology. The EY/KnowledgeWeb contains four coexisting environments: Lotus Notes messaging and groupware, Internal Web (Intranet), EY/Infolink that is a distributed searching capability, and Internet connections. A search engine searches across different sources of documentation with a single query. The bulk of data is stored in Lotus Notes databases on servers around the world. Employees are provided with portable equipment and CD-ROMs. Lotus Notes facilitates remote and disconnected use through built-in access control and good groupware functionality. Intranet is more scaleable and allows a

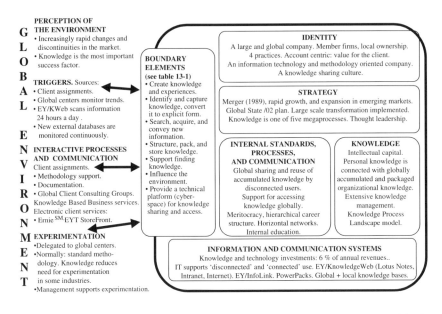

Figure 13.2: The strategic components of Ernst & Young (management consulting).

more efficient technical infrastructure and easier inter-enterprise connectivity. The two tech-nologies will merge "so that you don't know that they are separate" (John G. Peetz).

13.1.11   Summary of Ernst & Young's Strategic Components

Figure 13.2 summarizes the strategic components of Ernst & Young (Management Consulting).

13.2   Ernst & Young (Management Consulting) as a Living Organization

This section will analyze the dynamics of Ernst & Young's learning and renewal and sum-marize its functioning as a living organization.

13.2.1   'Sensing' and 'Memory' of Ernst & Young

Ernst & Young is motivated toward *openness* because the firm regards itself as a large, global, account-centric company that creates value for clients through thought leadership and know-ledge sharing. Openness is needed because global markets are characterized by increasingly rapid changes and discontinuities, and the environment is an arena of competition where knowledge is the most important competitive factor. Openness is facilitated by an extensive knowledge management organization, boundary elements, and information systems.

Ernst & Young needs efficient *access to accumulated knowledge* because it is a value creating and knowledge-sharing company that aims at thought leadership, and because knowledge is the most important success factor.

According to The Knowledge Process Landscape model, Ernst & Young's learning and renewal system affects the firm's new knowledge and vice versa. The global accumulation of knowledge into PowerPacks and knowledge bases enables global sharing. The methods to store and deploy knowledge influence the acquisition of new knowledge. Earlier experiences influence the strategic components, including the taxonomy used to structure knowledge for PowerPacks. Taxonomies can be purchased, but the available solutions did not fit the firm's business. Therefore, Ernst & Young created its own taxonomy, based on its own knowledge and needs (John G. Peetz). The 'knowledge content imperative' means that knowledge management has to take emerging needs into account instead of merely providing knowledge in a predetermined manner. Also, technical opportunities such as search engines decrease the dependence on predefined structures and taxonomies.

The firm's experience is also embedded in methodology (Fusion), standard work processes, documenting practices, and other procedures that influence learning capability. Also, the organizational solution, curriculum, education and learning, and renewal system itself are repositories of organizational knowledge. The firm's strategy (including the mega-processes and growth through acquisitions) as well as its identity as a value-creating thought leader company influence the creation and acquisition of new knowledge.

13.2.2 Summary of Ernst & Young as a Living Organization

Ernst & Young functions as a living organization, and its composition is of the form 'intentional fit' (Figure 13.3).

Ernst & Young's processes for learning and renewal have been consciously designed to support the achievement of the firm's strategic objectives, and are aligned to maintain the firm's identity and ongoing perception of its environment. Ernst & Young has purposely altered its image and identity through the merger in 1989 and the transformation process after that. The firm's identity as a rapidly growing and knowledge-sharing culture motivates the firm to learn from its environment (sensing) and from its earlier experiences through processes for global knowledge sharing (memory). This demonstrated capability has strengthened the firm's knowledge-sharing image and identity. Ernst & Young perceives its environment as one of increasingly rapid changes and frequent discontinuities in its knowledge-based market. This perception and its strategy of rapid growth and "thought leadership" have motivated the firm to develop communication and knowledge flows that facilitate openness and access to its knowledge. The firm supports these flows by an extensive knowledge management process and a global information and communication system. Ernst & Young supports connectivity internally and with its environment in a number of ways — for example, through a customized EY/KWeb (Ernst & Young Knowledge Web) tool, Ernie[SM] ,which is an 'artificial consultant' tool, and through access to the KBB (Knowledge Based Businesses) advisors via Internet.

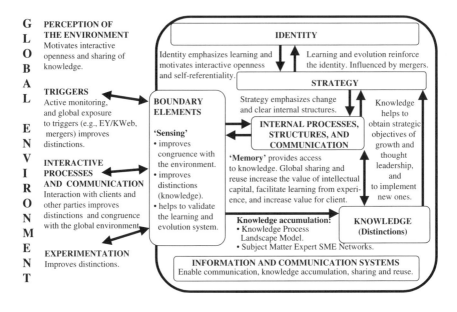

Figure 13.3: Ernst & Young (management consulting) as a living composition.

Through use of such tools, Ernst & Young improves its ability to coevolve in a multinational environment through interactions with clients in assignments, by identifying triggers from external sources through EY/KWeb, and by conducting research and experiments in its global knowledge centers. Boundary elements, such as local partner roles, employee roles, and global center roles, enable ongoing interactions with the environment. Information technologies facilitate communication with clients, and help to capture information and create knowledge from these relationships.

New knowledge is systematically structured and accumulated globally for knowledge sharing purposes. Internal standards and processes (such as work-processes and methodologies) are aligned with the firm's identity and strategy. Individual and organizational learning are linked together through standardized development curricula and education that are increasingly supplemented by 'chaotic' networks and communication.

The living composition of Ernst & Young combines interactive openness and self-referentiality. The result contributes to global performance (exploitation) and helps the company to learn and evolve continually (exploration). Extensive knowledge management processes help the company to collect, package, and store information and knowledge in PowerPacks and global knowledge bases. This structured knowledge accumulation process is supplemented by 'chaotic' networks, such as Subject Matter Expert Networks that help to create and collect new knowledge about specific topics into PowerPacks. Knowledge sharing, i.e. access to the globally accumulated knowledge (an example of self-referentiality) in client assignments provides new knowledge for consultants. Efficient processes for global knowledge sharing increase the value of globally accumulated knowledge capital.

Ernst & Young's learning and renewal system contributes to the firm's objectives to achieve consistency among local offices, reuse problem-solving experience, take advantage of its size and market dominance, accelerate the delivery of valuable knowledge to the marketplace, and broadly leverage its intellectual capital. In addition, interactive openness helps Ernst & Young to learn from its environment, to improve its knowledge about and congruence with the environment, and to validate its learning and renewal system. Improved knowledge developed through interactive openness has helped Ernst and Young to obtain its strategic objectives of growth and thought leadership. The earlier strategy work that resulted in the definition of mega-processes and implementation of extensive knowledge management systems increased the firm's performance dramatically by contributing to both current performance and continuous learning and renewal.

The application of the living composition model indicates that the major strengths of Ernst & Young's learning and renewal system are the efficient connecting of interactive openness and self-referentiality by information and communication technology and knowledge management. The principles are implemented throughout the company, and they are supported by broad commitment and extensive organizational and technical solutions. The knowledge management system is depicted in Ernst & Young's Knowledge Process Landscape model. The renewal system is aligned to meet the firm's identity and to be responsive toward the needs of the business environment.

Notes

1. Ernst & Young has established Centers of Business Knowledge (CBK) in Cleveland, Toronto, Paris, Sydney, Sao Paulo, London, Stuttgart, Rotterdam, and Singapore.
2. The career structure consists of the following steps: Consultant, Senior Consultant, Manager, Senior Manager, and Partner.

Chapter 14

The KaosPilots and KaosManagement

The KaosPilots[1] is a management educational institution, and KaosManagement a management consulting firm. They constitute a small, action-oriented, experimental interconnected value-chain. This chapter will illustrate the application of the living composition model to this value-chain. The first section of this chapter will analyze strategic components, and the second section will discuss major knowledge flows and overall dynamics. More detailed information can be found in Appendix 8. Two scientific evaluations have been made about The KaosPilots, but the conclusions can be largely applied also to KaosManagement.[2]

14.1 The Strategic Components of the KaosPilots and KaosManagement

14.1.1 The KaosPilots and KaosManagement's Identity

The KaosPilots and KaosManagement have a relatively short history but a strong identity. They regard themselves as two closely interconnected organizations that constitute a small, multinationally operating value-chain. They regard themselves as specialists in 'navigating in chaos'. Moreover, they want to be regarded as unique institutionalized platforms for experiments and market-oriented organizations. The KaosPilots and KaosManagement regard themselves as contributors to a Scandinavian leadership model.

The KaosPilots and KaosManagement constitute *a small, multinationally operating value-chain*. At the end of the 1980s, a network of culturally and socially conscious young persons in Aarhus, Denmark became aware of an increasingly chaotic world and growing unemployment in it. In 1987 the members of the group, including Uffe Elbæk, then a social pedagogue and journalist, established a media training program and an organization called Frontrunners.[3] They identified a need for 'pilots' who could navigate in chaos and structured a program to train these pilots. The KaosPilots was established in 1991 and KaosManagement in 1993. They are formally, legally, and financially distinct from each other and constitute a value-chain that combines their goals and resources. They have created a new niche in the management consulting and education market.

The KaosPilots is a three-year educational program in entrepreneurship and leadership, focusing on the professional spheres of creativity, innovation, and intercultural understanding. It educates and trains project leaders called 'kaospilots'. The curriculum includes experimental projects and internships mainly in the Nordic countries, the USA, and South Africa. Each annual team consists of 35 young men and women mainly from Denmark, Sweden, and Norway who are rich in resources and have different ranges of experience. The KaosPilots is a private educational institution, structured as an autonomous business entity. It is funded by the Danish Ministry of Education, student fees, and self-generated income. The KaosPilots regards itself as a learning organization and undergoes regular external evaluations. In 2000, the aggregate budget was US$1.2 million.

KaosManagement is a private, independent consultancy and project company that operates on a commercial basis. It was founded in 1993 as a commercial offshoot and distribution channel for The KaosPilots' knowledge. They share their cultural and social values, global awareness, methods, basic skills, and knowledge with corporate clients. KaosManagement has offices in Aarhus and Copenhagen (Denmark) and Oslo (Norway). KaosLab 1&2 is a training center in Aarhus. About half of the clients are Danish corporations, organizations, and institutions, and the other half represents other countries in Northern Europe. In 2000, the annual revenues were US$1 million. The firm has 14 full-time employees, some freelancers, and a wide network of trendsetters, resource persons, and collaborating partners.

KaosManagement realizes two missions through consulting, education, and projects. In the business environment it promotes development and community building. The broader objective is to increase global awareness and to make the world a better place to live. The firm combines profit and less-profit projects in order to maintain social and ethical priorities and create flexibility. KaosManagement helps firms and individuals use their talents and realize their innovative ideas. Based on The KaosPilots' principles and methods, it offers non-packaged services in the area of soft qualifications that are not available in the conventional consultancy market. Internally generated projects, realizing the ideas, are important because 'they give us energy' (Marianne Egelund Siig).

The KaosPilots and KaosManagement are *specialized in 'navigating in chaos'*. In 1992, The KaosPilots received UNESCO's prize for being a new, remarkable education concept that has two specific features.[4] It facilitates creating the skills that are needed when navigating in all kinds of countries in all sorts of conditions. The education also navigates itself along "the narrow channel between public administration and private trade and industry, aiming at new thinking in social and cultural understanding" (Langager, 1995, p. 8).

The KaosPilots wants to be an experimenting institution, *a unique institutionalized platform for experiments* (Uffe Elbæk). The objective is to set a new standard for education and personal development and become the best possible milieu for creativity, innovation, and learning. The KaosPilots is a laboratory of experimentation in the complex field of what is profitable and what is social (Langager, 1995).[5] It combines the wishes of trade and industry for creative, personal, and independent staff with the individual's interest in exploring life's many opportunities and in retaining a high degree of freedom at work and in private life. The KaosPilots introduces the social dimension into the sphere of capital and management.

> You cannot predict the future, but you can decide how you want to meet the future. This includes, for example, the mental skills, how you look at conflicts and problems, and how you prepare yourself (Uffe Elbaek).

The KaosPilots and KaosManagement are *market-oriented organizations*. They co-operate with international companies and the public sector, conduct projects in several countries, and utilize internal and external resources. The KaosPilots combines resources in a new way. This means, for example, combining educational objectives to experimental 'real life' projects in business environments (Uffe Elbæk).

The KaosPilots and KaosManagement have drawn attention in the media because of their fresh ideas of leadership and collaboration in organizations. They are familiar with cultural and societal trends and modern mass communication because the founders' original background is in media studies rather than in economics.

KaosPilots is closer to MTV than MBA (Uffe Elbæk).[6]

KaosManagement and The KaosPilots *contribute to a Scandinavian leadership model*[7] by combining a global vision with Nordic capabilities. Their objectives are based on Scandinavian welfare state values and the Nordic democracy, with an emphasis on social and environmental responsibility and decent family policy (Deichman-Sørensen, 1997).

14.1.2 The KaosPilots and KaosManagement's Perception of Their Environment

For The KaosPilots and KaosManagement, the environment means the whole society. They act as a part of this larger picture where social and ethical dimensions are highly relevant. For example, at KaosManagement projects are selected not only for their income potential. According to Wickie Meier Pedersen, there are also clients that KaosManagement does not want to work with, for ethical reasons.

The world is perceived as increasingly 'chaotic', complex, and quickly changing. The core philosophy that 'change is an opportunity and its potential is to be exploited' has two partially controversial implications (Deichman-Sørensen, 1997). It leads to exploring new challenges, environments, relationships, and projects, modifying the existing environment proactively, and abandoning existing solutions if necessary. Simultaneously it leads to development of dense relationships, trust, willingness to take risks, and investment in co-operation. The market is a collective that is defined by shared interests.

14.1.3 The KaosPilots and KaosManagement's Strategy

The KaosPilots organization has a compulsion to change: " … it is rare to meet an educational institution so willing to change as The KaosPilots" (Langager, 1995, pp. 36–37). The professional emphasis was changed from cultural projects to a project culture. An 'institution' changed itself into an 'organization' and further toward 'a learning organization'. In 1996, The KaosPilots started co-operation with The Chaordic Alliance™ and several big companies in the USA in order to develop and apply new management approaches based on self-organization. As a result of increasing global consciousness and systemic understanding, The KaosPilots decided to transform itself into a 'chaordic™' organization and 'the best possible milieu for creativity, innovation, and learning'. Seven basic principles were defined to achieve this objective.[8]

The KaosPilots has built its competence step-by-step. Each annual team has explored a new 'corner' of The KaosPilots' skills. The first team was practical and project oriented, the second one focused on personal development. The third team attempted to understand organization in a new way, and the fourth one explored entrepreneurship (Uffe Elbæk).

Growth is problematic and the two organizations have had serious ideological discussions about how to secure their identity. For example, the idea of franchising has not been accepted. Instead, The KaosPilots has planned to join a global network of sister schools and collaboration alliances.

The KaosPilots and KaosManagement have conducted numerous projects and internships in Australia, Europe, Africa, and the USA in order to increase global awareness among students and employees. They have created global presence through outposts and established cultural, professional, and political collaborations among selected regions. Scandinavia represents the historical and cultural roots, California demonstrates the new network economy and entrepreneurship, and South Africa represents leadership and the understanding of conflict. The students come mainly from the Nordic countries, and some of them from other European countries. Formal and informal networks, partnerships, projects, and internships in various countries have helped to expand the relationships into the business world and increase visibility.

14.1.4   The KaosPilots, KaosManagement, Knowledge, and Knowledge Management

Personal knowledge and skills   The 'Personal Mastery' model defines the competence structure of a Kaospilot. It is built around entrepreneurship, leadership, innovation, and interculturality. The ability to master a given situation is an integrated result of professional and social competencies and the abilities to act and innovate.[9] The emphasis is on practical skills, learning by doing, reflection, and personal development. Experimental projects support action-based learning.

> First, act before you know everything. It is OK to act before you know everything. Second, learn from action as soon as possible (Henrik Nitschke).

The KaosPilots' knowledge is largely tacit and personal. Their education should go into unknown territories and to the edge of the unknown, and students should feel like 'being sent to a training camp of the future'. However, there is also a need for a clear, specified, professional profile. It is acceptable that at least 10–20% of the professional content of the education is difficult to describe explicitly because it forces people to pay attention to the competence concept (Henrik Nitschke and The KaosPilots, Status Report 19.1.1998).

The KaosPilots and KaosManagement encourage various skills, such as network thinking and sharing ideas, in order to find resources that help to navigate in unknown situations. They encourage persons to trust themselves and to use intuition, " ... to define their own 'cosmology', to set their own personal goals and crystallize their own visions."[10] The KaosPilots' competency creation is about creating a new field, the one of will. It is about a new concept of knowledge, defined as handling and utilizing knowledge, not possessing it. It also means a new competence profile, something that is simultaneously very personal and exceptionally collective (Deichman-Sørensen, 1997)

The KaosPilots' capabilities can be compared to Reich's[11] four abilities of a symbol analyst: the ability to think in a systematic way, to abstract, to experiment, and to work with other people. The KaosPilots' practical, active, entrepreneurial, and project-producing abilities complement their experimental and co-operative skills. In contrast, the capacity for being analytical, reflective, abstract, and systematic is problematic for the intuitive and action-oriented Kaospilots (Langager, 1995). Marianne Egelund Siig, however, disagrees with this assessment.

> We (KaosManagement) are very abstract. Other firms have very concrete tools. We are talking about attitudes by using pictures, metaphors, and so on. We can be almost too abstract (Marianne Egelund Siig).

Reich's model may be too narrow to describe The KaosPilots' skills. Their broad concept of knowledge and competence is not attached to established sectors, and it does not focus on competition, benchmarking, and market power. This means "the core competence of The KaosPilots is aesthetical–ethical, based on an interplay between what we usually call human, social, and cultural capital, between personal and social resources, between experience, network(ing), and style." Instead of symbol analysts, The KaosPilots could be regarded as symbol artisans (Deichman-Sørensen, 1997, pp. viii–ix, 218–219).

Organizational knowledge and capability   The KaosPilots has a relatively unformalized structure and its organizational knowledge can be regarded as a stream of knowledge. Its everyday life is characterized by rapid change and new initiatives (Deichman-Sørensen, 1997). The emphasis of The KaosPilots and KaosManagement's knowledge has changed from cultural issues toward those of management and leadership and is tailored to each client in non-packaged projects and services. Marianne Egelund Siig mentions that KaosManagement creates new ideas, skills, and knowledge by including in every project at least one thing that has not been done before. The KaosPilots abandons outdated knowledge quickly and hires consultants and university people according to emerging knowledge needs.

The KaosPilots and KaosManagement also nurture a tacit organizational capability to act, learn, and evolve collectively. This means that they provide soft qualifications in an action-oriented manner, and it is often difficult and unnecessary to transform them into explicit form. Each new context forces participants to acquire new skills and knowledge and change their behavior. Once adopted, new knowledge becomes a point of departure for selecting new objectives and contexts. Knowledge is accumulated in staff members and embedded in the organizational culture and improved strategic objectives and competences. However, the accumulation of organizational competence is difficult because the staff consists largely of freelancers, and the Kaospilots leave the organization after finalizing their education.

The KaosPilots and partially also KaosManagement[12] have been analyzed in two external scientific evaluations. The mass media in the form of articles, interviews, and radio and TV-programs has also provided The KaosPilots and KaosManagement with opportunities for self-reflection and self-understanding. Moreover, some projects such as World Wide Chaos[13] in 1995 and Chaordic Explorations in 1996–1997 have produced documentation about the organizations' evolution.

Knowledge management   The KaosPilots and KaosManagement do not have a formal knowledge management system. Instead they have implemented the idea of *knowledge ecology*. This means learning from real life projects, not from fictional cases. Knowledge is utilized efficiently just-in-time, at the moment when it is new and has its highest value. Knowledge is abandoned quickly when new knowledge becomes available from experiments or other sources in society. According to Henrik Nitschke, it is expensive to renew knowledge through experiments because of curiosity about the next challenges and because The KaosPilots does not face the same situation again. However, Uffe Elbæk mentions that the organization learns from failures in order to develop new ways of functioning.

The KaosPilots' approach emphasizes the value-creation capability of knowledge. Knowledge is capital and its value is increased by handling and utilizing it, not by possessing it (Deichman-Sørensen, 1997).

According to Wickie Meier Pedersen, the sharing of knowledge is a normal practice. While KaosManagement "has not been especially good at evaluating accomplished projects and sharing knowledge (explicitly) about them", knowledge is also increasingly stored in explicit form. For example, KaosManagement saves documentation from earlier jobs and methods in a knowledge bank and sorts them into themes for further utilization. The KaosPilots' policy of 'Don't tell it — Show it' means that people have to present their ideas and concepts in written or visual form. All projects will be documented and evaluated explicitly.

14.1.5   The KaosPilots and KaosManagement's Boundary Elements

The KaosPilots and KaosManagement have created an extensive collection of boundary elements that help them interact with their environment. Many people — such as freelancers — have dual roles that enable them to act as knowledge bridges. The Kaospilots are very sensitive to changing trends in society. Through experiments they capture, evaluate, share, convey, and accumulate knowledge in tacit form. They increasingly convert it into explicit form when necessary. The boundary elements help them acquire knowledge from external sources and also influence the business environment and society. Finally, there are some technical links that support communication and information gathering (Table 14.1).

14.1.6   The KaosPilots and KaosManagement's interaction and Co-evolution with Their Environment

The KaosPilots and KaosManagement's clients consist of students, companies, and other organizations. They co-operate with their clients in the controversial framework of quick changes, chaos, trust, and dense relationships. The KaosPilots interacts with multiple official and unofficial networks that are defined in the *network policy*. KaosManagement is the closest partner in the network. The educational network consists of local, national, and international educational institutions. The Business Network consists of various companies such as Danish Telecom, Lego, and Oticon. Individual managers act as advisors. They are motivated to co-operate because they can test their own ideas and see the effects very quickly. The KaosPilots (but not KaosManagement) receives some financial support from its sponsors. The NGO network consists of various non-profit organizations.

The objective of KaosManagement is to operate in international, professional, and social networks. KaosManagement receives ideas from The KaosPilots and develops its own tailored service processes. The structure and content of each assignment are devised to meet the specific needs of the client. The key competences include leadership education, teambuilding, organizational development, entrepreneurship, project work, and coaching.

Table 14.1: The boundary elements of The KaosPilots and KaosManagement.

Boundary elements/Kaospilots & K.M.	Purpose of role/function
Permanent staff	Absorb and create new knowledge Scan for weak signals in society Maintain contacts with external networks Select individuals with rich resources
Freelance consultants	Collect experience from projects. Multi-skilled persons absorb knowledge from various fields
Hired teachers from universities, companies etc.	Provide The KaosPilots and KaosManagement with new knowledge
Teams in the KaosPilots' education program	Absorb and create new knowledge by interacting with companies and other organizations in unique experimental projects and internships
Group projects, internships. Co-operation with companies (profit and non-profit)	Act as platforms for exploration, experimentation, and creation of new knowledge about big themes, such as new organizational forms. Help to absorb new knowledge
Supporters, sponsors, company club Business network	Provide advice and knowledge for promoting ideas
Formal organization	Provide knowledge for strategic decision making and control
Scientific auditors	Provide feedback about development
Exposure to mass-media and publicity	Provide visibility
Contacts to universities and educational institutes	Provide access to new knowledge
Acting in networks of frontrunners, etc	Act as a source of inspiration and ideas
Internet connections Systems in the internet Knowledge bases on the server	Facilitate communication. Facilitate documentation and capturing of knowledge in explicit form. Support the accumulation of knowledge

The work consists of workshops, conferences, development programs, and internally created, less profit-oriented projects. The clients consist of organizations in various countries. Between 1993 and 1998 KaosManagement completed 1000 project tasks and organized workshops and educational programs of various sizes for 670 distinct clients inside and outside of Denmark. Each time there have been between 12–30 people attending workshops for at least 2–3 days. (Marianne Egelund Siig).

14.1.7 The KaosPilots, KaosManagement, and Triggers

KaosManagement and The KaosPilots use intuition and are sensitive to signals, trends, and tendencies in society in a way that differentiates them from most other consulting and educational organizations. Lifestyle, business, youth culture, music, and computers are relevant fields of interest. Being a kaospilot is largely a question of lifestyle and 24-hours-a-day commitment. The broad contact network provides kaospilots with new relevant information quickly. The experimental client projects and less-profit projects also provide triggers and surprises.

14.1.8 Experimentation at The KaosPilots and KaosManagement

Because The KaosPilots is not a commercial organization, its projects may contain more experimentation and risk taking than conventional consulting projects do. The knowledge and services of KaosPilots and KaosManagement are largely created by experimentation. The KaosPilots has evolved from an experiment to a project and further to an open experimenting institution (Deichman-Sørensen, 1997). The objective is to be an institutionalized platform for experiments. The investment strategy of KaosManagement aims to facilitate experimentation. "Our surplus is to be invested in experimental forms of education and training" (KaosPilots … crossing the Atlantic, 1996). The KaosPilots and KaosManagement want to experiment with what happens when three different cultural approaches — Scandinavian, North American, and African — interact. Each new version of the KaosPilots curriculum is a new experiment, and a considerable part of the education consists of action-oriented experiments. The KaosPilots and KaosManagement evolve experimentally, which involves acting 'before you know everything' and then rapidly implementing new knowledge in strategies, internal processes, and standards.

The move from experimentation to production is often difficult (Uffe Elbæk). KaosManagement and The KaosPilots operate in different markets, which may be one reason for the difficulty. KaosManagement competes in the consulting and business environment, whereas The KaosPilots is financed largely by public sources.

14.1.9 The KaosPilots and KaosManagement's Internal Standards, Processes, and Communication

Work processes and communication The KaosPilots and KaosManagement have separate internal processes and knowledge flows. The KaosPilots' work processes are regulated by the curriculum. KaosManagement sells and provides non-packaged service processes, which is time-, money-, and capacity-consuming. The purpose is to focus, make the results visible, and share knowledge in order to improve efficiency and avoid reinventing the wheel.

There is some exchange between The KaosPilots and KaosManagement. For example, KaosManagement takes students into project teams, provides role models, and shares knowledge with them. The projects act as non-paid internships for the students. In return KaosManagement receives The KaosPilots' knowledge from the students. "In a way they teach us". However, the transfer of knowledge is difficult and there is a need to tighten the co-operation (Marianne Egelund Siig).

Organization and career structure   The KaosPilots and KaosManagement are flat and flexible organizations. KaosManagement has a board, a CEO, and a core group of four persons that are responsible for leadership, management, administration, and knowledge development. Flexibility is important for the multiskilled consultants who want to utilize their capabilities also as freelancers outside their consulting capacity. There is no specified career structure.

The KaosPilots has a board, an educational council, and a core of permanent key personnel. Each class has 1–2 team managers/coaches from the professional and educational staff. The organization also includes a network of contracted teachers, consultants, and innovators who are grouped into four zones: Commitment, Learning, Development, and Performance.

Education and learning   The KaosPilots and KaosManagement require specific qualifications from their employees, such as independence, initiative, and open-mindedness. The majority of the employees have Kaospilot education and therefore share the same values and methods. One of their competences is the changing competence. Learning is based on individual motivation, intuition, and creativity.

> Someone just starts something. We do not remember how things happened — and we do not care. Ideas are like flowers: If you pick them they produce new ones. Things are just happening at this time. It is not merely accidental that they happen now. It is question of this time. We live in a network society, in an information society (Gitte Madsen).

14.1.10   The KaosPilots and KaosManagement's Information and Communication Systems

The KaosPilots and KaosManagement's information systems support work processes, communication, and knowledge sharing. The equipment consists of desktop computers and laptops. The KaosPilots has built its information systems on the Internet/Intranet as a part of the educational program. Documents are kept on a server, and sites are connected by e-mail and groupwork software. For example, a group project utilizes a homepage for planning, documentation, and knowledge sharing. An Internet connection also provides access to external sources of information.

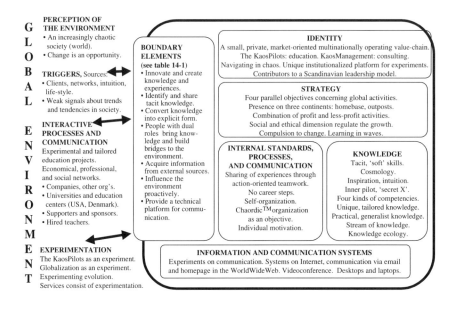

Figure 14.1: The strategic components of The KaosPilots and KaosManagement.

14.1.11   Summary of the The KaosPilots and KaosManagement's Strategic Components

The strategic components of The KaosPilots and KaosManagement are summarized in Figure 14.1.

14.2   The KaosPilots and KaosManagement as a Living Organization

This section will analyze the dynamics of The KaosPilots and KaosManagement's learning and renewal.

14.2.1   'Sensing' and 'Memory' of The KaosPilots and KaosManagement

The KaosPilots and KaosManagement are motivated toward *openness* because they are innovative, market-oriented, and experimenting navigators in chaos. Their strategic objective is to learn by accumulating experiences in various contexts. They see society as increasingly 'chaotic' and believe that it requires an open approach.

Weak signals and new 'impossible' ideas are adopted quickly because The KaosPilots and KaosManagement learn and evolve in an experimenting way. Their step-by-step curve of ambition aims at acquiring new experiences and satisfying curiosity. The key individuals' experience and visioning capability has helped them to identify weak signals and acquire new knowledge. Also, the teams process and interpret knowledge and give it meaning. Internal processes and standards, such as the 'knowledge ecology' principle, increase the opportunities to acquire new knowledge through real cases.

The identity, values, and ethical principles of The KaosPilots and KaosManagement, such as the organizations' relationship to money, influence their learning capability. These principles encourage the crossing of existing boundaries and categories and acquiring new knowledge from unknown territories rather than from familiar playgrounds. On the other hand, they may restrict the selection of projects and partners and the directions for growth. In spite of their orientation toward new global challenges, The KaosPilots and KaosManagement have a strong tendency to maintain their original Nordic and even Aarhusian roots and traditions.

The KaosPilots and KaosManagement *have not focused on accumulating explicit knowledge* and providing access to it because of their small size, identity as a 'navigator in chaos', strategy (experimentation), and perception of the environment as increasingly chaotic. Their knowledge is largely tacit, embedded in individuals and organizational practices. Knowledge is largely embedded in their core management group and internal processes, standards, and strategy, and it has influenced their methods of learning. There is, however, a need to improve access to knowledge through structuring, institutionalization, and accumulation in explicit form.

The KaosPilots has evolved step-by-step in a wave-like manner and occupied new corners of the competence model by utilizing earlier experiences as a point of departure. It has set new strategic objectives and developed new ways of functioning, which has also influenced KaosManagement. They have used their earlier experiences in creating global awareness, opening the education gradually to applicants, and expanding international networks and client relationships. Also, the external scientific evaluations have provided The KaosPilots and KaosManagement with an opportunity for self-reflection and self-understanding. They have helped to develop the identity, redefine the competence concept, and change the ways of functioning and learning.

14.2.2 Summary of The KaosPilots and KaosManagement as a Living Organization

It was assumed The KaosPilots and KaosManagement would represent emergent fit between the strategic components, which means unintended consistency among the strategic components. According to the previous discussion, their learning and renewal are largely based on 'experimenting evolution' and their composition is of the form 'emergent fit'. Their organizational capabilities have emerged step-by-step and the scope of their activities has expanded systematically. Therefore, it is possible that the emerged systematic pattern is merely hindsight. It is also possible that their evolution has been less based on luck than navigating in chaos would indicate. It may be that the founder's[14] vision has contributed to systematic testing of new aspects and accumulating of experiences. The KaosPilots and KaosManagement have thus adopted successes and failures quickly, which has in turn provided new opportunities for further experiments. Finally, The KaosPilots and KaosManagement have recognized increasing internal needs for structuring, for example by implementing the chaordic™ principles. The KaosPilots needs to strengthen its position as a unique institutionalized platform for experiments instead of its earlier status as an experiment. This means moving from an emergent fit toward an intentional fit (Figure 14.2).

The identity of The KaosPilots and KaosManagement as navigators in chaos drives their learning and renewal capacity. While the way in which the firms function has undergone several transformations, their common identity and basic values have remained the same.

Learning from the environment (sensing) is encouraged by the perception of the environment as a chaotic world where change is an opportunity. The objective of The KaosPilots and KaosManagement is not to achieve static congruence with an existing environment. Instead, they focus on future change and explore trends and opportunities proactively to be prepared to meet the future and influence society.

In order to explore unknown territories such as new geographic and business areas, The KaosPilots and KaosManagement improve knowledge through reciprocal interaction with their client organizations and wide contact networks. The KaosPilots and KaosManagement have leveraged their limited resources by creating attractive boundary element roles and by operating within networks in which 'external' persons, such as the freelancer consultants and Business Network members, have boundary roles in the two organizations.

The identity of KaosPilots and KaosManagement is centered around being curious, exploiting their experiences, improving knowledge, and quickly abandoning outdated knowledge. They explore and, where possible, seek to change the conditions of future congruence

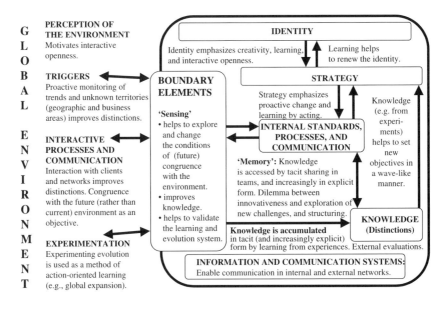

Figure 14.2: The KaosPilots and KaosManagement as a living composition.

with their environment and to create new ways of functioning. They do not try to accumulate explicit knowledge bases because their organization is small, and knowledge in their areas of activity quickly becomes outdated and is difficult to transform into explicit form. Instead, they compensate for perturbations caused by improving tacit knowledge, and by changing themselves quickly through action-oriented 'experimenting evolution'. Knowledge is accumulated as tacit personal knowledge and skills and as process-based organizational knowledge, such as groupwork skills. Part of its organizational knowledge, however, such as the curriculum offered by The KaosPilots, is explicit and forms the backbone for its functioning. Accumulated experience can be accessed via communication and sharing within teams, scientific evaluations, and increasingly via the information system that supports communication within teams (memory). Communication is used to actively create meanings rather than merely transfer facts. The KaosPilots and KaosManagement's learning and renewal processes are based largely on interactive openness that is sustained by their capability to learn from experiences.

People at The KaosPilots and KaosManagement are encouraged and trained to create, share, and exploit new knowledge in teams, projects, self-organizing communities of learners, and through personal communication. Motivation to learn is based on curiosity and individual willingness to grow, not on incentives or hierarchical career paths.

Their methods to interpret new knowledge are influenced by their culture, values, strategy, internal processes, standards, ways of communicating, and the Personal Mastery concept. Continuously improved knowledge helps The KaosPilots and KaosManagement to develop new strategic objectives. Their strategy has evolved in waves, through action-oriented learning and rapid implementation of new knowledge. Successful organizational evolution through periods of environmental turbulence has reinforced their identity as 'navigators in chaos' and promoted their role as a unique institutionalized platform for experiments.

The KaosPilots, and partly also KaosManagement, have been thoroughly investigated in two scientific evaluations. As a publicly financed educational institution, The KaosPilots is also subjected to regular external control.

The capacity of The KaosPilots and KaosManagement for learning and renewal enable them to be continually and proactively exposed to surprises and 'impossible' tasks, to learn how to handle such challenges, to stimulate creativity, and to implement necessary changes very quickly. The KaosPilots and KaosManagement develop new capabilities by utilizing the 'curve of ambition' and the 'inner pilot' concept. They multiply their resources and improve knowledge by attracting external people and organizations to boundary roles. They also validate the learning and renewal system via exposure to surprises and new territories, and via external evaluations.

Notes

1. In the USA, The KaosPilots has also used the term "The KaosPilots University". The term 'kaospilot' refers to a person who has successfully completed the 3–year management training program offered by The KaosPilots.

2. Søren Langager, The Royal Danish School of Educational Studies made the first external evaluation in 1995. It was based on observations during the first years, 1991–1994. Trine Deichman-Sørensen made the second external evaluation as a researcher at the Center for Cultural Studies, University of Aarhus in 1997. It was based on observations between the fall of 1993 and the spring of 1997. It was published by the Work Research Institute, Oslo.

 3. 'Frontløberne' in Danish. This is a culturally oriented non-profit project office that became the 'mother organization' for The KaosPilots and KaosManagement.

 4. The prize was related to UNESCO's program '90's — The Decade of The Culture'.

 5. The KaosPilots has some parallels with 'Kulturradikalisme', a liberal intellectual movement of the 1930s (Langager, 1995, pp. 38–39). One common feature is, for example, regarding individualization in the society as a positive challenge, not as a negative one.

 6. In Deichman-Sørensen (1997, p. 45).

 7. The model consists of (1) productivity and profitability requirements, (2) social requirements, (3) environmental requirements, and (4) ethical requirements.

 8. The seven principles of The KaosPilots are:

     1. Every person is unique and possesses infinite potential (Vision of a human being).
     2. Learning involves head, hand, and heart — and a life-long process (Vision of learning).
     3. Life is a prerequisite for change. Change is a prerequisite for life (Vision of life).
     4. Organizations are living systems that build on human relations and network (Vision of organization).
     5. Respect difference and value the common (Ethics).
     6. Live in the present — but respect the past and keep the eye on the future (Historical consciousness).
     7. Pursue quality in everything you do (Attitude to work).

 9. The competence structure of a kaospilot consists of:

     1. *Professional competence*: Project leadership and organization culture. Innovation and creativity. Entrepreneurship.
     2. *Social competence*: Capability to create contacts and trust. To understand other persons and their needs. To co-operate.
     3. *Handling/managing competence*: To set goals and priorities, and to make decisions. To demonstrate initiative and handling capability.
     4. *Changing competence*: Understanding of development and change personally and professionally. The capability to build on existing competencies and to control outdated knowledge and information. To bring together knowledge and information from different sources. To learn and intuitively accept new knowledge.

10. Internet 20.6.1997: http://www.kaospilot.com.

11. Reich, B. (1991). *The Work of Nations. Preparing Ourselves for the 21st Century Capitalism.*

12. KaosManagement was analyzed only in Deichman-Sørensen's evaluation.

13. World Wide Chaos was the name for projects and internships on four continents.

14. The principal, Uffe Elbæk, KaosPilots.

Chapter 15

Summary of Applying the Living Composition Model to Case Organizations

This chapter will summarize the results of the empirical analyses of the case firms. As with the cases themselves, the text here reflects the situation at the time of original analysis, and the situation of the company has possibly changed since then. The purpose is not to compare the case organizations to each other, but to present the variation of each component and the dynamics of the firms, and to show how the model helps to provide an overview of the complex enabling structure of an organization. The first section discusses the strategic components, and the second section summarizes the results concerning sensing and memory in the case organizations during the period of interviews and reporting. The dynamics and method of evolution will be discussed in the context of consistency/intentionality platforms and evolution models in Chapter 16.

15.1 Strategic Components of the Case Firms

15.1.1 Identities of the Case Firms

All case firms are distinguished from other entities in their environment, such as competitors and other actors. Based on the empirical analysis, they created and maintained continually their identity as a living organization. They have an integrated 'structure' that is composed of strategic components.

The case firms characterize themselves by a multidisciplinary approach (Arthur Andersen), emphasis on innovation and expertise (Arthur D. Little), methodology and IT-oriented services (Ernst & Young), and action-orientation (The KaosPilots and KaosManagement). They are influenced by their origins, history, driving force, motivational factors, and objectives. Arthur Andersen and Ernst & Young have their origins in the USA, and they have accumulated their knowledge largely in the U.S. because of cultural and language reasons. The KaosPilots and KaosManagement identify themselves as contributors to a Scandinavian leadership model.

These cases support the idea that the founders' personality and values are important for long-lived firms (de Geus, 1997a,b) and that professional service firms are often established and built around a person or a group of persons that are specialists in the field (Løwendahl, 2000). At Arthur Andersen, Arthur D. Little, and The KaosPilots/KaosManagement, the founder's values have an important role in the organizational values and stories about the firm's history. Ernst & Young was created through a merger, and the founders' names remain in the firm's name.

15.1.2   Perception of the Environment in the Case Firms

Because all case companies operate in the management consulting industry, they share quite similar views about the major trends. They perceive their environment as an increasingly chaotic knowledge society characterized by rapid changes, discontinuities, and an increasing volume of information. In general, multinational organizations operate in and co-evolve with a complex, diverse, and changeable environment, and they are increasingly dependent on it (Porter & Fuller, 1986; Whittington, 1993). In this kind of environment, change is an opportunity and knowledge is the most important success factor. According to Burns and Stalker (1994), the need of organizations to learn depends on their environment. The case organizations are motivated to implement solutions that support an open interaction with the environment.

15.1.3   Strategy in the Case Firms

The case firms' strategies are based on their identity, perception of their environment, and other relevant aspects that help to operationalize visions and objectives into internal standards and processes. For example, a strategy may emphasize the need for a continuous process improvement (Arthur Andersen), improvement of internal solutions (Ernst & Young), acting as one company (Arthur D. Little), or the capability to explore (The KaosPilots and KaosManagement). On the other hand, the firms modify their strategies because they have obtained improved knowledge through co-evolution with the environment, such as the GBPs of Arthur Andersen. The strategies are continually reproduced as a component in the firms' evolution processes. As White and Poynter (1990) write, strategy is an outcome of a collaborative process among organizational units.

The case firms' strategies emphasize the importance of learning and knowledge for a supplier of knowledge (Arthur Andersen), a specialist organization (Arthur D. Little), a value creating company (Ernst & Young), or a platform for experiments (The KaosPilots and KaosManagement). All case companies implement internal changes, for example, through transformations or continuous improvement.

The case firms grow organically or through mergers and acquisitions which help them to acquire new knowledge quickly. Arthur D. Little acquired Information Associates, and Arthur Andersen has established alliances with quickly moving firms. The KaosPilots and KaosManagement operate in networks and expand to new markets (the U.S. South Africa) in order to explore, experiment, and learn.

15.1.4   Knowledge and Knowledge Management in the Case Firms

All case companies regard knowledge as central to their success. Arthur Andersen, Arthur D. Little, and Ernst & Young regard knowledge as an asset (knowledge capital).

In the case organizations, knowledge changes continually. It helps to coordinate other components. Knowledge *facilitates and regulates* the self-production process. On the other hand, it is *continually produced* by the self-production process, which means that the evolutionary process facilitates the improvement of knowledge.

The case firms improve their knowledge through an exposure to the environment. They scan weak signals and acquire tailored information. Ernst & Young's EY/InfoLink that browses external databases regularly is a good example. Knowledge is created by interacting with clients and other parties, by establishing mobilizing projects (Arthur D. Little), and through specialized units such as the Next Generation Research Group (Arthur Andersen) and Global Centers (Ernst & Young).

Exposure and sensitivity to the environment, boundary elements, and work processes influence the availability of new experiences. For example, The KaosPilots and KaosManagement encourage intuition and sensitivity in their education program and monitor youth cultures, trends, and tendencies in society. The findings support the principle that perturbations lead to the improvement of distinctions and internal change (Mingers, 1995).

Some case companies accumulate knowledge into knowledge bases globally from internal and external sources. The employees and partially also the clients have global access to that knowledge. These firms create a shared meaning, share knowledge and experiences, and develop an organizational competence. They have implemented information and communication systems and solutions that facilitate interaction between people. The case companies also develop their capability to innovate (Arthur D. Little) and to change themselves quickly (The KaosPilots and KaosManagement). For a small, specialized organization that has limited resources, 'navigation skills' and an access to external sources of knowledge may be more relevant than the accumulation and maintenance of its own knowledge bases.

In the case companies, the conversations take place between individuals. They also take place between individuals and advanced information systems, such as Ernie[SM] the virtual consultant, and KnowledgeSpace[SM] (Arthur Andersen) and EY/KWeb (Ernst & Young) that are based on intranets. This extension is important because the socio-technical and neo-biological systems that integrate humans and new kinds of biological systems are increasingly important for human societies (Kelly, 1994).

Knowledge, competence management, learning, change, transformation, and renewal are distinct yet interconnected issues in the case companies. The study indicates that the perspective of 'living organization' helps to position them in the broader context of organizational survival and success. The case firms depict their knowledge management systems with various models, such as the divergent–convergent model and model of creating value (Arthur Andersen), Four Domains model (Arthur D. Little), Knowledge Process Landscape model (Ernst & Young), and the Personal Mastery and Knowledge Ecology principles (The KaosPilots and KaosManagement). They define the standards and rules for creating, accumulating, and sharing knowledge, providing an access to internal and external sources of knowledge, and controlling and measuring the knowledge management system.

The case companies facilitate the global accumulation, sharing, and application of knowledge (Arthur Andersen and Ernst & Young), provide an access to tacit specialist knowledge (Arthur D. Little), and emphasize efficient utilization of knowledge and abandoning it as soon as new knowledge is available (The KaosPilots and KaosManagement).

The case firms' learning and renewal capability is influenced by their career structure and recruiting policy (e.g. young versus experienced persons; generalists versus experts). The analysis of the case firms also reveals that individual employees' creativity and learning processes are influenced by organizational solutions such as career structure, recruitment policy, task definitions, measurement, rewards and incentives, and education. They influence individuals' motivation and capability to innovate, learn, and share their knowledge.

15.1.5   Boundary Elements in the Case Firms

Boundary elements consist of roles and functions that enable an organization's reciprocal interaction with its environment; they enable sensing (interactive openness). All of the case companies have established a wide variety of boundary elements, such as roles and functions of professionals, project managers, knowledge managers, knowledge stewards, Key Client Teams, electronic services, KnowledgeSpace[SM], and information and communication systems. They interact reciprocally with suppliers, clients, and the environment in general. The KaosPilots and KaosManagement have established a wide set of boundary elements that multiply their absorbing surface.

Persons may have boundary roles in an organization and other roles in some other organizations simultaneously. For example, the Company Club members contribute to The KaosPilots and KaosManagement's learning and renewal as supporters. They also have other roles, such as being the manager of a client company.

The boundary elements of the case organizations support survival and knowledge creation by interacting with their environments. They identify, capture, and convert knowledge into an explicit form. They search and acquire information from external sources and convey it to the company. They structure, pack, and store knowledge, and influence the environment proactively. They provide an access to various sources of information. Moreover, they act as information bridges and a cyberspace for internal and external interaction, and help to accumulate knowledge from it.

15.1.6   Interactive Processes and Communication in the Case Firms

In the case firms, interaction and communication with the environment enables interactive openness, facilitate learning, renewal, and creation of new knowledge, and improve congruence with their environment. The case firms interact with their environments through boundary elements. Interaction is guided by consulting approaches and tools that range from detailed methods to a model about personal qualities and skills (Personal Mastery model by The KaosPilots/KaosManagement).

15.1.7   Triggers (Exposure to Triggers) in the Case Firms

The case firms' specialists and employees are perturbed by their daily interaction with clients, competitors, and other aspects of their environments. The firms have proactively increased their potential to be perturbed by new information, for example, by co-operating with universities, research centers, and influential people, by scanning external databases, by monitoring emerging trends, events in the business world, and the world in general, and by accumulating best practices.

Task specifications may influence the opportunities to identify triggers. Detailed task definitions (Arthur Andersen, Ernst & Young) may restrict visions, but they may simultaneously help to identify new exceptional issues because the definitions and standards act as reference points. In innovation-oriented companies where the tasks are not pre-specified (Arthur D. Little, The KaosPilots and KaosManagement), the employees' visions are not restricted, but neither is there a reference point that would help to identify and accumulate new knowledge.

> I think we are definitely creating a lot of new things ... innovation, everybody is doing it. But sometimes without the consciousness behind it (Boudewijn Arts, Arthur D. Little, International, Inc.).

Scanning and identification of triggers may occur informally and intuitively (The KaosPilots/KaosManagement) or for specific needs (Arthur D. Little). Triggers can be scanned formally, regularly, and systematically by utilizing customized, pre-specified, and automated methods (Arthur Andersen, Ernst & Young). Boundary elements, such as 'cybrarian' and knowledge manager roles, help to screen sources of information and knowledge flows and to identify new triggers. Also the discussion groups in the intranet identify new knowledge and develop it further.

15.1.8   Experimentation in the Case Firms

Earlier experiences help the firms to conduct new experiments. Arthur Andersen has developed its knowledge management services gradually, starting from the GBPs solution. Arthur Andersen, Arthur D. Little, and Ernst & Young have units that conduct experimentation and research. The very purpose of an organization may be related to experimentation. The KaosPilots was established as an experiment, it evolves through experimentation, and it aims to be an institutionalized platform for experiments.

All case companies improve their knowledge by research and/or experimentation. For Arthur D. Little, KaosPilots, and KaosManagement, experimentation is an essential part of the assignments. It also serves the strategic purpose of creating new markets and services in all case companies. As von Krogh and Vicari (1993) have concluded, experiments are important for strategic learning. However, the case firms share best practices, success stories, and positive experiences but not erroneous actions and failures, which may indicate underutilized potential for learning.

15.1.9   Internal Standards, Processes, and Communication in the Case Firms

The case firms have aligned their work processes, knowledge flows, organization and career structure, task definitions, and education to support their identity and perception of their environments. They constitute firm-specific packages that help to learn and facilitate knowledge flows.

As to their work processes, the case firms differ from each other. Arthur Andersen and Ernst & Young have structured methodologies, specified tasks, and explicit knowledge. Arthur D. Little emphasizes innovation, expertise, and creativity in general, and The KaosPilots and KaosManagement stress the importance of personal qualities and the capability to improvise. These aspects are reflected in the task definitions, rules, routines, and in some cases in the lack of them. The production and management processes are supplemented by socio-technical solutions that help the employees and teams to communicate, co-operate, and share knowledge. Personal contacts and teamwork are important for large and small case companies alike. Standards — such as Arthur Andersen's Universal Process Classification Scheme map and Ernst & Young's methods — provide globally shared 'languages' that help employees to communicate in multinational teams and with multinational clients.

As to the traditional functional and organizational structure, the case firms vary considerably as measured by the number and location of subsidiaries (3–660 subsidiaries, 3–160 countries), form of ownership (private/partner-owned, private/employee-owned, public/'independent'), and age (less than 10 years to more than 100 years). The case firms consist of subsidiaries (Arthur Andersen, Arthur D. Little), local member firms (Ernst & Young), specified units (such as KnowledgeSpace^{SM} at Arthur Andersen and the Global Knowledge Centers at Ernst & Young), and a network (The KaosPilots and KaosManagement). They have grown organically (all case firms), through acquisitions (Arthur Andersen and Arthur D. Little), and through mergers (Ernst & Young). Career structures vary from a pyramid (Arthur Andersen, Ernst & Young) and cylinder (Arthur D. Little) to a small core organization that is connected to networks (The KaosPilots and KaosManagement). The case companies employ in varying proportions young, well-educated people and older experienced specialists who bring new knowledge into the organization. They provide very different opportunities for individual motivation and careers, accumulation and sharing of knowledge, and development of competencies. The firms have aligned their internal education to support their recruitment policy and career structures.

15.1.10 Information and Communication Systems in the Case Firms

For the case firms, the communication networks have an enabling role. They act as strategic components and facilitate other strategic components. The large methodologically oriented firms have implemented extensive, advanced information and communication systems that enable global knowledge accumulation and sharing (Arthur Andersen, Ernst & Young, recently also Arthur D. Little). The ICT systems provide an access to accumulated knowledge and external sources of information and facilitate creativity, analysis, and communication. The case firms have also implemented solutions that facilitate communication among people around selected topics in groups and networks (communities of practice at Arthur Andersen, SME networks at Ernst & Young), including interaction with clients in virtual cyberspaces. Groupware and collaboration have an important role, especially for the methodology-oriented management consulting companies (Reimus, 1996, 1997). These findings support studies which claim that large organizations can also become organized anarchies, adhocracies, and free-form organizations (Hedlund, 1993).

15.2 Major Knowledge Flows of the Case Firms

15.2.1 'Sensing' in the Case Firms

The case firms have developed various solutions that help them to continually align their functioning with their rapidly changing environments. They utilize their boundary elements in the process of mutual co-evolution, compensate for triggers, improve their knowledge, and develop their internal 'structure' (components in their living composition) when necessary.

As to their sensing capability, the case companies are engaged in experiments, they create knowledge in close interaction with their clients, and they interpret and utilize information that they acquire through their boundary elements, such as specified positions and professions for individuals, groups, and organizational units.

15.2.1.1 Benefits of sensing Interaction and co-evolution with the environment causes structural changes to the living composition, for example, to an organization's internal standards and workflows. Interactive openness helps the case companies to refine knowledge, to improve congruence with the environment, and to validate the learning and evolution system.

The case companies *refine their knowledge and create and accumulate new knowledge* through an exposure to external variety. They have accelerated their learning and renewal processes by implementing knowledge management, by monitoring triggers and trends, and by increasing their exposure to relevant 'disturbances' from the business environment. For example, Arthur Andersen utilizes GBP as triggers for its own development and creates alliances with quickly moving firms. Ernst & Young scans knowledge about its business environment through its extensive knowledge management system and by numerous information professionals and sophisticated tools. The KaosPilots and KaosManagement improve their knowledge through experiments and by exploring unknown geographic or business territories. They search for new solutions to unique and 'impossible' problems by transcending existing categories and combining contrasting objectives. Arthur D. Little creates new knowledge side by side with its clients. All case companies capture knowledge for future purposes from the interaction. They accumulate it into global knowledge bases (Arthur Andersen, Ernst & Young, Arthur D. Little) and facilitate specialization (Arthur D. Little). The KaosPilots and KaosManagement accumulate tacit knowledge in networks through action-oriented methods.

According to the law of limited variety (Pondy & Mitroff, 1979), a system will exhibit no more variety than the variety to which it has been exposed in its environment. The case firms have actively searched for an exposure to new knowledge. However, adopting an external variety can also lead to considerable diversification (Arthur D. Little). The selection and development of the operating environment may be critical for knowledge development.

The case firms *improve congruence with their environments* through their boundary elements that increase their capability to acquire new knowledge and make sense of the surrounding world. The findings support Luhmann's (1983) conclusion that interactive openness helps organizations to coordinate their functioning with their environments. All case companies also influence their environments proactively. For example, Arthur D. Little improves congruence with its environment through 'organic' approaches and internal change, such as a transformation. The firm also influences its environment proactively, conducts experiments, organizes high-level executive programs, contributes to international conferences, and co-operates with universities. Ernst & Young improves congruence by scanning external information, by identifying weak signals, by responding to changes in its environment through internal changes such as the major transformation process, and through the Center for Business Innovation™. The Knowledge Process Landscape model depicts how the company evolves in its environment, facilitated by client projects. The KaosPilots and KaosManagement do not only aim to survive in the chaos, but they specialize in navigating successfully in it. They proactively change their *conditions of future congruence* through challenging profit and less-profit projects and openness to weak signals from their environment. They have adapted to their environment by going through several transformations.

The case companies *validate their learning and evolution system* by measuring and developing its functioning and features. They also develop their learning and renewal methods, such as the methods to screen and interpret new knowledge, to meet the changing external and internal requirements. Arthur Andersen utilizes GBP to develop its knowledge management. New external knowledge provides reference points for evaluating the firm's living composition and individual components. At Ernst & Young, the Center of Business Knowledge™ (CBK) measures the usage and other characteristics of the knowledge management system and its value for clients. The KaosPilots and KaosManagement utilize external evaluations for improving their functioning. They test and validate their learning and renewal system by exposing it purposely to surprises, by taking it to unknown territories, and by stretching people's consciousness and intuition to cover a broad range of issues that extend the traditional consulting skills.

15.2.1.2 Challenges concerning sensing   As to the *refinement of knowledge*, it is challenging to identify, filter, and interpret information. The capacity of the knowledge management organization and the motivation of employees to contribute to learning may be limited as the volume of information increases. For example, it is difficult to encourage project teams to accumulate information.

> They want to get out what they need to serve their client, and they just don't have the time to put the knowledge back again. We have a real challenge ahead of our system to find out what are the unique techniques and procedures we can use to encourage people to be more generous with all their personal knowledge capital (Robert J. Hiebeler).

It is also problematic to meet increasingly sophisticated client needs in a profitable way. For example, Arthur D. Little's niche of consulting, innovation, and specialism sets high demands on the quality of knowledge. The client cases are unique and it is difficult to know beforehand what knowledge should be accumulated from them for future purposes. Therefore, it is challenging to balance between the specialists' tacit knowledge that requires communication, and an explicit organizational knowledge that requires global screening and accumulation of knowledge.

The increasing volume of information and the need to maintain its relevance and quality are also challenges for Ernst & Young. It is difficult to accumulate knowledge from local sources in the multilingual and multicultural organization. Also, managing the large number of Small and Medium-size Enterprises (SME) Knowledge Networks that prepare and update PowerPacks is a demanding task.

It is problematic to change an organization's focus, to tailor new approaches frequently, and to create new knowledge and skills profitably. However, it is The KaosPilots and KaosManagement's success at these processes that make them attractive to their clients and other parties. As they continue to develop their expertise, they also have to find a balance between diversification and a clear professional profile. A further challenge arises from the difficulty of accumulating knowledge in an explicit form, because the organizations are small and their services are 'soft' and action oriented.

It is challenging to *maintain congruence with* the business environment because it is multinational and multicultural, and the needs of clients and the conditions of competition change continually. In specialist organizations such as Arthur D. Little, employees have to learn fast and acquire new knowledge in order to maintain their specialism. An access to external sources is important because brand positions are changing in the industry and 'generalist' competitors are increasing their innovativeness and the sophistication of their assignments. Moreover, it is challenging for Arthur D. Little to grow in its current niche and to answer its clients' unique needs. It is difficult balancing between diversity and freedom on one hand, and focus, structure, and discipline on the other.

Ernst & Young has proactively changed its competitive situation rather than adapted to it. The firm has invested considerably in knowledge management. However, the high costs of information technology development are a major challenge for the company. Other major challenges include maintaining standard offerings while anticipating clients' needs for new offerings (Digrius, 1997). It is also challenging to support consultants so that they can improvise approaches that suit the particular client situation (Davenport, 1996).

The KaosPilots and KaosManagement escape static congruence with the environment and prefer exploring the unknown. The KaosPilots depends on the market in a paradoxical way, by being against it. It was a loosely connected 'parasite organization' during its first years of operation. It is also 'parasitic' by nature, and this parasitic relationship is problematic because of The KaosPilots' excessive dependency on the market. On the other hand, The KaosPilots is 'going against' the market by being untraditional. This is paradoxically in consonance with the environment's expectations of The KaosPilots because it is supposed to change its focus and boundaries continually and to represent something new. This expectation has created pressure on the organization (Deichman-Sørensen, 1997).

As to validation, it is difficult to measure the employees' contribution to and utilization of the knowledge management system as well as the system's value for employees and clients. This need for validation is partially addressed by peer evaluations, where measurement is linked to incentives. Ernst & Young has successfully measured the contribution and access to knowledge, but measuring the benefits for clients is difficult. Moreover, measuring the reuse of knowledge is difficult because 'disconnected' use does not create statistics.

As to the broader picture, it is a challenge to measure the functioning and benefits of the learning and renewal system from the angle of survival and success. The impact of investments is often immaterial and indirect.

15.2.2   'Memory' in the Case Firms

As to memory, the case firms utilize their existing knowledge, rules, standards, and other accumulated resources in many ways. Memory means that *an organization's accumulated knowledge affects its functioning and learning.* In the case firms, the availability of globally accumulated knowledge enables their daily functioning and facilitates their learning and evolution. The case companies support access to knowledge by Intranets, efficient search mechanisms, and classification of knowledge (Arthur Andersen and Ernst & Young).

Memory also means that *an organization's functioning affects the acquisition and creation of new knowledge.* For example, the interpretation rules and the methods to accumulate knowledge influence the acquisition of new knowledge. The companies that use packaged knowledge have developed screening mechanisms to identify knowledge 'nuggets' that could act as sources for such packages. Companies that are based on specialist knowledge and unique client assignments create new knowledge by facilitating cooperation among experts and clients (Arthur D. Little).

The case firms' motivation to develop solutions that improve their memory arises largely from their identities as learning organizations and suppliers of knowledge. Also, the notion of knowledge as the most important success factor in the rapidly changing environment, and the objective to share and reuse knowledge globally (Arthur Andersen, Ernst & Young, increasingly Arthur D. Little) motivate the building of self-referential structures and processes.

The case firms have organized their access to accumulated knowledge in various ways. They find expert knowledge through communication systems and form explicit knowledge into global knowledge bases — such as Ernst & Young's PowerPacks. They also utilize shared culture, strategies, rules, and practices.

15.2.2.1   Benefits of memory   An access to the existing knowledge provides several benefits for the case firms. Global sharing and reuse increase the value of knowledge. Organizational memory helps them to learn from earlier experiences, to accelerate the provision of services, and to improve the quality, sophistication, and innovative content of those services. Arthur Andersen's organizational memory enables the reuse of earlier knowledge (temporal aspect) and helps the consultants utilize each other's globally accumulated knowledge (sharing aspect). Memory facilitates innovation because it reduces the time needed for routine tasks and helps to meet the increasing needs of client assignments. Arthur D. Little benefits from diversified specialist knowledge because the global information and communication system improves access to tacit, specialist knowledge and accumulated, explicit knowledge. Access to knowledge improves efficiency, decreases 'reinventing the wheel', and strengthens the firm's identity. According to the Knowledge Process Landscape model, the 'application circle' provides Ernst & Young with an access to accumulated knowledge. It enables the company to share and reuse knowledge on a global scale and to create value for clients by providing them with relevant knowledge quickly.

Learning from shared experiences has improved Ernst & Young's global performance considerably and strengthened the firm's identity. Memory helps the firm to achieve consistency across its relatively loose multinational and multicultural organization that has grown rapidly.

At KaosManagement and The KaosPilots, people access an accumulated tacit knowledge largely via communication. This supports shared culture and organizational identity. Embedded knowledge, such as the Personal Mastery model, improves competence and helps the organization use scarce resources efficiently. The decision to move toward more explicit knowledge improves the visibility of knowledge and facilitates sharing.

Access to knowledge that is embedded in organizational solutions also helps to build and utilize shared standards, processes, and strategies, to create consistency and shared culture across the organization, to create historical perspective, continuity and identity among its employees, and to strengthen the identity through improved self-understanding. This facilitates value-creation on a global scale and improves global performance.

15.2.2.2 Challenges concerning memory Maintaining the relevance and quality of knowledge is important because low-quality knowledge would not have value. It is challenging to provide rapid access to globally accumulated knowledge for various user groups because the volume of knowledge is increasing (Arthur Andersen, Arthur D. Little, Ernst & Young). Even if search engines help to find knowledge, Arthur Andersen and Ernst & Young structure knowledge by using taxonomies. Arthur Andersen updates its knowledge bases regularly.

Avoiding rigidity may be a particular challenge for large organizations that act as one global integrated company and have a collective company culture. The risk of rigidity may affect, for example, task definitions, curriculum, and the ways to identify, interpret, and structure knowledge. The continuous improvement of processes and the utilization of best practices from external sources decrease the risk.

At Arthur D. Little, the sharing of tacit expert knowledge is not easy. The specialists may be reluctant to share their expertise. It is also difficult to maintain the specialists' freedom, creativity, and innovativeness while simultaneously implementing necessary rules and structures. Arthur D. Little's shared values represented in the One-Company Management platform aim at unifying the diversified company. However, maintaining the firm's invaluable traditions while avoiding dependence on the past are challenges for the firm.

For Ernst & Young, access to knowledge is a challenge because the knowledge bases constitute a complex system. For an employee it can be difficult to find the needed knowledge from the 470 databases that include 150 PowerPacks and 62,000 documents. Moreover, new databases are released frequently. The firm's high growth rate and the 15–20% annual turnover of people, make the system's complexity an even more critical issue. Ernst & Young minimizes the difficulty by structuring the content of PowerPacks in a standardized way, by utilizing search engines that help to find knowledge from a variety of sources, and by providing tools, methods, and services (such as Knowledge Navigation and E&Y Knowledge Services Group) that help people to find needed knowledge.

Ernst & Young's and Arthur Andersen's best practices knowledge is purposely biased toward good examples and success stories instead of failures or 'bad practices'. This distortion is motivated because it helps employees to learn from good examples and reduces the total volume of knowledge, but it does not provide potentially valuable learning from failures.

For Ernst & Young, a firm that is characterized by meritocracy, hierarchy, and discipline, it is challenging to build a sharing culture, to facilitate creativity and improvisation, and to avoid rigidity. This question concerns several aspects such as internal processes, standards, culture, methodology, working practices, communication, career structure, and education. It also concerns the firm's extensive knowledge management system, such as the ways to interpret information, and the taxonomies that are used for structuring knowledge into the PowerPacks and global knowledge bases. Gaining global access to local knowledge is a challenge. Cultural differences prevent consultants from utilizing globally accumulated knowledge in cases where it is regarded as too US oriented.

For small action-oriented organizations like The KaosPilots and KaosManagement, it is problematic to balance between tacit and explicit knowledge and to convert knowledge into an explicit form. Self-understanding is also an intriguing question for them. KaosManagement and The KaosPilots attract positive attention in the mass media and actively promote themselves. These are invaluable skills for small organizations. Self-understanding helps them to match the promises and expectations to their capabilities and resources, even when many of their successful projects were originally regarded as 'impossible'. They can tackle unknown situations and therefore it is difficult to draw a line between realism and exaggeration in their projects and identity.

While KaosManagement and The KaosPilots have an increasing need for efficiency and a clear, specified professional profile, they are attractive to clients because of their future-orientation, intuition, and willingness to explore new, unknown issues. Their very image is about avoiding rigidity, and it does not favor looking for earlier documentation. They are not expected to provide knowledge about yesterday or today but 'from a training camp in the future'. The relevance of their knowledge is not measured by its capability to reflect earlier experiences but by its contribution to the creation of a new future. Therefore, the emphasis of The KaosPilots and KaosManagement is on exploration instead of exploitation.

15.2.3   The Linkage between 'Sensing' and 'Memory' in the Case Firms

In the case firms, sensing and memory are interconnected. For example, Arthur Andersen and Ernst & Young have built solutions that support the acquisition and accumulation of knowledge (interactive openness), provide global access to it (self-referentiality), and connect these two aspects within one integrated system that is continually monitored, developed, and validated. The linkage between interactive openness and self-referentiality has a crucial role for the case firms' capability to co-evolve with their environment. "Components in general and basic elements in particular can be reproduced only if they have the capacity to link closure and openness" (Luhmann, 1990, p. 12).

The analysis of the case firms reveals that the sensing (interactive openness) and memory (self-referentiality) are not contradictions but:

1. *They coexist simultaneously* and complement each other. This finding is compatible with earlier literature (von Krogh & Roos, 1995; Luhmann, 1983, 1990).
2. *They are linked to each* other via knowledge flows.
3. *They facilitate each other, creating a dynamically evolving pattern.*
4. *They enable each other.* The result is compatible with earlier literature which says that societies in general are systems capable of maintaining closure under the condition of

openness (Luhmann, 1983, 1990) and that the "autopoietic systems are 'organization-ally closed' but interactively open. They interact with their environment through their structure" (Mingers, 1995, p. 33).

All case companies regard themselves as learning organizations. The relationship between learning and knowledge is twofold. On the one hand, learning is a process of creating and adding value to the knowledge asset (Arthur Andersen, Ernst & Young). On the other, knowledge is used as a raw material for learning.

'Action' has different and even controversial roles for organizational knowledge, learning, and renewal.

1. Methodologically oriented organizations apply pre-defined activities in order to produce new knowledge that is collected, stored, and applied in a future action.
2. For an experimental organization, action has a different role. The KaosPilots and KaosManagement utilize action as a method to create and accumulate new experiences and tacit knowledge and to learn from them. They act first and then learn, mainly without an explicit knowledge. They implement quickly what is possible rather than use predefined rules or accumulated knowledge.

Argyris and Schön's (1996) model of learning has only a limited capability to explain learning in the future-oriented case companies that operate in rapidly changing environments and express their values in dynamic and highly abstract terms. Instead, the autopoiesis model can better explain the dynamics of learning in the case firms.

The case firms supplement their evolutionary processes with mergers and acquisitions (Arthur Andersen, Arthur D. Little, Ernst & Young), action-oriented 'experimenting evolution' (The KaosPilots and KaosManagement), coordinated, company-wide transformation (Arthur D. Little, Arthur Andersen and Ernst & Young), and long-term improvement of organizational solutions (all case organizations). Some case companies have had exceptionally high growth rates. For example, Ernst & Young (Management Consulting) grew 29% in 1997 and 38% in 1996. In addition to growth and profit maximization, the case firms also have other objectives such as intellectual challenge (Arthur D. Little) and curiosity and impact on society (The KaosPilots and KaosManagement).

PART IV

PLATFORMS AND IMPLICATIONS

This part of the book utilizes a normative approach. It is divided into two chapters. Chapter 16 analyzes the opportunities to position and develop organizations by using the living composition model. Chapter 17 summarizes the ideas of living composition, and thereafter reframes the controversies and dilemmas presented in the beginning of this book. The chapter also discusses the implications for managers, consultants, researchers, and teachers.

Chapter 16

Improving Living Organizations

This chapter first discusses opportunities to proactively improve organizations by applying the model of living composition. The experiences of the case firms are also reviewed when needed. Then it presents four consistency/intentionality platforms and evolution models that help to position an organization according to its method of evolution. Finally, this chapter suggests six steps for improving the evolutionary processes of organizations by influencing their living compositions.

16.1 Proactive and Passive Approaches

The theory of self-production can be interpreted either in a proactive or in a passive way. *The proactive interpretation* emphasizes an organization's possibilities to co-evolve with its environment by utilizing its boundary elements as well as the capability to learn from interactions and to influence its own fate. The proactive interpretation may lead to methods, processes, and managerial practices that help to continually improve the organization in the larger context of a business ecosystem. *The passive interpretation* emphasizes an organization's closure, separating boundaries, isolation, and a limited capability to react to external triggers. It may lead to a pessimistic picture about an organization's ability to learn and renew. Table 16.1 summarizes the differences between the proactive and passive interpretations.

The case companies interact with their environments and change themselves proactively, yet in different ways. They facilitate changes in their client organizations and their business environments. They improve the prospects for their future success by continuously evolving their current service offerings, research, and public visibility. The case firms proactively develop their conditions for co-operation, for example, through new services and 'mobilizing projects' (Arthur D. Little), specialized units (the Next Generation Research Group of Arthur Andersen, Global Centers of Ernst & Young), and virtual forums (KnowledgeSpace[SM] of Arthur Andersen; Ernie[TM] of Ernst & Young). However, The KaosPilots and KaosManagement choose not to focus on achieving congruence with today's environment, because paradoxically their clients expect them to 'be against the market'. Instead they focus on exploring the conditions for achieving congruence with future environments.

The case firms also change themselves proactively. They continuously improve their learning and evolution capabilities, intentionally seek to increase their exposure to triggers, develop new boundary elements, and thereby improve their capacity to absorb knowledge. They also evaluate and measure their capability to learn and evolve — for example, by evaluating employees' contribution to knowledge sharing.

These observations support earlier findings that organizations have to build systematic practices in order to manage self-transformation (Drucker, 1992, 1993) and that there must be increasing focus on processes of collective learning and proactive experimentation to

Table 16.1: Proactive and passive interpretation of living organizations.

	Proactive interpretation	**Passive interpretation**
Boundary	Connects an organization to its environment through reciprocal interaction.	Separates an organization from its environment.
Relationship to the environment	Interactively open toward the environment. An organization learns and renews itself through experimentation, reciprocal interaction, and exposure to triggers from the environment. It selects autonomously whether to change or not	Closed (isolated) toward the environment. An organization cannot change itself, and the environment cannot directly instruct the organization
Knowledge and self referentiality	Enable learning from earlier experience	Limit learning
Internal 'structure' (living composition)	Provides an enabling infrastructure for learning and continuous renewal	Is a source of rigidity?

create new competences (Grant, 1991; Boisot, 1995). They also support the view that a proactive stance toward the environment can 'excite' the organization as a system, and that the system can increase its own 'excitability' by increasing its cognitive complexity, thereby better preparing itself to observe deviations in its environment and thereby to notice and process more information (Luhmann, 1995).

16.2   Consistency/Intentionality Platforms

16.2.1   *Four Consistency/Intentionality Platforms*

As mentioned earlier in Chapter 3, consistency among strategic components can be defined by two dimensions, consistent/inconsistent and intended/unintended. These dimensions give rise to four types of consistency: intentional fit, stretch, emergent fit, and misfit. These characteristics can be described further as different types of consistency/intentionality platforms that characterize an organization's method for maintaining its living composition and renewal capability (see Table 16.2).

Table 16.3 summarizes the variation in their living compositions of the case firms. They were originally selected to represent three of the consistency types. It became evident that

Table 16.2: The four consistency/intentionality platforms concerning the living composition.

		INTENTIONALITY	
		Intended	**Unintended**
CONSISTENCY OF THE LIVING COMPOSITION	**Consistent**	**1.** **Intentional fit** A tailored and consistent composition that connects interactive openness and self-referentiality. It facilitates company-wide learning and renewal	**2.** **Emergent fit** Incidental changes, experiments, or action-oriented evolution, with a consistent outcome
	Inconsistent	**3.** **Stretch** A planned and controlled transformation or change, or a sequence of them. Temporarily inconsistent	**4.** **Misfit** Incidental changes, experiments, or action-oriented evolution, with an inconsistent outcome

in a special case an organization can represent two types of consistency. Arthur D. Little is an example of such a situation.

1. *The intentional fit platform* is an intended and consistent composition that facilitates continuous learning and renewal in the short and long term. The strategic components are aligned so that they facilitate interactive openness and self-referentiality. The empirical findings from Arthur Andersen, Ernst & Young, and Arthur D. Little suggest that the intentional fit composition constitutes a subtle package of components, a carefully designed 'puzzle'. However, the content of the individual components can vary considerably among organizations, depending on an organization's identity, perception of its environment, and its overall composition.

The composition may have evolved unconsciously during co-evolution with the business environment. However, sophisticated socio-technical solutions are generally results of conscious design, aimed at competence and survival in changing conditions. Therefore, developing intentional fit composition further may require tailored and holistic coordination of multiple components. The improvement of one strategic component only, for example an information and communication system without understanding the content of and

Table 16.3: The compositions of the case organizations.

		INTENTIONALITY	
		Intended	Unintended
		1. **Intentional fit**	**2.** **Emergent fit**
CONSISTENCY BETWEEN STRATEGIC COMPONENT	**Consistent**	Arthur Andersen (Business Consulting) Ernst & Young (Management Consulting) Arthur D. Little (Europe) (improves the intentional fit Scomposition)	← KaosPilots and KaosManagement
		3. **Stretch**	**4.** **Misfit**
	Inconsistent	Arthur D. Little (Europe) (the temporary transformation process)	

relationships among other components in the composition, would not necessarily improve a firm's learning and renewal dynamics.

The cases reveal that intentional fit is a useful concept because it helps in understanding the internal logics of very different organizations and their compositions. For example, Arthur Andersen and Ernst & Young have defined and aligned consistent packages of career paths, specified tasks, methods, curriculums, knowledge management, information and communication systems, and other aspects to support their success and survival. However, their solutions differ considerably from each other. Arthur D. Little has created a consistent package for a diversified specialist organization. Strategic components, such as the cylindrical organization model, multiple alternative career opportunities, and interactive co-operation with clients, have been aligned to meet the firm's specific identity.

The cases also reveal that a firm may be positioned into two consistency/intentionality platforms simultaneously. Arthur D. Little applies basically a carefully designed intentional fit approach in its composition. However, it also represents the stretch approach, because during the interviews it was in the midst of a considerable transformation process. The purpose was to move the organization from the current intentional fit composition to an improved intentional fit.

2. *The emergent fit platform* refers to incidental changes, experiments, and action-oriented evolution that lead to consistent outcomes and congruence among strategic components. It

provides new insights, supports rapid changes, and enables spontaneous learning and evolution processes mainly in the short term. Knowledge is accumulated as individual and organizational experiences rather than in explicit form. This platform may not be easy to predict and measure. Reviewing earlier history helps the organization to learn from experiences. The KaosPilots and KaosManagement are an example of a company that has evolved by using the emergent fit platform.

3. The *stretch platform* is an intended and temporarily or partially inconsistent composition. It provides a platform for a conscious, planned, and controlled large-scale transformation. Arthur D. Little represents this platform in relation to its ambitious transformation process.

4. The *misfit composition* refers to incidental changes, experiments, and action-oriented evolution that lead to inconsistent outcomes. This platform provides an opportunity to learn from errors and possibly from a crisis.

16.2.2   How to Use Consistency/Intentionality Platforms

The consistency/intentionality platforms can be used for positioning an organization's renewal method and capability. This can occur by using two variables: the consistency of the strategic composition, and the intentionality of the consistency. The platforms can also be used for comparing the organization to others, such as competitors. The platforms help to understand earlier evolution and changes, caused for example by increasing intentionality. Moreover, the evolution models help to improve the infrastructure that is needed to enable further evolutionary processes.

There is no one right platform of living composition. Each platform can be feasible for an organization, depending on its life cycle, size, specific change situation, and other aspects. However, the findings emphasize the importance of the composition and its conscious design for an organization's learning, renewal capability, survival, and success.

Organizations may have a tendency toward *intentional fit*. In particular, they may have a tendency to move from the emergent fit platform that is a result of natural drift to the intentional fit platform. This tendency is indicated by some case firms' willingness to increase structures and standardization, and by the need to establish a more solid basis for long-term development.

Organizations that have learned to learn may also have a tendency to improve their existing intentional fit composition. There is room for many different intentional fit compositions depending on a firm's specific identity and other relevant aspects. Therefore an achieved intentional fit does not mean that organizational development has ended.

It is possible that the *emergent fit platform* is a feasible and productive choice mainly for relatively small and young organizations. As an organization becomes larger, the need and opportunities for more structured solutions emerge. The questions that are related to the size of an organization will be discussed in Section 17.4.

Stretch can be regarded as a transition category that depicts a move from one platform to another, or a radical improvement within a platform. The relationship of the stretch category to other categories would require further analysis. The concept also deserves further specification because it may indicate three different aspects. First, it may refer to ambitious engagements, services, employees, and challenges in general. Second, it may refer to continuous development as a permanent characteristic of an organization. Third, it may refer to a considerable temporary transformation, as was the case in Arthur D. Little (Europe).

16.3   Evolution Models

16.3.1   Four Evolution Models

It is also possible to position an organization's method of evolution by reviewing the various combinations of sensing and memory. The four alternatives are depicted in Table 16.4.

1a. *The systematically exploring and accumulating evolution model* means that an organization can learn effectively from perturbances from its environment and from co-evolution with it. The organization identifies new knowledge through boundary elements and then also utilizes its earlier and continually accumulating experiences. This alternative resembles the 'connected open and closed system' (open boundary; internal closure) that was presented in Section 16.2.

1b. *The original, innovative evolution model* is a variation of the previous alternative. This means that instead of responding to external perturbations, an organization utilizes its knowledge and other internal resources proactively, combines them in a creative way, acts first, and then receives the response from its environment. It produces original, self-generated, and innovative outcomes with potential to influence the environment with a time delay. An organization can facilitate endogenous development and originality and use

Table 16.4: The evolution models concerning the living composition.

		'MEMORY', SELF-REFERENTIALITY Accessing earlier experiences and knowledge, and learning from them	
		Memory is utilized	Memory is not utilized
'SENSING', INTERACTIVE OPENNESS Interaction and co-evolution with the environment	**Sensing is utilized**	**1a.** Systematically exploring and accumulating organization	**2.** Exploring and adapting organization ('ad hoc')
		1b. Original, innovative organization	
	Sensing is not utilized	**3.** Isolated organization	**4.** Passive organization

accumulated knowledge creatively. Based on the responses from its environment, an organization may react according to its internal rules.

In both alternatives (1a and 1b), an organization uses its boundary elements and their sensing capability to co-evolve with its environment and to learn from it. It also uses its accumulated knowledge that is stored in its memory as a source for creativity and learning.

2. *The exploring and adapting evolution model* means efficient exploration and co-evolution with the environment and inefficient utilization of earlier experiences. This organization is double-open. It uses its sensing but not its memory. This kind of organization continually seeks new experiences and changes itself at a rapid tempo. However, it cannot learn from its experiences and utilize them.

3. *The isolated evolution model* means that an organization uses its memory but not its sensing capability. Interaction with its environment is weak or missing, and the organization is isolated. Knowledge is based on organizational memory only. This evolution model may result in endogenous, self-generated outcomes that lack viability.

4. *The passive evolution model* means that an organization does not learn from the perturbations from its environment, i.e. it does not have sensing capability. Moreover, it does not learn from its own accumulated experiences. Therefore the organization is not coordinated with its environment, it does not function in an efficient way, and it does not have the capability to co-evolve with its environment.

16.3.2   How to Use Evolution Models

The evolution models can also be used for positioning an organization's renewal method and capability by using sensing and memory as variables. The evolution models also help to compare an organization's learning and renewal method to others'.

Measured by the evolution models, all case firms combine interactive openness and self-referentiality in their own specific way. The findings suggest that the living composition can be composed in various ways within the 'systematically exploring and accumulating' model type. Arthur Andersen and Ernst & Young can be regarded as 'systematically exploring and accumulating' companies. They facilitate interactive openness and self-referentiality by extensive information and communication systems and knowledge management. Arthur D. Little evolves as an original, innovative company. Interactive openness results in specialization and diversification. The company attempts to strengthen its self-referential capabilities with an information and communication system and knowledge management. The company is increasingly adopting characteristics of the 'systematically exploring and accumulating' model. The KaosPilots and KaosManagement evolve as an exploring/adapting organization. Their sensing means exploring the unknown and implementing changes quickly through action. The focus is on new experiences rather than on earlier ones.

16.3.3   Comparison of Consistency/Intentionality Platforms and Evolution Models

The consistency/intentionality platforms and evolution models cannot be directly compared because they are based on different dimensions. Consistency/intentionality platforms are based on consistency and intentionality of the strategic composition, and evolution models on sensing and memory. However, there is some correlation that would require additional research. For example, the 'systematically exploring and accumulating' evolution model may correlate positively with the intentional fit platform, the exploring/adapting evolution model may correlate positively with the emergent fit platform, and the passive evolution model may correlate positively with the misfit platform.

16.4   Six Steps for Improving a Living Composition

According to the basic principles of autopoiesis, it is not possible to control a living organization and its members from outside. Instead an organization may implement changes that its members regard as relevant and in line with the organization's identity, existing knowledge, and other relevant components. Therefore it is important to plan a possible intervention so that it begins by strengthening awareness and clarifying the identity.

The living composition model helps in understanding *how to create an infrastructure that enables innovativeness, learning, and continuous renewal in an organization.* The core issue is to coordinate, clarify, and strengthen the strategic components into a composition so that the two major knowledge flows, sensing and memory, function better. This may imply changes in individual components or more comprehensive changes in the whole 'puzzle'.

Table 16.5 presents the process to systematically identify, evaluate, and improve an organization's living composition. The process consists of six steps.

16.4.1   Step 1: Create Awareness and Communicate the Need for Change

The empirical findings indicate that people in organizations are more or less conscious of strategic compositions and methods of learning and evolving. Therefore, the first step is to create shared awareness and to communicate the potential need for change. Because the development process should be based on shared understanding of the strengths, problems, objectives, and methods, it is necessary to ensure that there is also sufficient awareness of the general principles of living organizations and living compositions. Next, it is useful to position the organization by using the current consistency/intentionality platform and evolution model. In this context it may also be possible to make comparisons to competitors. This analysis helps the management of an organization to preliminarily identify the basic strengths and weaknesses in the strategic composition and evolutionary process. The analysis may result in the finding that the organization is living, but that there is space for improvement. Based on these activities, it is possible to describe the preliminary strengths, problems, development needs, and objectives, and to decide whether further steps are necessary.

16.4.2   Step 2: Analyze the Strategic Components

An organization's living composition type largely determines its current capability to renew itself and to co-evolve with its environment. The needs and opportunities for improvement can be identified by using the living composition model as a framework, creating the basis

Table 16.5: The process for improving an organization's living composition.

Step 1: Create awareness and communicate the need for change
- Create shared awareness of the principles of living organizations
- Identify the current position of the organization on the consistency/intentionality platform and evolution model
- Describe preliminary strengths, problems, development needs, and objectives

Step 2: Analyze the strategic componentsIdentity
- Perception of the environment
- Strategy
- Knowledge and knowledge management
- Boundary elements
- Interactive processes and communication
- Triggers
- Experimentation
- Internal standards, processes and communication
- Information and communication systems

Step 3: Analyze the knowledge flows and knowledge processes
- Analyze two major knowledge flows: (1) Sensing, (2) Memory
- Analyze four knowledge processes: (1) Highly structured explicit/digital knowedge, (2) Less-structured explicit/digital knowledge, (3) Highly structured tacit knowledge, (4) Less-structured tacit knowledge

Step 4: Describe the current living composition of the organization and analyze its dynamics
- Describe and analyze the relationships among the strategic components, knowedge flows, and knowledge processes
- Analyze the strengths and weaknesses in the dynamics of the living composition

Step 5: Design and implement the improved or new living composition
- Select the future consistency/intentionality platform and evolution model for the organization
- Design the improved living composition and align the strategic components, knowledge flows, and knowledge processes to support the selected future state
- Prioritize the changes to maximize systemic effects. Communicate the plans in the organization
- Implement changes in the strategic composition

Step 6: Utilize, measure, and improve the living composition
- Utilize the improved living composition
- Create methods to measure the most critical aspects of its functioning and its impact on learning and renewal
- Improve continually the structure and functioning of the composition and the co-evolution with the environment

for further steps. For this purpose, an analysis of strategic components and their relationships is needed. Their systematic analysis helps in depicting the composition and communicating the specific development needs in an organization, and helps organizational members in different positions to understand the strengths and weaknesses in the individual components and their relationships.

16.4.3   Step 3: Analyze the Knowledge Flows and Knowledge Processes

This step includes two different methods to analyze the dynamics of organizational knowledge: (1) analysis of the two major knowledge flows and (2) analysis of the four knowledge processes.

Analysis of the two major knowledge flows. The analysis of *sensing* benefits from careful investigation of existing and potential boundary elements and their functioning. The sensing activities — exposure to triggers and responding to them, interactive processes and communication with the environment, and experimentation — also have to be mapped and evaluated. Organizational *memory*, especially the type and location of critical knowledge and access to it, is also a target for analysis at this stage. Therefore it is useful to conduct in parallel the analysis of the four knowledge processes.

Analysis of the four knowledge processes covers highly structured explicit/digital knowledge, less-structured explicit/digital knowledge, highly structured tacit knowledge, and less-structured tacit knowledge. Their analysis helps organizational members to recognize the variety of different kinds of knowledge in the organization and the rapid development in digital technologies that are available. This stage may also help to identify the structured and less-structured tacit knowledge and its importance for the organization.

16.4.4   Step 4: Describe the Current Living Composition of the Organization and Analyze its Dynamics

In this step the organization's strategic composition and its dynamics are described and analyzed. The purpose is to consider the larger picture that constitutes the composition by analyzing the relationships among individual components, knowledge flows, knowledge processes, and other details that have been identified in earlier steps. Based on these relationships, the dynamics of the whole composition can be evaluated. This analysis helps in understanding the enabling infrastructure, its impact on the learning and renewal of an organization, and its strengths and development potential.

16.4.5   Step 5: Design and Implement the Improved or New Living Composition

The purpose of this step is to design the improved or new composition and its implementation process, and to successfully conduct the implementation process. The first task is to select the future consistency/intentionality platform and evolution model for the organization.

There is no standard content for the components and composition to be implemented. Taking the current composition as a point of departure, the second task is to design the improvements to the living composition or to design a new composition, and to align the strategic components so that the composition becomes a functioning entity. Sometimes the better coordination of current individual components may be sufficient, and sometimes the composition may require a more thorough revision and alignment. This is the case, for example, in organizations that have resulted from mergers and acquisitions, because they may have two different organizational cultures that have to be coordinated and streamlined into a functioning entity.

The third task is to prioritize the improvements to the composition so that their systemic effects can be maximized. Communicating the improvement plans in the organization may increase the systemic effects. The improvements may also cause systemic effects in the business environment. It may therefore be useful to test the systemic impact of the new composition, for example on a smaller scale before launching it on a larger scale.

Implementation of the changes to a strategic composition probably causes changes in organizational culture and attitudes of people. The current composition may have evolved during a long period, and therefore the acceptance and development of the new enabling infrastructure may face some resistance and take a long time, possibly years or decades. Therefore it is important to utilize the systemic effects and to build the process by accumulating successes. It is also important to communicate the commitment to long-term development of the enabling infrastructure.

16.4.6   Step 6: Utilize, Measure, and Improve the Living Composition

The final step includes the utilization of the new improved infrastructure, the new living composition of the organization. In order to facilitate the evolutionary process properly, it is useful to create methods to measure the most critical aspects of its functioning and the impact of the composition on the organization's learning and renewal. Measurement should focus mainly on aspects that are systemically important and enable and facilitate learning and renewal. It is also useful to continually improve the structure and functioning of the composition and the co-evolution of the organization with its business ecosystem.

16.5   Summary

Autopoiesis theory can be interpreted in a proactive or passive way. This book suggests the proactive interpretation, which underlines an organization's possibilities to co-evolve with its environment by utilizing boundary elements. It also emphasizes the capability to learn from the interaction and to influence its own fate.

The relationships among strategic components can be defined by two dimensions, consistent/inconsistent and intended/unintended. The combinations of these dimensions result in four types of consistency/intentionality platforms that help to analyze an organization's method for maintaining its living composition and renewal capability:

1. Intentional fit platform
2. Stretch platform
3. Emergent fit platform
4. Misfit platform.

The four evolution models also help to position an organization according to its method of evolution. They are based on various combinations of sensing and memory:

1a. The systematically exploring and accumulating evolution model
1b. The original, innovative evolution model
2. The exploring and adapting evolution model
3. The isolated evolution model
4. The passive evolution model.

Living compositions are complex and *unique packages* of strategic components. No standard solutions can be applied that would be feasible for every organization. Therefore, it is useful to design an improved living composition and to prioritize the necessary changes. The *six steps for improving living composition* include:

Step 1: Create awareness and communicate the need for change.
Step 2: Analyze the strategic components.
Step 3: Analyze the knowledge flows and knowledge processes.
Step 4: Describe the current living composition of the organization and analyze its dynamics.
Step 5: Design and implement the improved or new living composition.
Step 6: Utilize, measure, and improve the living composition.

Chapter 17

Conclusions

This chapter summarizes the findings of the earlier chapters and makes conclusions. First it presents a summary and evaluation of the living composition model. Then it revisits the concepts of control and creativity in light of the living composition model and empirical evidence. After that the five dilemmas, presented in the beginning of this book, will be reframed in light of the model developed in this book. This chapter also presents managerial implications, discussing the impact of size, growth, and technological level on an organization's evolution. Finally, this chapter presents theoretical implications and suggestions for further research and teaching.

17.1 Summary of the Living Composition Model

The main objective of this book is to explain organizations as living systems that can learn and renew themselves continually, thereby improving their chances of survival and success. This book attempts to show that the firm can be regarded as a living composition that learns and evolves by producing itself. For this purpose this book has provided a new, original interpretation of an organization as a self-producing, living system. This was accomplished by analyzing and interpreting the ideas of self-production (autopoiesis) in the context of organizations or their subunits. The living composition model, its theoretical justification, and empirical testing in the case firms are thereby the main contributions of this book. These contributions include the formulation of the living composition concept and positioning it centrally in the model, as well as the identification of strategic components, boundary elements, two major knowledge flows, and four knowledge processes. They enable the self-producing and co-evolutionary dynamics of organizations.

The main propositions implicit in the living composition model are:

1. The evolutionary capability of a living organization is derived from the functioning of its living composition.
2. A successful organization is likely to have found ways to utilize the complexity phenomena of self-organization and emergence through its living composition.
3. A living organization improves its chances of co-evolving with its complex environment within its business ecosystem by creating and utilizing boundary elements.

The living organization and living composition are defined in the following way:

> *The living composition model* specifies the essential characteristics of living organizations. A living organization is a self-producing (autopoietic) system that is composed of ten different non-physical strategic components. Boundary elements are included as one component type. The living composition model describes the 'structure' of a living organization in which the strategic components and their interrelationships determine an organization's

evolutionary capability. An organization evolves by continually producing its strategic components as simultaneous tracks with a pattern of interactions. The production and interaction of the components and their relationships facilitate sensing (interactive openness) and memory (organizational/internal closure) in an organization. Sensing and memory are simultaneous and interconnected phenomena. They enable both an organization's current efficiency and its capability to learn, to renew itself, and to co-evolve with its changing environment within its larger business ecosystem.

The model analyzes and develops organizations through several components and their interconnected functioning. The basic principles of living organizations are relatively simple and easy to communicate. In the context of organizations, the model can be supplemented with other system models, such as transformation and system dynamics models. However, alone they are not sufficient for explaining an organization as a learning and evolving entity.

A living composition enables learning and renewal processes. It may also respond to triggers from the environment, but according to an organization's internal rules and cognitive capacity. These findings are compatible with earlier studies, which claim that learning is a systems-level phenomenon (Nevis et al., 1995) and that an organization itself can be regarded as a response to its environment (Pfeffer & Salancik, 1978).

Based on the empirical evidence, the case organizations produce their non-physical, strategic components continually. Their learning and renewal dynamics can be described and explained by their compositions, which are self-producing 'packages'. Their compositions are aligned with their identity and perception of their environments, and they facilitate co-evolution with their environments. The organizations' accumulated knowledge about themselves and their environments is embedded in their compositions.

Knowledge is a regulator for the dynamic processes and a result of them. The two interlinked knowledge flows, sensing and memory, enable interactive openness and self-referentiality. The emphasis on four knowledge types and knowledge processes varies from one firm to another.

The *consistency/intentionality platforms and evolution models* help to position the organizations' method of evolution. They also help to compare an organization to others and to develop its method of evolution and enabling infrastructure further.

Autopoiesis theory does not originally deal with learning but rather with structural coupling and drift. However, an interpretation of the theory explains organizations as creative, learning, and renewing entities. Because system theories can be applied in many ways, this interpretation is one of several potential alternatives. Autopoiesis theory is not only a fruitful metaphor, but it can be extended to cover the non-physical production of organizations as well, i.e. organizations are truly autopoietic systems.

17.2 Re-framing of Control and Creativity in Light of the Living Composition Model

The results of the empirical analysis indicate that the controversy between control and creativity can be re-framed by using the living composition model. In Part I of this book the question of control and efficiency versus creativity and freedom was preliminarily discussed. It was also mentioned that exploitation of old certainties and exploration of new possibilities is a classic dilemma in economics, and that organizations tend to favor exploitation over exploration (March, 1991). This section will revisit these concepts in light of the research on the case organizations. This section suggests that the organizations attempt to create a balance between control and creativity.

17.2.1   Are Organizations Moving toward Creativity or Control?

In the case organizations, two trends can be identified. They seem contradictory at first sight, but a closer investigation reveals that they represent a need to re-frame the concepts of control and creativity.

Structured companies aim at increasing creativity Companies that are characterized by structured, methodological approaches (Arthur Andersen and Ernst & Young) apply the principles of autonomy and self-organization in a controlled way in their hierarchies to foster creativity and inspiration among their employees. This occurs for example by implementing communities, networks, knowledge management solutions, and information and communication systems that facilitate creativity.

Paradoxically at the same time *innovative and self-organizing companies aim at implementing structures and standards.* The companies that specialize in innovation and creativity (Arthur D. Little, The KaosPilots, and KaosManagement) aim to implement standards, structures, knowledge-management methods, and information and communication systems in order to become more efficient and ensure their competitiveness.

17.2.2   The Living Composition Enables Simultaneous Efficiency and Creativity

The analysis of the case organizations reveals that it is possible and even necessary to manage the relationship between control and creativity or order and self-organization. The principles of autopoiesis and the living composition model can help in understanding and managing the controversy between creativity and efficiency. These aspects have been highlighted in Figure 17.1.

Observations from the case firms suggest that the organizations' living compositions facilitate simultaneous creativity and efficiency in three ways:

1. *The organization acquires and creates new knowledge by using its boundary elements.* The organization explores its external environment, and co-evolves with its business ecosystems through reciprocal interaction. It is not possible to manage the external environment. However, it is possible to explore it and to influence it proactively. Through the boundary elements, the firm responds to triggers and thereby navigates in the unknown and continually changing environment. Without that capability, the organization would be isolated at the mercy of external changes and not capable of influencing its own fate. Co-evolution with the business ecosystem may lead to new emergent properties in the larger environmental context.

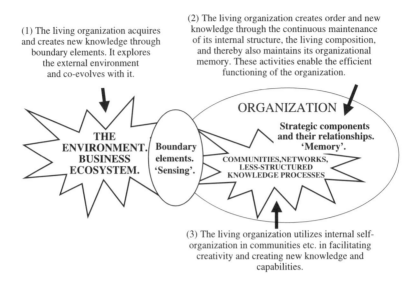

(1) The living organization acquires and creates new knowledge through boundary elements. It explores the external environment and co-evolves with it.

(2) The living organization creates order and new knowledge through the continuous maintenance of its internal structure, the living composition, and thereby also maintains its organizational memory. These activities enable the efficient functioning of the organization.

ORGANIZATION

THE ENVIRONMENT. BUSINESS ECOSYSTEM.

Boundary elements. 'Sensing'.

Strategic components and their relationships. 'Memory'.

COMMUNITIES,NETWORKS, LESS-STRUCTURED KNOWLEDGE PROCESSES

(3) The living organization utilizes internal self-organization in communities etc. in facilitating creativity and creating new knowledge and capabilities.

Figure 17.1: The living composition enables creativity and efficiency.

2. *living organization creates order and new knowledge through the continuous mainte-nance of its internal structure, the living composition, and thereby also its organiza-tional memory. These activities enable the efficient functioning of the organizations.* The maintenance of the internal structure is a continual self-organization process, a characteristic of complex systems. The case firms learn and renew themselves through their living compositions that define their components and relationships. Some case companies operate in a methodological, structured, and predefined way, whereas oth-ers act in a more diversified or action-oriented way.

3. *The living organization utilizes internal self-organization in communities to facilitate cre-ativity and create new knowledge and capabilities.* The organization tolerates and even facilitates internal self-organization and controlled, 'productive chaos' in self-organizing teams, internal communities, discussion groups, networks, and less-structured knowledge processes. Examples are Subject Matter Expert Networks at Ernst & Young and Communities of Practice at Arthur Andersen. The knowledge management systems uti-lize the results of the creative processes and accumulate valuable information.

Thus, the case companies utilize creativity and efficiency as well as exploration and exploitation simultaneously. Knowledge sharing helps them to meet their clients' increas-ing needs for tailored solutions, because it releases time for the specific aspects of the assignment (Arthur Andersen) and facilitates improvisation (Ernst & Young). Knowledge accumulation and sharing help to identify and develop new knowledge (Arthur Andersen, Arthur D. Little, Ernst & Young). These processes provide, in the long term and on a global scale, opportunities for new, customized, higher margin services. The companies that spe-cialize in innovation (Arthur D. Little) or explore 'on the edge of chaos' (The KaosPilots and KaosManagement) aim to benefit from their creative processes through structuring and standardization. The synthesis is largely enabled by information and communication technology. However, technology alone does not explain the fusion. It is also based on a comprehensive alignment of organizational variables, including human resources management and business processes.

The cases indicate that an organization can benefit simultaneously from creativity and control, which helps it to evolve without a crisis. The principles of living composition can be compared to a good heating system that helps to maintain a proper temperature in the house and to adapt to the seasonal variation in the environment. For example, The KaosPilots and Arthur D. Little show that it is possible to implement innovative atmospheres and continual creative processes, which create trust among employees and clients and help to build organizational culture. In contrast, a crisis would bring destructive powers into an organization, especially if it is repeated or artificially generated by management with the purpose of fostering innovation among employees. In a crisis-oriented environment, the fire would burn the house down at regular intervals.

17.3   Reframing the Five Dilemmas

Chapter 1 presented five dilemmas in strategic management. In the following discussion they will be reviewed in light of the living composition model (Table 17.1).

Dilemma 1: The goal: knowledge or learning and renewal?

New view: Survival is the main goal. It is obtained through continual self-production and successful co-evolution with the environment. Knowledge helps to operate adequately in an individual or cooperative situation. Knowledge is a strategic component in the living composition. In this role, knowledge is continually reproduced among other strategic components and in interaction with them. Knowledge is an enabler for learning and renewal, and thereby for survival and evolution. It is also necessary to investigate the processes of knowing. The core activities in knowing are distinction making and shared understanding through communication.

Dilemma 2: Is knowledge objective or subjective?

New view: There are two simultaneous realities: ontological reality and experiential reality. Logical accounting helps to differentiate between them. Objective knowledge is assumed to represent the reality 'out there', whereas subjective knowledge is relative and changing. In the living composition model, it is not possible to know the environment directly. Instead triggers from the environment 'excite' the organization and individuals. We do not know whether our knowledge is objective, correct, or true, but we may know whether it is viable.

Dilemma 3: Is knowledge located in an organization or in several brains?

New view: Knowledge is located in an organization and in the brains. Some recent approaches assume that organizations consist only of people, of 'several brains' that communicate with each other. Interaction among individuals is important for renewal, learning, and creativity.

Table 17.1: Third worldview: Re-framing the five dilemmas.

The five dilemmas	Worldview 3: Re-framing the dilemmas by using the assumptions of the living composition
Dilemma 1: The goal: knowledge, or learning and renewal?	Survival is the goal. It is obtained through continual self-production, facilitated by knowledge flows, and through successful co-evolution with the environment. Knowledge helps to operate adequately in an individual or cooperative situation. Knowledge is a strategic component in the living composition
Dilemma 2: Is knowledge objective or subjective?	Logical accounting helps to differentiate between two simultaneous realities: ontological reality and experiential reality
Dilemma 3: Is knowledge located in an organization or in several brains?	Knowledge is located in the organization and in the brains In a living composition both organizational and technical solutions as well as human skills and competencies have their role
Dilemma 4: Control, order, efficiency or self-organization, emergence, and creativity?	In the living composition memory (self-referentiality) facilitates efficiency, and sensing (a condition for interactive openness) facilitates creativity. They are interconnected phenomena and necessary for learning and renewal
Dilemma 5: Detailed long-term planning or chaos, crisis, and revolution?	Utilization of unfolding opportunities. Building the learning and renewal capability by developing the living composition

However, their activities and capabilities are facilitated and limited by organizational solutions. Knowledge is created through distinction making and it is shared through communication. Knowledge can therefore reside in individuals and also in an organization's composition, including knowledge bases. An organization's capability to renew itself influences the individuals' capability to act and learn, and vice versa. In a living composition, both organizational and technical solutions as well as human knowledge and skills have their specific role.

Dilemma 4: Control, order, and efficiency, or autonomy, self-organization, emergence, and creativity?

New view: In a living composition, memory (self-referentiality) facilitates efficiency, and sensing (a condition for interactive openness) facilitates creativity. They are interconnected phenomena and necessary for learning and renewal. Control, order, and efficiency are not necessarily opposites of autonomy, self-organization, emergence, and creativity. Instead, continuous learning and renewal may require all of them, yet within a structured composition.

Dilemma 5: Detailed long-term planning or chaos and revolution?

New view: Utilization of unfolding opportunities. Building the learning and renewal capability by developing the living composition. Competitive organizations can utilize unfolding opportunities. However, they do not drift without any clear vision from a crisis or revolution to another, but instead improve their capability to utilize these unfolding opportunities by investing in the development of a consistent, responsive living composition.

To summarize, it can be concluded that the dilemmas presented in Chapter 1 can be reframed in a new, productive way by utilizing the living composition model.

17.4 Living Composition — Managerial Implications

17.4.1 New Shared Framework for Managers, Consultants, and the Whole Organization

One objective of this book is to help managers and consultants to improve the composition of a firm. The model therefore presents a detailed description of the living composition model, platforms for positioning a firm, as well as six steps that are needed for improving a firm's composition.

The model provides the perspective that organizations can in general be regarded as living, thus freeing managers from the sense that they must start generating the 'life' of an organization. However, managers can proactively apply the model to help identify inconsistencies in an organization's living composition and compose a well-functioning 'package' with improved renewal capability.

Discussions with managers indicate that the living composition model is close to their natural way of thinking. It emphasizes the identity of an organization and its perception of its environment, and thereby describes and explains various aspects from an internal perspective, 'from within the company'. The model helps managers to identify and develop strategic components from their own perspective but in a larger framework so that they can support learning, renewal, and co-evolution better.

People in organizations have different views, attitudes, and fields of responsibility. It is often difficult for them to see their own role in the larger picture. The living composition model may provide a new shared framework for understanding the role of various persons, functions, and activities in the whole organizational composition.

Changing and competing strategies, ongoing and planned development projects, and consulting fads and technical solutions often constitute a fragmentary approach to organizational development. The living composition model may serve as a comprehensive framework and tool for planning and communication, and may help to coordinate these various aspects within a larger shared and holistic framework. Without such a framework, they risk being treated as separate activities that are not linked to each other.

An organization's competitiveness and capability to survive and succeed depend on open co-evolution with its environment. When organizing change processes, managers should recognize that a living organization cannot be changed from the outside. Rather it can only be triggered to change internally by outside stimuli. Managers can increase interactive openness by improving sensitivity to triggers and supporting greater interaction and experimentation (sensing), as well as by defining and resourcing the roles and functions (boundary elements) and practices that enable that interaction.

17.4.2   Coping with Size, Growth, and Technological Level

It is also necessary to take into account the size, growth, and technological level of an organization. It is likely that small and large companies, fast-growing and stable organizations, as well as high-tech and low-tech firms utilize different methods to organize their internal structures and to communicate with their environment. The living composition model helps to systematically analyze and improve the web of organizational characteristics. This is useful especially because there are differences among small and large, fast and slow, and high-tech and low-tech organizations. The differences influence a firm's identity, its perceptions about the environment, and overall resources available. In particular, they may influence a firm's need for knowledge (Table 17.2).

Size: large and small organizations   *Large organizations* have a broad, influential contact network and the capability to influence their business environments. Standards and structures are available and they enable efficiency and reliability. In a large organization, communication methods and tools are necessary because people do not know each other. It is important to make employees aware of the organization's composition and the dynamics of learning, because they help them understand the impact of their own activities in the larger picture. However, large organizations may also be relatively bureaucratic and slow to move. They are influenced by their own identity that has been developed over a long period. Their perception of the environment may have become outdated.

In a large organization, internal accumulation and sharing of knowledge and its transformation into explicit form may be more profitable than in a small organization. Profitability depends on the number of people who accumulate and utilize knowledge. The type of knowledge dictates whether it can be shared in explicit form. Also, access to external sources of knowledge is often necessary.

Large organizations may benefit from an open and proactive organizational culture. With such a culture they could identify, tolerate, and utilize 'disturbances' such as feedback from clients. Socio-technical solutions may make interaction with the environment more efficient. Experimentation and cross-border communication speed up innovativeness and improve the capability to implement changes.

Table 17.2: Knowledge-related needs in different kinds of organizations.

	Knowledge-related needs in different kinds of organizations	
Size of organization	*Large:* Internal accumulation and sharing of knowledge Transformation of knowledge into explicit form	*Small:* Access to external knowledge Communication in networks Utilization of tacit knowledge
Growth rate	*Fast-growing:* Knowledge about market and competition New knowledge via recruiting, acquisitions, and mergers Rapid utilization of existing knowledge. Development of new knowledge Access to external knowledge	*Slow-growing:* Knowledge about market opportunities Analysis of existing resources, capabilities, and knowledge Development of new Knowledge ICT as a tool Access to external knowledge
Technological level	*High-tech:* Scientific knowledge and technological innovations Access to networks Access to external expert knowledge Timing	*Low-tech:* Knowledge about market Commercial innovations concerning the product, process, and service Social innovations Knowledge about collaborators

For *small organizations* the basic principles are the same. However, small organizations may be more flexible. There are fewer users for accumulated knowledge and, therefore, the creation of explicit knowledge and internal knowledge bases may be less profitable. Instead, they may benefit from access to external sources of knowledge and efficient utilization of tacit knowledge.

Small, young organizations may be inexperienced in organizing. They have a short history, limited memory, and a flexible organization. They have few employees and all the employees know each other. For these reasons, communication is important. New and emerging business models enable interaction with the horizontal network of partners and vertical networks of clients, suppliers, and other parties. Connecting these business models to knowledge management and major knowledge flows may considerably improve the capability of a relatively small organization to absorb new knowledge.

Growth rate: fast-growing and slow-growing organizations   *Fast-growing organizations* may need access to external sources of knowledge such as commercial knowledge bases. They may develop their own existing knowledge base, but also acquire new knowledge through mergers and acquisitions. Fast growth and expansion emphasize the need for accurate market information. There is pressure for rapid utilization of existing knowledge, competence development through recruiting, and creation of new knowledge. Because the organization grows fast, it is necessary that the employees understand the logic of change and are able to implement even radical changes rapidly.

Slow-growth organizations may be small or large and operate in conventional industries. In order to facilitate growth, they need knowledge about new opportunities in the market. Acquiring external knowledge may trigger the organization. Slow-growth organizations may also benefit from analysis of their own resources and capabilities and from identifying their knowledge. Utilization of Information and Communication Technology (ICT) and other technologies may create the potential to improve their market situation.

Technological level: high-tech and low-tech organizations   *High-tech organizations* depend on access to research and scientific knowledge that is available from universities and research institutes. Knowledge is also increasingly produced in networks. In their rapidly changing market, which does not allow failures, high-tech organizations need quick results. On the other hand, they should continually create new knowledge, which requires experimenting and learning from failures. Success of a high-tech organization may depend on timing and on the capability to renew knowledge and itself. The boundary elements should therefore be directed to acquire specialist knowledge from external sources.

Low-tech organizations may improve their learning and renewal capability by acquiring knowledge about markets. Moreover, their success depends on their access to knowledge about commercial innovations concerning services, products, processes, and distribution channels. Low-tech organizations may also benefit from knowledge concerning social innovations. The boundary elements should therefore be directed to interact with a potentially broad group of collaborators (in networks), clients, and other parties.

17.5   Living Composition — Theoretical Implications and Suggestions for Further Research

For researchers this book illustrates how to interpret and utilize the theory of self-producing systems in the context of organizations. It also clarifies the relationship between autopoiesis and some other complexity-related concepts such as control, self-organization, and emergence. The model helps in understanding the difference between detail complexity and dynamic complexity, and the critical role of knowledge flows in an organization's survival and success.

As to the theoretical implications of this book, it is necessary to emphasize the importance of the living composition as the internal enabling infrastructure and the major contribution of this book. All other implications are subordinated to this major finding.

The main theoretical implications of this book are:

1. Positioning the autopoiesis theory among other paradigms and theories.
2. Interpreting and applying autopoiesis theory in an organizational context.
3. Describing the underlying dynamics of organizational learning and renewal in terms of living composition, including the strategic components and major knowledge flows.

17.5.1   Positioning of Autopoiesis Theory

The theoretical requirements of autopoiesis theory must be taken into account when autopoiesis is applied in an organizational context. Therefore, the common ontological and epistemological domain that was developed in this book is useful. However, further analysis would be needed to position autopoiesis theory among the main philosophical paradigms, because the specifications could have implications for the definitions of concepts and available methodologies.

17.5.2   Interpreting and Applying Autopoiesis Theory to Organizations

It had not been self-evident earlier that organizations could be regarded as autopoietic and thus living. However, the increasing interest in complex evolving systems and the changes in the business environment have increased the need to apply the concepts of complexity and also those of autopoiesis theory to organizations.

Autopoiesis theory has been applied to organizations in several ways. Many of the earlier interpretations focus on second- and third-order autopoiesis, concentrating on interaction among people and viewing organizations as social systems. Also, the term 'living company' has often been used in a metaphorical way that is not based on autopoiesis theory. In this book, organizations are living in terms of self-production (autopoiesis), which is based on the production of multiple different non-physical components. More specifically, this means that organizations are not merely 'metaphorically' autopoietic systems, 'organizationally closed' (autonomous) systems, or 'consensual' domains where other autopoietic systems (such as human beings) exist and interact. The model developed in this book as well as alternative interpretations of autopoiesis theory would be fruitful topics for further research.

17.5.3   Describing the Underlying Dynamics of Organizational Learning and Renewal in Terms of Living Composition

The living composition model reframes an organization's dynamics and underlying structures. It analyzes evolution capability in terms of major knowledge flows. The composition is positioned centrally in the autopoietic interpretation. Therefore organizations can be regarded as autopoietic entities in their own right. While several earlier studies have focused on communication among people (social autopoiesis), this book defines multiple strategic components that explain an organization as a learning and evolving unit. However, more research is needed on different compositions and their impact on creativity, learning, and renewal, as well as on the consistency/intentionality platforms and evolution models. Also, the impact of an organization's size and life cycle on the consistency/intentionality platform or evolution model could be a relevant subject for further study.

In addition, analysis of individual components as a part of a larger composition would be useful, as well as studies about the development of the composition. The model of living composition provides opportunities to review conventional organizational issues in a new way from the angle of strategic components. This means, for example, that 'identity', 'knowledge', and 'strategy' that are conventional subjects for research could be treated as components of a larger interconnected self-production system. The sensitivity of an organization to changes in specific components (such as boundary elements) could be a fruitful target for research. Experimentation, exposure to external knowledge, and measurement of the components and functions also call for further research.

The empirical findings provide new insights into the nature of openness and closure and may contribute to theories of business administration, organization and strategic management, systems theory, and information systems science. The findings concerning openness and closure in this book add to the research concerning organizations as open systems. Also other system models, such as system dynamics models, are useful for explaining diverse organizational phenomena, and they can supplement the living composition model. However, they alone are not sufficient for explaining firms as learning and evolving entities.

Because the living composition model is based on modern concepts of complexity and on thorough theoretical analysis of the principles that concern dynamic evolution of an organization, it can be compared to models that concern learning organization, knowledge management, competence-based management, and other relevant scientific and pragmatic approaches to organizations.

Also the interpretations and findings concerning self-referentiality and organizational (internal) closure are important and require further research because these concepts are easily misunderstood. Interactive openness and self-referentiality provide a new and fruitful point of departure for investigating knowledge flows and communication.

The relationships between autonomy, self-organization, emergence, and creativity, and control and efficiency are important fields for research. Their simultaneity is an especially interesting target for research.

This book places knowledge into a key role in the living composition, demonstrates the functioning and interconnection of two major knowledge flows, and illustrates their impact on learning and evolution. The concept of less-structured explicit/digital knowledge may have far-reaching implications for organizational learning and information systems. The analysis indicates that the conventional division into explicit and tacit knowledge should be re-evaluated in light of modern technology.

The autopoietic interpretation can be applied to various levels of an organization, such as teams, groups, departments, the organization as a whole, or even a region. The empirical material for this book originates from management consulting firms that are multinational, knowledge-intensive service companies. Some additional studies have been made in other industries and sectors. This research indicates that the model may be successfully applied to various kinds of organizations, such as other service companies, manufacturing firms, and public sector organizations. Moreover, the living composition model may help in understanding how the larger populations of organizations — the business ecosystems — evolve.

17.6   Living Composition — Implications for Teaching

The living composition model provides many benefits for teachers and students. It brings new thinking and material to be applied in educational contexts. The model is based on new, systematic interpretations of selected concepts of complexity that may otherwise be difficult to explain and easily misunderstood. On the other hand, it is based on empirical research, and the cases help to illustrate the diversity of renewal and learning dynamics in various kinds of organizations. The case descriptions in this book can act as material for further analysis in classrooms. They may also be used as examples and as a reference, for example when student teams analyze local companies for educational purposes.

Experience from educational situations has shown that the model, after a relatively short introduction, provides a relatively simple framework that helps students to understand the basic enabling structures and dynamics of a living organization in a holistic way. It also provides a useful classification in the form of ten strategic components and two major knowledge flows, which help students to identify, describe, analyze, and evaluate the 'simple renewal logic' behind the diversity of details in different kinds of organizations. Moreover, the platforms provide the opportunity to develop the empirical cases further.

In practice, the living composition model has proved to be an efficient tool for analyzing and communicating the complex characteristics and dynamics of organizations. Student teams have been able to successfully analyze various firms in different industries, and to make a reasonable analysis of the strengths, weaknesses, and development needs of their learning and renewal systems.

References

Aadne, J. H., von Krogh, G., & Roos, J. (1996). Representationism: The traditional approach to cooperative strategies. In: G. von Krogh & J. Roos (Eds), *Managing knowledge. Perspectives on cooperation and competition* (pp. 9–31). London: Sage.

Abrahamson, E. (1996). Management fashion. *Academy of Management Review*, *21*(January), 254–285.

Aldrich, H. (1999). *Organizations evolving.* London: Sage.

Anttiroiko, A.-V. (1993). Systeemiteoria kunnallistieteellisen tutkimuksen paradigmaattisena lähtökohtana. In: A.-V. Anttiroiko, O. Kallio & P. Rönkkö (Eds), *Systeemiteoria kunnallistieteellisen tutkimuksen lähestymistapana*(pp. 2–29). [*Systems theory as a pragmatic point of departure for municipal research.*] Tampere: Tampereen yliopisto, Julkaisusarja 4. (In Finnish).

Argyris, C., & Schön, D. A. (1996). *Organizational learning II.* Reading, MA: Addison-Wesley.

Baden-Fuller, C., & Volberda, H. W. (1995). Strategic renewal within complex organizations: Four dynamic mechanisms. Paper submitted to The Third International Workshop on Competence-Based Competition. Ghent, Belgium November 16–18.

Bailey, K. D. (1994). *Sociology and the new systems theory. Toward a theoretical synthesis.* New York: State University of New York Press.

Bank, D. (1996). The new worker know-it-alls, *The Wall Street Journal*, November 18.

Barney, J. (1991). Firm resources and sustained competitive advantage. *Journal of Management*, *17*(1), 99–120.

Barr, P. S., Stimpert, J. L., & Huff, A. S. (1992). Cognitive change, strategic action, and organizational renewal. *Strategic Management Journal*, *13*(Special Issue), 15–36.

Barthès, J.-P. (1996). ISMICK and knowledge management. Keynote speech at the *Fourth international ISMICK symposium, Rotterdam,* 21–22 October (*International symposium on the management of industrial and corporate knowledge*). In: J. F. Schreinemakers (Ed.), *knowledge management. Organization competence and methodology*. Advances in knowledge management (Vol. 1). Würtzburg: Ergon Verlag .

Bartlett, C. A., & Ghoshal, S. (1989). *Managing across borders — the transnational solution*. London: Hutchinson Business Books.

Baum, J. A. C., & Singh, J. V. (1994a). Organizational hierarchies and evolutionary processes: Some reflections on a theory of organizational evolution. In: J. A. C. Baum & J. V. Singh (Eds), *Evolutionary dynamics of organizations*. Oxford: Oxford University Press.

Baum, J. A. C., & Singh, J. V. (1994b). Organization-environment coevolution. In: J. A. C. Baum, & J. V. Singh (Eds), *Evolutionary dynamics of organizations*. Oxford: Oxford University Press.

Beer, S. (1994). Preface to autopoiesis: The organization of the living. In: R. Harnden & A. Leonard (Eds), *How many grapes went into the wine? Stafford Beer on the art and science of holistic management* (pp. 345–354). New York: Wiley.

Bhaskar, R. A. (1989). *Reclaiming reality*. London: Verso.

Blackler, F. (1995). Knowledge, knowledge work and organizations: An overview and interpretation. *Organization Studies, 16*(6), 1021–1046.

Bogaert, I., Martens, R., & van Cauwenbergh, A. (1994). Strategy as a situational puzzle: The fit of components. In: G. Hamel & A. Heene (Eds), *Competence-based competition* (pp. 57–74). New York: Wiley.

Bohm, D., & Peat, F. D. (1987). *Science, order and creativity*. London: Routledge.

Boisot, M. H. (1995). Is your firm a creative destroyer? Competitive learning and knowledge flows in the technological strategies of firms. *Research Policy, 24*, 489–506.

Boisot, M., Griffiths, D., & Moles, V. (1995). The dilemma of competence: Differentiation versus integration in the pursuit of learning. A paper prepared for the third international workshop on competence-based competition. Ghent, Belgium, November 16–18.

Boulding, K. (1956). General systems theory: The skeleton of science. *Management of Science, 2*(3), 197–208.

Burns, T., & Stalker, G. M. (1994). *The management of innovation*. London: Oxford University Press Inc. (Published originally in 1961).

Burrell, G., & Morgan, G. (1979). *Sociological paradigms and organizational analysis. Elements of the sociology of corporate life.* Brookfield: Ashgate Publishing Company.

Bøgh Andersen, P. (1995). Constructivism and truth. A comment on John Mingers: Self-producing systems. *Cybernetics and Human Knowing, 3*(3), 53–57.

Campbell, A. J., & Verbeke, A. (1996). A note on networks: How service multinationals exploit cross-border synergies. A presentation at the EIASM Workshop on Global Logistics. Brussels, May 24.

Chakravarthy, B. S., & Doz, Y. (1992). Strategy process research: Focusing on corporate self-renewal. *Strategic Management Journal, 13*(Special Issue), 5–14.

Chandler, A. D., Jr. (1962). *Strategy and structure: Chapters in the history of the industrial enterprise*. Cambridge, MA: MIT Press.

Chandler, A. D., Jr. (1986). The evolution of modern global competition. In: M. E. Porter (Ed.), *Competition in global industries* (pp. 405–448). Boston, MA: Harvard Business School Press.

Checkland, P. (1995). Systems theory and management thinking. In: K. Ellis, A. Gregory, B. R. Mears-Young & G. Ragsdell (Eds), *Critical issues is systems theory and practice.* Fourth international conference of the United Kingdom Systems Society, July 10–14, Hull, England.

Christensen, J. F., & Foss, N. J. (1996). *Dynamic corporate coherence and competence-based competition*. Copenhagen Business School and Technical University of Denmark, 1996-1.

Choo, C. W. (1998). *The knowing organization. How organizations use information to construct meaning, create knowledge, and make decisions*. Oxford: Oxford University Press.

Collis, D. J. (1996). The management consulting industry. In: K. Speicher & S. Stump (Eds), *Management consulting 199* (pp. 1–3). In cooperation with the Management Consulting Club. Boston, MA: Harvard Business School Publishing.

Consultants' News, 1997.

Crossan, M. M. (1996). Review of: Nonaka Ikujiro and Takeuchi, Hirotaka: The knowledge-creating company: How Japanese companies create the dynamics of innovation. *Journal of International Business Studies,* (First Quarter), 196–201.

Cyert, R., & March, J. (1963). *A behavioural theory of the firm.* New York: Prentice-Hall.

Czerniawska, F. (1999). *Management consultancy in the 21st century.* London: MacMillan Business.

Daft, R. L., & Weick, K. E. (1984). Toward a model of organizations as interpretation systems. *Academy of Management Review,* 9(2), 284–295.

D'Aveni, R. A., & Gunther, R. (1994). *Hypercompetition — managing the dynamics of strategic maneuvering.* New York: Free Press.

Davenport, T. (1996). Ernst & Young champions knowledge management, *Knowledge Inc. The Executive Report on Knowledge, Technology and Performance,* Vol. 1, No. 3. July, pp. 1.4.

De Leo, F. (1994). Understanding the roots of your competitive advantage. From product/market competition to competition as a multiple-layer game. In: G. Hamel & A. Heene (Eds), *Competence-based competition* (pp. 35–55). New York: Wiley.

Dierickx, I., & Cool, K. (1989). Asset stock accumulation and sustainability of competitive advantage. *Management Science,* 33(12), 1504–1513.

Digrius, B. (1997). Knowledge management consultants: Ernst & Young. *External services providers (ESP).* Research Note, Gartner Group, May 13.

Dodgson, M. (1993). Organizational learning: A review of some literatures. *Organization Studies,* 14(3), 375–394.

Doz, Y. L., & Prahalad, C. K. (1993). Managing DMNCs: A search for a new paradigm. In: S. Ghoshal & E. D. Westney (Eds), *Organization theory and the multinational corporation* (pp. 24–50). New York: St. Martin's Press.

Drazin, R., & Van de Ven, A. H. (1985). Alternative forms of fit in contingency theory. *Administrative Science Quarterly,* 30, 514–539.

Drucker, P. F. (1992). The new society of organizations. *Harvard Business Review,* (SeptemberOctober), 95–104.

Drucker, P. F. (1993). *Post-capitalist society.* Oxford: Butterworth Heinemann.

Duncan, R., & Weiss, A. (1979). Organizational learning: Implications on organizational design. In: B. M. Staw (Ed.), *Research in organizational behavior,* 1, (pp. 75–123). Greenwich, CT: JAI Press.

Egelhoff, W. G. (1991). Information processing theory and the multinational enterprise. *Journal of International Business Studies,* 22(3), 341–368.

Egelhoff, W. G. (1993). Information-processing theory and the multinational corporation. In: S. Ghoshal & E. D. Westney (Eds), *Organization theory and the multinational corporation* (pp. 182–210). New York: St. Martin's Press.

Emerson, J. C. (1997). Ernst & Young LLP: Setting the new knowledge sharing standard. *Emerson's Professional Service Review,* March/April.

Essers, J., & Schreinemakers, J. (1996). The conceptions of knowledge and information in knowledge management. In: J. F. Schreinemakers (Ed.), *Knowledge management. organization competence and methodology. Advances in knowledge management* (Vol. 1, pp. 93–104). Würtzburg: Ergon Verlag.

Forrester, J. W. (1980). *Principles of systems. 2.* Cambridge, MA. (Second preliminary edition, Published originally in 1968).

Foss, N. J., Knudsen, C., & Montgomery, C. A. (1995). An exploration of common ground: Integrating evolutionary and strategic theories of the firm. In: C. A. Montgomery (Ed.), *Resource-based and evolutionary theories of the firm: towards a synthesis* (pp. 1–18). London: Kluwer Academic Publishers.

Galbraith, J. R., & Kazanjian, R. K. (1986). *Strategy implementation. Structure, systems and process* (2nd ed.). St. Paul, MN: West Publishing.

Garvin, D. A. (1993). Building a learning organization. *Harvard Business Review*, *71*(A), 78–91.

de Geus, A. P. (1997a). The living company. *Harvard Business Review,* (March–April), 51–59.

de Geus, A. (1997b). *The living company. Growth, learning and longevity in business.* London: Nicholas Brealey Publishing.

Ghoshal, S., & Bartlett, C. (1988). The multinational corporation as a network. perspectives from interorganizational theory. *INSEAD, research working papers* No. 88/28, Fontainebleau.

Ghoshal, S., & Nohria, N. (1993). Horses for courses: Organizational forms for multinational corporations. *Sloan Management Review*, (Winter), 23–35.

Gibbons, M., Nowotny, H., Limoges, C., Trow, M., Schwartzman, S., & Scott, P. (1994). *The new production of knowledge.The dynamics of science and research in contemporary societies.* London: Sage.

von Glasersfeld, E. (1991). Knowing without metaphysics: Aspects of the radical constructivist position. In: F. Steier (Ed.), *Research and reflectivity* (pp. 12–29). London: Sage.

Goguen, J. A., & Varela, F. J. (1979). Systems and distinctions: Duality and complementarity. *International Journal of General Systems*, *5*, 31–43.

Govindarajan, V. (1988). A contingency approach to strategy implementation at the business-unit level: Integrating administrative mechanisms with strategy. *Academy of Management Journal, 31*(4), 828–853.

Grant, R. M. (1991). Porter's advantage of nations': An assessment. *Strategic Management Journal, 12*, 535–548.

Grant, R. M. (1996). Toward a knowledge-base theory of the firm. *Strategic Management Journal, 17*(December), 109–122.

Gupta, A. K., & Govindarajan, V. (1993). Coalignment between knowledge flow patterns and strategic systems and processes within MNC's. In: P. Lorange, B. Chakravarthy, J. Roos & A. Van de Ven (Eds), *Implementing strategic processes: Change, learning and co-operation* (pp. 329–346). Oxford, UK: Blackwell.

Hagström, P. (1992). Inside the 'Wired' MNC. In: C. Antonelli (Ed.), *The economics of information networks* (pp. 325–345). London: North-Holland.

Hamel, G., & Prahalad, C. K. (1993). Strategy as stretch and leverage. *Harvard Business Review*, (March–April), 75–84.

Hamel, G., & Prahalad, C. K. (1994a). *Competing for the future.* Boston, MA: Harvard Business School Press.

Hamel, G., & Prahalad, C. K. (1994b). Competing for the future. *Harvard Business Review*, (July–August), 122–128.

Hannan, M. T., & Freeman, J. (1997). The population ecology of organizations. *American Journal of Sociology, 82*(5), 929–964.

Hedlund, G. (1986). The hypermodern MNC — a heterarchy? *Human Resource Management, 25*(1), 9–35.

Hedlund, G. (1993). Assumptions of hierarchy and heterarchy, with applications to the management of the multinational corporation. In: S. Ghoshal & E. D. Westney (Eds), *Organization theory and the multinational corporation* (pp. 211–236). New York: St. Martin's Press.

Hedlund, G. (1994). A model of knowledge management and the N-form corporation. *Strategic Management Journal, 15*, 73–90.

Hildén, S. (2004). *Does organizational change improve organizational functionality? Intentions and experiences in a frequently changing organization.* Doctoral dissertation, Tampere University of Technology.

Hirschheim, R., Klein, H. K., & Lyytinen, K. (1995). *Information systems development and data modeling. Conceptual and philosophical foundations.* London: Cambridge University Press.

Holland, J. H. (1995). *Hidden order. How adaptation builds complexity.* Cambridge: Perseus Books.

Holland, J. H. (1998). *Emergence from chaos to order.* Cambridge: Perseus Books.

Itami, H., & Roehl, T. W. (1987). *Mobilizing invisible assets.* Cambridge, MA: Harvard University Press.

Jennings, D. F., & Seaman, S. L. (1994). High and low levels of organizational adaptation: An empirical analysis of strategy, structure and performance *Strategic Management Journal, 15*, 459–475.

Kallio, O. (1993). Systeemiteoria kunnallistieteellisessä tutkimuksessa. In: A.-V. Anttiroiko, O. Kallio & P. Rönkkö (Eds), *Systeemiteoria kunnallistieteellisen tutkimuksen lähestymistapana* (pp. 30–48). [*Systems theory in municipal research.*] Tampere: Tampereen yliopisto, Julkaisusarja 4. (In Finnish)

Kast, F. E., & Rosenzweig, J. E. (1981). *Organization and management. A systems and contingency approach* (3rd ed.). 7th printing 1984. London: McGraw-Hill.

Katz, D., & Kahn, R. L. (1978). *The social psychology of organizations* (2nd ed.). New York: Wiley. (Published originally in 1966.)

Kauffman, S. A. (1993). *The origins of order: Self-organization and selection in evolution.* University of Pennsylvania and the Santa Fe Institute: Oxford University Press.

Kelly, K. (1994). *Out of control: The rise of neo-biological civilization.* New York: Addison-Wesley.

Kim, D. H. (1993). The link between individual and organizational learning. *Sloan Management Review*, (Fall), 37–50.

Kofman, F., & Senge, P. M. (1993). Communities of commitment: The heart of learning organizations. *Organizational Dynamics, 22*(2), Autumn, 5–23.

Kogut, B. (1993). Learning, or the importance of being inert: Country imprinting and international competition. In: S. Ghoshal & E. D. Westney (Eds), *Organization theory and the multinational corporation* (pp. 136–154). New York: St. Martin's Press.

Kogut, B., & Zander, U. (1993). Knowledge of the firm and the evolutionary theory of the multinational corporation. *Journal of International Business Studies,* (Fourth Quarter), 625–645.

Kolb, D. A. (1984). *Experiential learning — experience as the source of learning and development.* Englewood Cliffs: Prentice-Hall.

von Krogh, G. and Roos, J. (1995). *Organizational epistemology.* London: MacMillan Press Ltd.

von Krogh, G., & Roos, J. (Eds). (1996a). *Managing knowledge. Perspectives on cooperation and competition.* London: Sage.

von Krogh, G., & Roos, J. (1996b). Conversation management for knowledge development. In: G. von Krogh & J. Roos (Eds), *Managing knowledge. perspectives on cooperation and competition* (pp. 218–225). London: Sage.

von Krogh, G. Roos, J., & Slocum, K. (1996a). An essay on corporate epistemology. In: G. von Krogh & J. Roos (Eds), *Managing knowledge. perspectives on cooperation and competition* (pp. 157–183). London: Sage.

von Krogh, G., Roos, J., & Yip, G. (1996b). A note on the epistemology of globalizing firms. In: G. von Krogh & J. Roos (Eds), *Managing knowledge. perspectives on cooperation and competition* (pp. 203–217). London: Sage.

von Krogh, G., & Vicari, S. (1993). An autopoiesis approach to experimental strategic learning. In: P. Lorange, B. Chakravarthy, J. Roos & A. Van de Ven (Eds), *Implementing strategic processes: Change, learning and co-operation,* (pp. 394–410). London: Basil Blackwell.

Kubr, M. (1996). *Management consulting. A guide to the profession* (3rd revised ed.). Geneva: International Labour Office.

Kyrö, P. (1996). *Liikkeenjohdon konsultoinnin rakenteet muuttuvat.* [*The structures of management consulting are changing.*] Helsingin kauppakorkeakoulun julkaisuja D-231. Helsinki. (In Finnish. English Summary).

Langager, S. (1995). *The KaosPilots —evaluation of a course of training.* (English Summary) April. Århns: The Royal Danish School of Educational Studies.

Lawrence, P. R., & Lorsch, J. W. (1969). *Organization and environment. Managing differentiation and integration.* London: Irwin-Dorsey International. (Published originally in 1967).

Levinthal, D. A., & March, J. G. (1993). The myopia of learning. *Strategic Management Journal, 14,* 95–112.

Liebeskind, J. P. (1996). Knowledge, strategy and the theory of the firm. *Strategic Management Journal, 17*(December), 93–108.

Luhmann, N. (1983). Retssystemets enhed. In: J. C. Jacobsen (Ed.), *Autopoiesis II. Udvalgte tekster af Niklas Luhmann,* (1995) (pp. 134–164). Copenhagen: Forlaget politisk revy.

Luhmann, N. (1990). *Essays on self-reference.* New York: Columbia University Press.

Luhmann, N. (1995). Why "systems theory"? *Cybernetics and human knowing, 3*(2), 3–10. (Translated by Lars Qvortrup).

Luostarinen, R. (1979). *Internationalization of the firm.* Doctoral dissertation. Series A:30. Helsinki: Helsinki School of Economics.

Lyles, M., von Krogh, G., Roos, J., & Kleine, D., (1996). The impact of individual and organizational learning on formation and management of organizational cooperation. In: G. von Krogh & J. Roos (Eds), *Managing knowledge. perspectives on cooperation and competition* (pp. 82–99). London: Sage .

Lyytinen, K., & Klein, H. (1985). The critical theory of Jürgen Habermas as a basis for a theory of information systems. In: E. Mumford, R. Hirschheim, G. Fitzgerald & A. T. Wood-Harper, (Eds), *Research methods in information system* (pp. 219–236). Amsterdam: North-Holland.

Løwendahl, B. R. (2000). *Strategic management of professional service firms* (2nd ed.). Copenhagen: Copenhagen Business School Press.

March, J. G. (1991). Exploration and exploitation in organizational learning. *Organization Science, 2*(1), 71–87.

March, J. G., & Olsen, J. P. (1975). The uncertainty of the past: Organizational learning under ambiguity. *European Journal of Political Research, 3,* 147–171.

Martinez, J. I., & Jarillo, J. C. (1989). The evolution of research on coordination mechanisms in multinational corporations. *Journal of International Business Studies,* (Fall), 489–514.

Maturana, H. R., & Varela, F. J. (1980). *Autopoiesis and cognition. The realization of the living.* London: D. Reidel Publishing Company.

Maturana, H. R., & Varela, F. J. (1987). *The tree of knowledge.* London: New Science Library, Shambhala.

Maula, M. (1999). M*ultinational companies as learning and evolving systems. A multiple-case study of knowledge-intensive service companies. An application of autopoiesis theory.* Doctoral dissertation. Helsinki School of Economics and Business Administration, Helsinki.

Maula, M. (2000a). The senses and memory of a firm — implications of autopoiesis theory for knowledge management. *Journal of Knowledge Management, 4*(2), 157–161.

Maula, M. (2000b). Three parallel knowledge processes. *Knowledge and Process Management, 7*(1), 55–59.

Maula, M., & Poulfelt, F. (2002). Fit and misfit between codes of conduct and reality in management consulting. In: M. L. Pava & P. Primeaux (Eds), *Re-imagining business ethics: Meaningful solutions for a global economy. Research in ethical issues in organizations* (Vol. 4, pp. 125–143). Amsterdam: Elsevier Science.

McGee, K. (1997). Book review: Self-producing systems: Implications and applications of autopoiesis. John Mingers. Plenum Press, 1995. *The Observer.* Issue no. 13. http://wwww.informatik.umu.se/~rwhit/Obs13.html. (22.1.1998).

Mesarovic, M. D., & Takahara, Y. (1989). *Abstract systems theory.* Lecture notes in control and information sciences 116. New York: Springer.

Miles, R. E., & Snow, C. C. (1984). Fit, failure and the hall of fame. *California Management Review, XXVI*(3), 10–28.

Miller, D. (1981). Toward a new contingency approach: The search for organizational gestalts. *Journal of Management Studies, 18*(1), 1–26.

Mingers, J. (1995). Self-producing systems. *Implications and Applications of Autopoiesis.* London: Plenum Press.

Mingers, J. (1997). Systems typologies in the light of autopoiesis: A reconceptualization of Boulding's hierarchy, and a typology of self-referential systems. A research paper. *Systems Research and Behavioral Science*, *14*, 303–313.

Mingers, J., & Stowell, F. (1997). *Information systems: An emerging discipline*, London: McGraw-Hill.

Mintzberg, H. (1996). Five P's for strategy. In: H. Mintzberg & J. B. Quinn (Eds), *The strategy process. Concepts, contexts, cases* (pp. 10–17). New Jersey: Prentice-Hall, Inc. (Originally published in *The California Management Review* (Fall 1987)).

Mitleton-Kelly, E. (1997). *Organisations as co-evolving complex adaptive systems*. A paper presented at the BAM97 British Academy of Management Annual Conference, London, September, 8–10.

Mitleton-Kelly, E. (2003). Ten principles of complexity and enabling infrastructures. In: E. Mitleton-Kelly (Ed.), *Complex systems and evolutionary perspectives on organisations. The application of complexity theory on organizations* (pp. 23–50). London: Elsevier Science, Advanced Series of Management.

Montgomery, C. A. (Ed.). (1995). *Resource-based and evolutionary theories of the firm: Towards a synthesis*. Dordrecht: Kluwer Academic Publishers.

Morgan, G. (1986). *Images of organization*. London: Sage. About autopoiesis: Unfolding Logics of Change. Organization as flux and transformation (pp. 233–272).

Morgan, G. (1994). Organization as flux and transformation. In: H. Tsoukas (Ed.), *New thinking in organizational behaviour. From social engineering to reflective action* (pp. 135–146). Oxford: Butterworth Heinemann.

Murdoch, A. (1996). The insider's guide to management consultants. *World Link*, September/October, 14–25.

Mäki, U. (1989). On the problem of realism in economics. In: *Ricerche Economiche*, *43*. Reprinted In: B. Caldwell (Ed.), *The philosophy and methodology of economics* (pp. 176 –198). Aldershot: Edward Elgar.

Mäki, U. (1992). Scientific realism and some Peculiarities of Economies. Paper presented in the conference on realism and anti-realism in science, Beijing, 15–17 June, Draft.

Nelson, R. (1994). Why do firms differ, and how does it matter? In: R. P. Rumelt, D. E. Schendel & D. J. Teece (Eds), *Fundamental issues in strategy* (pp. 247–269). Boston, MA: Harvard Business School Press.

Nelson, R. R. (1995). Recent evolutionary theorizing about economic change. *Journal of Economic Literature*, *XXXIII*, March, 48–90.

Nelson, R. R., & Winter, S. G. (1982). *An evolutionary theory of economic change*. Cambridge, MA: The Belknap Press of Harvard University Press.

Nevis, E. C., DiBella, A. J., & Gould, J. M. (1995). Understanding organizations as learning systems. *Sloan Management Review*, *36* (Winter), 73–85.

Nonaka, I. (1988). Creating organizational order out of chaos. *California Management Review*, (Spring), 57–73.

Nonaka, I. (1990). Managing globalization as a self-renewing process: Experiences of Japanese MNCs. In: C. A. Bartlett, Y. Doz & G. Hedlund (Eds), *Managing the Global Firm* (pp. 69–94). London: Routledge.

Nonaka, I., & Takeuchi, H. (1995). *The knowledge-creating company*. Oxford: Oxford University Press.

Ohmae, K. (1983). *The mind of the strategist.* London: McGraw-Hill.

Pantzar, M., & Csányi, V. (1990). *The replicative model of the evolution of the business organization.* Labour Institute for Economic Research Discussion Papers 98, Helsinki.

Peltoniemi, M. (2004). *Cluster, value network and business ecosystem: Knowledge and innovation approach.* A paper presented at the Conference "Organisations, Innovation and Complexity: New perspectives on the knowledge economy", University of Manchester, 9–10th September 2004. NEXSUS, The Complexity Society and CRIC Centre for Research on Innovation and Competition

Peteraf, M. A. (1993). The cornerstones of competitive advantage: A resource-based view. *Strategic Management Journal, 14*, 179–191.

Pfeffer, J., & Salancik, G. R. (1978). *The external control of organizations. A resource dependence perspective.* New York: Harper & Row.

Pondy, L. R., & Mitroff, I. I. (1979). Beyond open system models of organization. In: B. M. Staw (Ed.), *Research in organizational behavior* (Vol. 1, pp. 3–39). Greenwich, CT: JAI Press.

Porter, M. E., & Fuller, M. B. (1986). Coalitions and global strategy. In: M. E. Porter (Ed.), *Competition in global industries* (pp. 315–343). Boston: Harvard Business School Press.

Prahalad, C. K., & Doz, Y. L. (1987). *The multinational mission. Balancing local demands with global vision.* New York: The Free Press.

Prahalad, C. K., & Hamel, G. (1990). The core competence of the corporation. *Harvard Business Review*, (May-June), 79–91.

Prahalad, C. K., & Hamel, G. (1994). Strategy as a field of study: Why search for a new paradigm? *Strategic Management Journal, 15*, 5–16.

Pöyhönen, A. (2004). *Modeling and measuring organizational renewal capability.* Doctoral dissertation, Lappeenranta University of Technology.

Quinn, J. B. (1996). Strategies for change. In: H. Mintzberg & J. B. Quinn (Eds), *The strategy process. Concepts, contexts, cases* (pp. 3–10). New Jersey, Prentice-Hall, Inc. Excerpted from James Brian Quinn (1980) *Strategies for change: Logical incrementalism*, Chapters 1 and 5.

Reimus, B. (1996). Does knowledge sharing reflect a firm's identity? *Consultants News*, March, 1 and 7; May, 8.

Reimus, B. (1997). *Knowledge sharing within management consulting firms.* Executive summary. Fitzwillian, New Hampshire: Kennedy Publications.

Roos, J. (1996). Distinction making and pattern recognition in management. *European Management Journal, 14*(6), 590–595.

Roos, J., & Oliver, D. (1997). *The poised organization: Navigating effectively on knowledge landscapes.* Internet 4.5.1997 (http://www.imd.ch/fac/roos/paper_po.html). Earlier versions of the paper were presented, e.g. at The Strategy and Complexity Seminar, London School of Economics, London, February 12.

Roth, K., & Ricks, D. A. (1994). Goal configuration in a global industry contest. Strategic Management Journal, *15*, 103–120.

Roth, K., Schweiger, D. M., & Morrison, A. J. (1991). Global strategy implementation at the business unit level: Operational capabilities and administrative mechanisms. *Journal of International Business Studies, 22*(3), 369–402.

Rumelt, R. (1974). *Strategy, structure and economic performance.* Boston: Harvard University Press.

Rumelt, R. (1996). Evaluating business strategy. In: H. Mintzberg & J. B. Quinn (Eds), *The strategy process*, (3rd ed., pp. 55–63). New Jersey: Prentice-Hall.

Sanchez, R. (1997). Strategic management at the point of inflection: Systems, complexity and competence theory. *Long Range Planning, 30*(6), 939–946.

Sanchez, R. (2001a). Managing knowledge into competence: The five learning cycles of the competent organization. In: R. Sanchez (Ed.), *Knowledge management and organizational competence* (pp. 3–37). Oxford: Oxford University Press.

Sanchez, R. (2001b). Product, process and knowledge architectures in organizational competence. In: R. Sanchez (Ed.), *Knowledge management and organizational competence* (pp. 227–250). Oxford: Oxford University Press.

Sanchez, R., & Heene, A. (1996). A systems view of the firm in competence-based competition. In: R. Sanchez, A. Heene & H. Thomas (Eds), *Dynamics of competence-based competition: Theory and practice in new strategic management* (pp. 3962). Oxford, UK: Pergamon. Elsevier Science Ltd.

Sanchez, R., & Heene, A. (1997). A competence perspective on strategic learning and knowledge management. In: R. Sanchez & A. Heene (Eds), *Strategic learning and knowledge management* (pp. 3–15). Chichester: Wiley.

Sanchez, R., & Heene, A. (2004). *The new strategic management. Organization, competition and competence.* Chichester: Wiley.

Sanchez, R., Heene, A., & Thomas, H. (Eds), (1996). *Dynamics of competence-based competition: Theory and practice in new strategic management.* Oxford, UK: Pergamon, Elsevier Science Ltd.

Sarvary, M. (1999). Knowledge management and competition in the consulting industry. *California Management Review, 41*(2), 95–107.

Schein, E. H. (1993). How can organizations learn faster? The challenge of entering the green room. *Sloan Management Review*, (Winter), 85–92.

Schoonhoven, C. B. (1981). Problems with contingency theory: Testing assumptions hidden within the language of contingency "theory". *Administrative Science Quarterly, 26*, 349–377.

Scott, W. R. (1992). *Organizations: Rational, natural and open systems* (3rd ed.). Englewood Cliffs: Prentice-Hall.

Senge, P. M. (1990). *Fifth discipline.* London: Doubleday.

Simon, H. A. (1991). Bounded rationality and organizational learning. *Organization Science, 2*(1), 125–134.

Sivula, P., van den Bosch, F. A. J., & Elfring, T. (1997). Competence building by incorporating clients into the development of a business service firm's knowledge base. In: R. Sanchez & A. Heene (Eds), *Strategic learning and knowledge management* (pp. 121–137). Chichester: Wiley.

Spender, J.-C. (1996). Making knowledge the basis of a dynamic theory of a firm. *Strategic Management Journal, 17*(December), 45–62.

Spender, J.-C., & Grant, R. M. (1996). Knowledge and the firm: Overview. *Strategic Management Journal, 17*(December), 5–10.

Starbuck, W. H. (1992). Learning by knowledge-intensive firms. *Journal of Management Studies, 29*(6), 713–740.

Steier, F. (1991a). Reflexivity and methodology: An ecological constructionism. In: F. Steier (Ed.), *Research and reflexivity* (pp. 163–184). London: Sage.

Steier, F. (1991b). Research as self-reflexivity, self-reflexivity as a social process. In: F. Steier (Ed.), *Research and reflexivity* (pp. 1–11). London: Sage.

Ståhle, P. (1998). *Supporting a system's capacity for self-renewal.* Doctoral dissertation, The University of Helsinki.

Teece, D., & Pisano, G. (1994). The dynamic capabilities of firms: An introduction. *Industrial and Corporate Change, 3*(3), 537–556.

Thyssen, O. (1995). Some basic notions in the systems theory of Niklas Luhmann. *Cybernetics and Human Knowing, 3*(2), 13–22.

Tsoukas, H. (1993). Analogical reasoning and knowledge generation in organization theory. *Organization Studies, 14*(3), 323–346.

Tsoukas, H. (1996). The firm as a distributed knowledge system: A constructionist approach. *Strategic Management Journal, 17*(December), 11–26.

Tuomi, I. (1996). The communicative view on organizational memory: Power and ambiguity in knowledge creation systems. *Proceedings of the 29th Annual Hawaii International Conference on Systems Sciences* (pp. 147–155). Hawaii.

Tuomi, I. (1999). *Corporate knowledge. Theory and practice of intelligent organizations.* Helsinki: Metaxis.

Van de Ven, A. H. (1992). Suggestions for studying strategy process: A research note. *Strategic Management Journal, 13*(Special Issue), 169–188.

Van de Ven, A. H., & Drazin, R. (1985). The concept of fit in contingency theory. In: B. M. Staw & L. L. Cummings (Eds), *Research in Organizational Behavior, 7,* (pp. 333–365). Greenwich, CT: JAI Press.

Varela, F. (1979). *Principles of biological autonomy.* New York: Elsevier.

Varela, F., Maturana, H., & Uribe, R. (1974). Autopoiesis: The organization of living systems, its characterization and a model. *Biosystems, 5*(4), 187–196.

Varela, F., Thompson, E., & Rosch, E. (1993). *The embodied mind. Cognitive science and human experience.* London: The MIT Press.

Vicari, S. (1991). *L'impresa vivente. Itinerario in una diversa concezione.* Milano: Etas libri.

Vicari, S., von Krogh, G., Roos, J., & Mahnke, V. (1996). Knowledge creation through cooperative experimentation. In: G. von Krogh & J. Roos (Eds), *Managing knowledge. Perspectives on cooperation and competition* (pp. 184–202). London: Sage.

Wernerfelt, B. (1984). A resource-based view of the firm. *Strategic Management Journal, 5,* 171–180.

Wheatley, M. J. (1994). *Leadership and the new science. Learning about organization from an orderly universe.* San Francisco: Berrett-Koehler Publishers, Inc.

Wheatley, M. J., & Kellner-Rogers, M. (1996). *The simpler way.* San Francisco: Berrett-Koehler Publishers, Inc.

White, R. E., & Poynter, T. A. (1990). Organizing for world-wide advantage. In: C. A. Bartlett, Y. Doz & G. Hedlund (Eds), *Managing the global firm* (pp. 95–113). London: Routledge.

Whittington, R. (1993). *What is strategy — and does it matter?* London: Routledge.

Winograd, T., & Flores, F. (1986). *Understanding computers and cognition. A new foundation for design.* Nerwood: Alex Publishing Corporation.

Appendix 1: Glossary

NOTE: The sign (*) means that the concept has been defined specifically for the model of living composition.

Allopoietic system. A system that produces something other than itself (Mingers, 1997, p. 305).

Autonomous system. An organizationally closed system that does not necessarily produce its own components. Its 'organization' is characterized by processes that (1) are related as a network so that they recursively depend on each other in the generation and realization of the processes themselves, and (2) constitute the system as a unity recognizable in the space (domain) in which the processes exist (Varela, 1979, p. 55). Autopoietic systems (that produce their own components) are a special case of autonomous systems.

Autonomy. In the context of systems theory: the condition of subordinating all changes to the maintenance of the 'organization'.

Autopoietic system. A special case of organizationally closed autonomous systems. An autopoietic system is characterized by boundaries and the production of its own components. A composite unity whose organization can be described as a closed network of productions of components that through their interactions constitute the network of productions that produce them, and specify the network's extension by constituting boundaries in their domain of existence (Maturana in Mingers, 1997, p. 305). An autopoietic system can be identified by a six-point key.

Boundary element (*). A specific role or function that maintains a system's reciprocal interaction and co-evolution with its environment. It can be embedded, for example, in employees, groups, and information systems. Boundary elements act as 'senses' of an organization and enable sensing (interactive openness).

Chaos. Confusion, or confused mass of formless matter and infinite space, supposed to have existed before the ordered universe; any mixed mass, without due form or order — (from Greek chaos, empty space, abyss). The term 'chaos' is often used metaphorically in an organizational context. Chaos is not identical to complexity.

Chaos theory. Describes non-linear dynamics based on the iteration of a mathematical algorithm or a set of simple rules of interaction and the iterated formula remains constant. Especially in a social context, the applying of chaos theory may not always be appropriate because humans have cognitive capabilities that may enable them to change their rules of interaction (Mitleton-Kelly, 2003).

Closed system. A system that is influenced by its own behavior by feedback loop structures that bring results from the past to control future action (Forrester, 1980).

Closure. See organizational closure; self-referentiality.

Co-evolution. The evolution of one domain or entity partially depends on the evolution of other related domains or entities (e.g. Kauffman, 1993).

Communication (in autopoiesis theory). Communication takes place in a domain of social behaviors each time there is behavioral coordination in a realm of structural coupling. The phenomenon of communication depends not on what is transmitted, but on what happens to the person who receives it (Maturana & Varela, 1987, pp. 193–196).

Complex adaptive system (CAS). A complex system where the adaptation to changing conditions is essential. Complex adaptive systems have the capacity to create order from chaos and to generate new emergent properties in an accumulative manner. The roots of CAS are in evolutionary biology (Kauffman, 1993; Holland, 1995, 1998).

Complex evolving system (CES). A complex system where the adaptation to changing conditions and the co-evolution of the system with its environment are essential. CES includes five main areas of complexity research: dissipative structures, complex adaptive systems, autopoiesis (self-production), chaos theory, and increasing returns (Mitleton-Kelly, 2003).

Complex system. A system that may be capable of adapting and evolving and changing its rules of interaction.

Complexity. 'Plexus' (Latin) means braided or entwined. 'Complexus' means braided together, being interconnected and intertwined internally and in connection to the environment. Complexity is a source of order creation (Kauffman, 1993). Detail complexity refers to a large number of details and variables. Dynamic complexity refers to cause and effect relationships that are subtle and where the effects of interventions are not obvious (Senge, 1990). Complexity is not identical to chaos.

Composite system. A system consisting of components and relations (structure) (Mingers, 1997, p. 305). All composite systems are structure-determined, which means that all changes are structural changes (Maturana in Mingers, 1995, p. 30).

Connectivity. Inter-relatedness among the system elements such as individuals.

Consistency relationship (*). A relationship between strategic components. Types of consistency: intentional fit, emergent fit, stretch, or misfit. They also represent different types of living composition.

Contingency theory. Contingency theory emphasizes the dependence of an organization on environmental contingencies and the fit between it and its environment. The basic principles are: (1) There is no one best way to organize, which means that there are many ways to end up with the same result. (2) Any way of organizing is not equally effective under all conditions.

Distinction. The indication of any being, object, thing, or unity involves making an act of distinction, which distinguishes what has been indicated as separate from its background (Maturana & Varela, 1987, p. 40).

Emergent fit composition (*). Unintended consistency (fit) among strategic components.

Emergence means that coherent new patterns, structures, and behaviors emerge from prior ones. Self-emergent properties provide possibilities for unexpected new solutions (Kauffman, 1993; Holland, 1995, 1998).

Enabling infrastructure. A system's infrastructure that is based on socio-cultural and technical conditions that facilitate rather than inhibit learning and the sharing of knowledge. Also: enabling environment (Mitleton-Kelly, 2003).

Epistemology. The study or theory of the nature and grounds of knowledge. Origins of the term: 'episteme' (knowledge) and 'logos' (discourse) (Greek).

Experimentation. Helps an organization to create new knowledge and learn about its environment through successes and failures. A company can shift from adaptive rational learning to experimental learning in order to facilitate learning and knowledge creation (Vicari et al., 1996; von Krogh & Roos, 1995).

Far from equilibrium. The breaking of the symmetry of established patterns. 'Edge of chaos'.

Feedback. In the scientific context (e.g. engineering), feedback mechanisms. In the social context, feedback processes. Positive feedback: reinforcing and amplifying. Negative feedback: balancing, such as a thermostat. Feedback-loops may be intertwined and interacting on several levels.

First-order autopoietic system. Living systems, characterized by continuous self-production. The relationships consist of autopoietic relations. Example: a cell (Mingers, 1997, p. 307).

Four parallel knowledge types and processes (*).

1. Highly structured explicit/digital knowledge
2. Less-structured explicit/digital knowledge
3. Highly structured tacit knowledge
4. Less-structured tacit knowledge

Identity (in autopoiesis theory). (1) The system is able to maintain the integrity of its 'structure,' and (2) The system is distinguishable from the background and from other units (von Krogh & Roos, 1995, pp. 33–42). Identity of an organization (*) refers to the way the organization defines itself, its history, mission, and essential characterizing features.

Information (in autopoiesis theory). In the context of organizations: A firm creates information from data through application of established norms and distinctions (von Krogh & Vicari, 1993, p. 398).

Information and communication systems. May include a variety of more or less structured digital information systems.

Intentional fit composition (*). Intended consistency ('fit') among strategic components.

Interactive openness. See sensing (*).

Interactive processes (structural and social coupling externally) (*) include the methods used by an organization to communicate reciprocally and co-evolve with its environment, for example with clients. They also include social coupling that refers to communication with individuals in the external environment of an organization.

Interactively open autopoietic system. A system that interacts with its environment through its structure (Mingers, 1995, p. 33).

Interdependence. A decision or action of a system element may affect other elements of the system.

Internal closure. A system is internally (organizationally) closed if all its possible states of activity must always lead to or generate further activity within itself (Mingers, 1995, p. 32). Internal (organizational) closure refers here especially to an autopoietic system's self-referential capabilities. See self-referentiality.

Internal standards, processes, and communication (structural and social coupling internally) (*). May include various elements that influence the motivation and capability to learn, such as production processes, career structure, task definitions, and education that constitute firm-specific 'packages'.

Knowing (in autopoiesis theory). Effective action, which means operating efficiently in the domain of the existence of living beings (Maturana & Varela, 1987, p. 29).

Knowledge (in autopoiesis theory). Effective or adequate behavior in a given context, i.e., in a realm or domain, which we define by an explicit or implicit question (Maturana & Varela, 1987, p. 174). Knowledge enables distinction making. Distinctions, in turn, enable the development of knowledge (von Krogh & Roos, 1995, p. 53). Knowledge (distinctions) facilitates and regulates the autopoietic self-production process. A living composition is characterized by two major knowledge flows and four parallel knowledge processes.

Knowledge management. Approaches to knowledge management include, e.g. (1) the perspective on knowledge based systems (based, for example, on artificial intelligence, knowledge representation, cognitive sciences, psychology, and sociology), (2) the managing of intellectual assets in organizations, and (3) facilitating knowledge management with information technology (Barthès, 1996). See also languaging.

Knowledge processes. See four parallel knowledge types and processes.

Language. An ongoing process that only exists as languaging, not as isolated items of behavior (Maturana & Varela, 1987, p. 210).

Languaging. A domain of consensual coordinations of action (Mingers, 1997, p. 305). Languaging is the nexus of organizational knowledge development (von Krogh et al., 1996a, pp. 170–171). It includes bringing people together, experimenting in the realm of the unknown, and aiming at shared understanding by discussions. It is also the process in which language is not only maintained but is constantly being created, based on previous language (p. 167).

Law of limited variety. A system will exhibit no more variety than the variety to which it has been exposed in its environment (Pondy & Mitroff, 1979).

Law of requisite variety. A system's internal diversity must match the variety and complexity of the environment in order to deal with challenges posed by it (Ashby, 1956).[1]

Learning (in autopoiesis theory). Learning is an expression of structural coupling, which always maintains compatibility between the operation of an organism and its environment (Maturana & Varela, 1987, pp. 171–172).

Linkage between sensing and memory (interactive openness and self-referentiality (*) means that they are simultaneous and interconnected phenomena in a living organization. Sensing helps to coordinate the viable functioning of an organization within its environment, while memory maintains an organization's efficient functioning.

Living composition model (*) specifies the essential characteristics of living organizations. A living organization is a self-producing (autopoietic) system that is composed of 10 different non-physical strategic components. Boundary elements are included as one component type. The living composition model describes the 'structure' of a living organization in which the strategic components and their interrelationships determine an organization's evolutionary capability. An organization evolves by continually producing its strategic components as simultaneous tracks with a pattern of interactions. The production and interaction of the components and their relationships facilitate sensing (interactive openness) and memory (a condition for organizational/internal closure) in an organization. Sensing and memory are simultaneous and interconnected phenomena. They enable both an organization's current efficiency and its capability to learn, to renew itself, and to co-evolve with the changing environment within its larger business ecosystem.

Living composition model is a registered trademark also: Strategic composition.

Memory (*) means here that:

- The organization has access to its existing knowledge.
- Old accumulated knowledge affects the organization's 'structure' and operation.
- The organization's 'structure' and operation affect the acquisition of new information and the creation of new knowledge. This can occur, for example, through an organization's use of accumulated knowledge to interpret new signals in its environment. Self-referentiality facilitates access to and learning from earlier experience and knowledge.

Here *self-referentiality*, a feature of organizational closure, is also used to refer to organizational memory. See also self-referentiality.

Misfit composition (*). Unintended inconsistency among strategic components.

Observer. A (human) being capable of making distinctions and descriptions through language and whose lived experience is always within language (Mingers, 1997, p. 304).

Ontogeny. The origin of the term: 'ontos' (being) and 'genes' (born of) (Greek). In autopoiesis theory: the history of structural changes in a particular living being (Maturana & Varela, 1987, p. 95).

Ontology. A theory about the nature of being. The origin of the term: 'ontos' (being) and 'logos' (discourse) (Greek).

Open system. Organization as an open system: An organization viewed as a system in which resources flow into and out of the organization (Sanchez & Heene, 2004).

Organization (in management literature). A system of independent actors who collectively share the same goals for creating and realizing value through their interactions (Sanchez & Heene, 2004).

'Organization' (in autopoiesis theory). The relations that must exist among the components of a system for it to be a member of a specific class (Maturana & Varela, 1987, p. 47).

The relations among components and the necessary properties of the components that characterize or define the unity in general as belonging to a particular type or class. 'Organization' is the idea behind all its potential embodiments (structures). Example: the idea and description of the requirements for an airplane that it can fly and be identified as a plane (Mingers, 1995, p. 14). See also 'structure.'

Organizational closure. Every autonomous system is organizationally closed (Varela, 1979, p. 58). See also internal closure.

Perception of the environment (*). Living organizations respond to triggers (perturbations) and create distinctions (knowledge) about their environments according to their own internal rules.

Perturbations. See triggers.

Phylogeny. The evolutionary history of a kind of organism or a genetically related group of organisms. The origin of the term: 'phylogenie,' 'phulon' (race), and 'geneia' (birth, origin) (Greek). In autopoiesis theory: a succession of organic forms sequentially generated by reproductive relationships (Maturana & Varela, 1987, pp. 103–104).

Replication. The repeated generation of unities of the same class (like cars in a factory) (Maturana & Varela, 1987, p. 39).

Reproduction. A fracture that results in two non-identical unities of the same class. Reproduction necessarily gives origin to historically connected unities (Maturana & Varela, 1987, pp. 56–65).

Second-order autopoietic system. A multicellular system, characterized by functional differentiation. The relations consist of structural coupling between cells. Example: plants (Mingers, 1997, p. 307).

Second-order cybernetics. 'Cybernetics of cybernetics,' 'observing an observer'. Conventional 'first-order cybernetics' deals with simpler forms of feedback. (Cybernetics and Human Knowing, 1996, 3(4)).

Self-organization. A property of complex systems. The capability of a system to create order from chaos. 'A structural change from a system type to another, not a specific system type' (Mingers, 1995).

Self-referentiality. Self-referentiality facilitates access to and learning from the earlier experience and knowledge. See also memory (*).

Self-referential systems make some form of reference to or impact on themselves. Their organization must have some form of closure in the sense that one or more of the major relations characterizing the system must be circular, a relation between the system and itself. The following classification does not include self-referential systems at the social level. Some levels contain two alternatives (Mingers, 1997, pp. 309–312).

1. *Self-referring systems* refer structurally to themselves by position or pictorial or linguistic symbolism (e.g. the sentence 'This is a sentence').
2. *Self-influencing systems* are dynamic systems that involve circular causality and causal loops (e.g. inflation).
3. *Self-regulating systems* maintain a particular variable at a particular level (e.g. a thermostat).
4. *Self-sustaining systems* mean that all parts of the system are necessary and sufficient for the operation of the whole, but do not produce each other (e.g. a gas pilot light in a heating boiler).
5. *Self-producing (autopoietic) systems* are characterized by autonomy. The system both produces and is produced by itself (e.g. a cell).
6. *Self-recognizing systems* are able to recognize their own parts and reject others (e.g. immune systems within an organism).
7. *Self-replicating systems* build replicas of themselves (e.g. computer viruses).
8. *Self-cognizing systems* generate cognitive identity through recursive neuronal activity (e.g. animals with nervous systems interacting symbolically).
9. *Self-conscious systems* are able to interact with descriptions of themselves (e.g. a person saying 'I acted selfishly today').

Sensing (a condition of interactive openness) (*) means here that an organization interacts with its environment by being aware of and compensating for perturbations, by improving its knowledge (distinctions), and by changing internally. As an organization is exposed to the environment, its boundary elements and components are engaged in a process of mutual co-evolution (structural coupling) with the environment. An organization conducts experiments, interacts reciprocally with the environment, and compensates for triggers by making specific compensations in its living composition (internal structure). Some degree of interactive openness is thus necessary in creating and accumulating new knowledge that helps an organization sense and respond to its evolving environment. See also interactive openness.

Six-point key (Varela et al.,[2] in Mingers, 1995, pp. 16–17):

1. The system is a unity with identifiable boundaries.
2. The system can be broken into components and is analyzable as a whole.
3. The component properties satisfy certain relations that determine their interactions and transformations in the unity.
4. The system is maintained by interactions of its components.
5. The system is contained within and produces a boundary.
6. The system's modus operandi is a dynamic network of interacting processes of autopoietic production.

Social coupling. The domain of discourse in the social context. A social domain refers to the linguistic domain (adapted from Maturana & Varela, 1987, pp. 230–235).

Strategic components (*). According to the living composition model, an organization evolves by producing different kinds of components as simultaneous tracks in an interacting pattern. In the model 10 specific components are identified that constitute the strategic composition, the enabling structure of an organization, and thereby have a central role for the evolutionary capability of an organization. The components and their relationships are defined so that their production and interaction facilitate sensing (interactive openness) and memory (organizational closure) of the organization. The strategic components are: (1) identity, (2) perception of the environment, (3) strategy, (4) knowledge, (5) boundary elements, (6) interactive processes and communication (with the environment), (7) triggers, (8) experimentation, (9) internal standards, processes, and communication, and (10) information and communication systems.

Strategic composition (*). See also living composition model (*).

Strategic gap. The perception of a difference between the current state of a system element and the desired state of the system element (Sanchez & Heene, 2004).

Strategy. A pattern or plan that integrates an organization's major goals, policies, and action sequences into a cohesive whole (Quinn, 1996). A strategy helps to operationalize visions and objectives into internal standards and processes. Here: Strategy is based on the identity, perception of the environment, and other relevant aspects.

Stretch composition (*). An intentional difference between strategic components or between their current and future states.

Structural coupling. The history of recurrent interactions leading to the structural congruence between two (or more) systems (Maturana & Varela, 1987, p. 75).

'Structure' (in autopoiesis theory). The components and relations that actually constitute a particular unity and make its organization real (Maturana & Varela, 1987, p. 47) Example: a real physical plane. See also 'organization.'

System. In abstract system theory; a set of interrelated objects (Mesarovic & Takahara, 1989).

System dynamics. A branch of general systems theory that explains feedback and the dynamic and complex nature of systems. The system dynamics approach builds on recognizing patterns of behavior, structures that recur again and again (Senge, 1990).

Third-order autopoietic system. A social system, such as an organization, characterized by rules, meanings, norms, and power. The relations consist of structural coupling among organisms (Mingers, 1997).

Triggers (exposure to triggers, compensating for perturbations). In autopoiesis theory: data/signals from the environment. An autopoietic system, such as a living organization, accepts triggers only as perturbations that may lead to compensations in its 'structure.' It does not treat them as input into the organization. An autopoietic system can also be triggered internally.

Unity. An entity or whole that is distinguished by an observer in relation to a background or medium. A unity may be simple (unanalyzed) or composite (analyzed into components by further distinctions) (Mingers, 1997, p. 304).

Notes

1. Ashby, W. R. (1956). The effect of experience on a determinant system. Behavioral Science, 1, 35–42.
2. Varela, F., Maturana, H., & Uribe, R. (1974) Autopoiesis: The organization of living systems, its characterization and a model. *Biosystems*, 5(4), 187–196.

Appendix 2: Fit, Order, Consistency, and Efficiency

This appendix will discuss the implications of fit, order, and consistency for an organization's efficiency. This discussion helps in understanding the importance of consistency for an organization's composition. First, this appendix will review literature about the positive correlation between fit and efficiency, and then it will present some mixed results concerning the relationship between fit and efficiency.

Fit and Efficiency

Conventional strategy literature emphasizes *organizational efficiency and order*. Creating fit between an organization's components and avoiding inconsistency improves efficiency (Chandler, 1962). Contingency theory claims that fit between environmental complexity, internal differentiation, and integration contribute to organizational success (Katz & Kahn, 1978; Lawrence & Lorsch, 1969). The primary managerial role is to seek congruence among an organization, its environment, and its various subsystems (Kast & Rosenzweig, 1981). While contingency theories vary widely on the subject, they all propose that an organizational outcome is a consequence of fit between two or more factors (Van de Ven & Drazin, 1985). Obtaining the fit among multiple organizational dimensions is the most important factor for economic effectiveness. "The design problem is more than matching strategy and structure and matching processes and strategy. It requires matching all these dimensions to one another as well as to strategy in order to achieve a fit, a consistency, or congruence among all organizational dimensions. We regard the achievement of fit as the most important feature of the contribution of organization to economic effectiveness" (Galbraith & Kazanjian, 1986, pp. 11, 108).

Strategic thinking, consistency, and coherence are weapons of a strategist (Ohmae, 1983). Consistency is also one of the main criteria of strategy evaluation (Rumelt, 1996).[1] Fit between organizational objectives and the values of the management group provide coherence to organizational action. A good fit between international strategy and organizational design improves the effectiveness of a business unit (Roth, Schweiger, & Morrison, 1991).

Some combinations of the environment and structure fit better than others. "What drives fit is the principle of requisite complexity — the complexity of a firm's structure must match the complexity of its environment" (Ghoshal & Nohria, 1993, p. 23). For improving fit between a firm's strategic capability and the dominant industry demand (efficiency, responsiveness, or transfer of knowledge), it is necessary to build multiple sources of competitive advantage that can be managed in a complementary and flexible manner. "The basic problem underlying companies' search for a structural fit was that it focused on only one organizational variable — formal structure — that could not capture the complexity of the strategic task facing the worldwide company" (Bartlett & Ghoshal, 1989, pp. 32–33).

During the 1980s, the process school in strategic management challenged the traditional static resource-based notion of fit among strategic assets and introduced dynamic capability, the continuous maintenance of fit. It means that the strategy is a situational puzzle of linking internal assets with external contingencies (Bogaert et al., 1994). Strategic assets refer to a set of resources and capabilities that are scarce, appropriable and specialized, and difficult to trade and imitate. Situational fit refers to the congruence between strategic assets and external elements in relation to the dynamic time component. Strategy creation is an ongoing puzzle game where uncertainty is an inherent characteristic. As managers' perception of the situation and their judgment of strategic assets differ over time, the puzzle patterns constantly change. This calls for flexibility: the deployed pieces have to fit into multiple places. Synergy between various strategic assets enables an organization's superior performance.

Corporate coherence refers to the fit between a firm's competences and its overall strategy. While the static notion of coherence is useful for short-term operational efficiency, the dynamic notion is relevant for corporate strategic management. The static notion focuses on the existing portfolio of product or business lines. It is concerned with competence-leveraging and short-term operational efficiency. The dynamic notion refers to the corporate capacity to successfully exploit and explore synergies or new combinations from a diversity of competences, capabilities, and other assets (Christensen & Foss, 1996). It depends on the successful management of competence-building from a corporate-level perspective.

Mixed Results Concerning Fit and Efficiency

From the viewpoint of efficiency, fit (consistency) is a state to be achieved, and inconsistency is a state to be avoided. However, there are also mixed and contrasting results about the implications of fit. The variation depends in part on the methods used.[2]

The degree of fit (minimal, tight, early, or fragile fit)[3] and nature of fit (fit or misfit) should be differentiated. The degrees of fit are associated with an organization's survival, excellence, and performance. Firms can survive for some time and under some circumstances despite misfit in their industry, but in a competitive environment minimal fit will be required in the long term. Fit is the hallmark of successful organizations. Tight fit is the causal force at work when various managerial and organizational characteristics produce organizational excellence. The difference between minimal fit and misfit is not obvious. However, losing the fit refers to general decline and deterioration (Miles & Snow, 1984).

Several studies compare the importance of internal and external consistency. It may be difficult to obtain internal consistency and alignment with external contingencies simultaneously. Therefore, a tradeoff may be required. Proper balance between external and internal consistency improves performance. It implies the adoption of an internally consistent structure that lies within the feasible context-design set (Van de Ven & Drazin, 1985).

High-performing organizations adopt internally consistent structural patterns that are largely unresponsive to external contingencies. Studies of manufacturing firms and airlines concluded that high-performing organizations had consistent internal structures that matched a single contingency, whereas low-performing firms had inconsistent structures that attempted to respond to multiple contingencies (Child in Van de Ven & Drazin, 1985). Also, Jennings and Seaman (1994) report that internal consistency may be more important than external consistency. Top managers who did not adopt new (external) powers performed as well as those who did. They could defend an existing approach, even in the face of substantial environmental change, as long as their strategy-structure alignment was consistent. On the other hand, a study of four American tobacco companies that attempted to maintain alignment with shifting environments indicates that good internal fit does not alone guarantee performance. External fit (the alignment of external contingencies) has a strong impact on performance as well (Miles & Snow, 1984). Some studies indicate that there is no relationship between (internal) consistency and performance (Roth et al., 1991; Bourgeois in Roth & Ricks, 1994).

The previous results mean that the conventional fit concept does not unambiguously explain the performance of organizations. Moreover, the research on fit and consistency has focused on performance rather than on creativity, innovativeness, learning, and renewal.

Notes

1. The other main criteria are: consonance, advantage, and feasibility.
2. Bivariate analysis and the systems approach (examination of many variables) of contingency have provided more reliable results than the examination of pairs of organizational context and design factors (Van de Ven & Drazin, 1985; Govindarajan, 1988).
3. Miles and Snow (1984): (1) *Minimal fit* is required of all organizations in competitive environments, (2) *Tight fit* is associated with long-term effectiveness, (3) *Early fit* can create significant competitive advantage, and (4) *Fragile fit* leaves the organization vulnerable to external changes and internal ineffectiveness.

Appendix 3: Research Objectives and Method

Research Objectives and the Nature of the Study

This book is based on a study entitled *"Multinational Companies as Learning and Evolving Systems. A Multiple-Case Study of Knowledge-Intensive Service Companies. An Application of Autopoiesis Theory"* (Maula, 1999). The objective was to investigate how knowledge-intensive multinational companies (MNCs) learn and evolve as systems in their turbulent, globalizing, multinational environment.

Based on a comparison between various approaches, autopoiesis theory was selected as a theoretical basis for explaining the learning and evolution of MNCs. The study formulated an initial model and propositions to guide the empirical research, which led to a final model. The ontological and epistemological implications of autopoiesis theory were taken into account by defining the chain of interpretation and by evaluating the validation criteria of the study.

The study was multidisciplinary, because it was related to business administration (international business, strategic management, and organization theory), systems sciences and cybernetics, and philosophy (philosophy of science). It was an instrumental case study, which means that its purpose was to provide insight into an issue and to refine a theory. It applied a holistic multiple-case approach as a research method. The unit of analysis was a company, a knowledge-intensive service MNC, seen as an autopoietic learning and evolving system. The autopoietic processes were investigated as a systemic pattern, not as a longitudinal and historical process. The study examined, by applying a pattern-matching mode of analysis, whether the assumed components and relationships of the initial model could be identified in the case firms' learning and evolution. It also examined whether the case companies function as autopoietic learning and evolution systems as assumed, and whether the variation of their renewal patterns was related to their compositions.

Research Process, Schedule, and Method

The theoretical part of the study compared five theories and models — congruence model, contingency theory, conventional open system model, system dynamics model, and autopoiesis theory — that could potentially explain a firm's learning and evolution from the consistency perspective. The empirical part of the study was conducted in 1997–1999. A pilot case study was conducted in PBS (Danish Payment Systems Ltd.) jointly with a Danish management consulting company Progrès A/S as part of a bigger development project. The pilot study provided useful methodological information but was not included in the multiple-case study.

The empirical material was collected from four case companies during 1997 and 1998. The case companies were selected by applying literal replication logic that is comparable to multiple experiments. The selected companies — Arthur Andersen (Business Consulting), Arthur D. Little (Europe), Ernst & Young (Management Consulting), and

KaosPilots and KaosManagement vary along the dimensions of age, size, technology intensity, and orientation. They were compared to the initial model, not to each other. The case descriptions were finalized in 1999 and approved by the participating organizations for publishing.

Altogether 42 top managers at global and regional levels and consultants at the local level were interviewed in the USA, UK, France, Netherlands, Belgium, Germany, Sweden, and Denmark. In addition, group meetings and an internal event provided feedback about the selected approach. Other sources of information consisted mainly of printed company documentation.

All case organizations had created models about organizational learning, change, and/or knowledge management for their clients and themselves. The firms provided the opportunity to interview persons who had been creating them and were thus exceptionally experienced in the research problem of this study.

The pattern matching process included three stages. The first stage analyzed strategic components. The second stage investigated whether the case company functions, from the perspective of learning and evolution, as an autopoietic system. It analyzed interactive openness, self-referentiality, and the role and consistency of the living composition. The third stage of pattern matching consisted of a cross-company analysis.

Appendix 4: Openness and Closure: Three Approaches

This appendix analyzes the relationship between openness and closure by using three approaches. The analysis helps in understanding the nature of self-referential systems, such as self-producing (autopoietic) systems. Openness and closure can be analyzed by:

- Using the conventional concepts of boundaries and feedback as a point of departure.
- Analyzing the relationship between organizational closure and inputs.
- Evaluating existing definitions of simultaneous openness and closure in autopoiesis.

Conventional Concepts of Boundary and Feedback as an Analogy

Boundaries and feedback have conventionally been used to characterize the openness and closure of a system. As was concluded in Chapter 8, they result in four combinations:

- Connected open and closed system (open boundary, internal closure).
- Double-open system (open boundary, 'open feedback' via environment).
- Isolated, double-closed system (closed boundary, internal closure).
- Passive, closed and open system (closed boundary, 'open feedback' via environment).

Conclusion: Defined by the two variables, boundary and feedback, openness and closure can be simultaneous features of a simple system. By analogy, it can be assumed that openness and closure may also exist simultaneously in more complex systems such as autopoietic systems.

Organizational Closure and the Role of Inputs

'Closure' is a relevant feature of self-referential systems, in the sense that one or more of the major relations characterizing these systems must be circular, a relation between the system and itself. "A system is organizationally closed if all its possible states of activity must always lead to or generate further activity within itself" (Mingers, 1995, p. 32, 1997, p. 310). Autopoietic systems can only be perturbed by their environment. Two questions can be presented about inputs and outputs in autopoietic systems (Mingers, 1995):

1. *The organizational question:* Is the system closed or open?
2. *The structural question:* Are we interested in the unity itself in its own right (the autopoiesis perspective), or in the unity as a part of some wider system (the control perspective)? If we describe the system *in its own right* (autopoiesis perspective), all interactions should be described as perturbations that lead to particular compensations. If we describe the system *as a part of a larger system* (the control perspective, an allopoietic system), the interactions may be seen as inputs and outputs (Mingers, 1995; Goguen & Varela, 1979). This reduces the system to a simple conventional open system model.

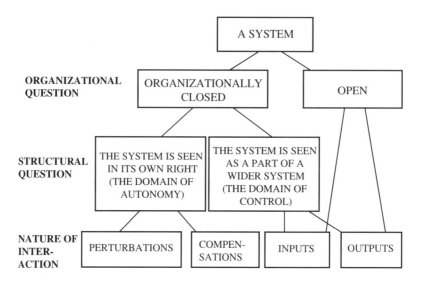

Figure A4.1: Inputs/outputs and perturbations/compensations (based on Mingers, 1995).

These questions imply the differentiation between inputs, outputs, perturbations, and compensations. Autopoietic systems belong to organizationally closed systems, whereas the conventional simple open systems belong to open systems. (see Figure A4.1).

Conclusion: A system can be regarded as an open input-transformation-output system if it is seen as a part of a larger system. Simultaneously it can be regarded as organizationally closed system with the capability of reciprocal interaction with its environment, if it is described in its own right (autopoietic).

Simultaneity of Openness and Closure in Autopoiesis: Existing Definitions

Some researchers claim that organizations as autopoietic systems are simultaneously open and closed but on different issues. For example, an organization is open with respect to data, but closed to information and knowledge that are created internally (von Krogh & Roos, 1996b). Organizations can also be regarded as open on some scales (such as formal structure) and closed on others (such as norms and beliefs) (von Krogh & Roos, 1995).

According to Luhmann, social systems are autopoietic and therefore open and closed. In his view, autopoietic systems must be understood as the recursively-closed organization of an open system, that is, beyond the traditional dichotomy of open vs. closed regarding the linkage of the two (von Krogh & Roos, 1995). This new insight means that closure is a condition of openness. Components can be reproduced only if they have the capacity to link closure and openness (Luhmann, 1990). Social systems are basically open systems, and closure is a necessary precondition for their openness and functioning. "Communication is an evolutionary potential for building up systems that are able to maintain closure under the condition of openness" (p. 13).

A legal system is a normatively closed and cognitively open system (Luhmann, 1983). *Normative closure* refers to the production of decisions concerning legal cases. The legal system is normatively (organizationally) closed because only the legal system itself can justify the constitution of its components. *Cognitive openness* means that the legal system relates its solutions simultaneously to the environment and solves how the preconditions for each legal case have been met. For this reason, the behavior of the legal system can be changed if the facts from the environment create sufficient pressure for change. Also, an economic system is an autopoietic system. It is closed because all activities are connected to payments or money-related terms. All activities facilitate new activities and maintain the system's autopoiesis. However, it is exactly this closure that facilitates its openness, because every payment necessitates a motive and the satisfaction of a need.

Normative closure and cognitive openness coexist and interact. Normative closure maintains the system's autopoietic functioning, and cognitive openness helps to coordinate its functioning within the environment. Self-referential operations and system/environment differences imply each other mutually and logically (Luhmann, 1983, 1995).

Mingers also emphasizes the simultaneity of organizational closure and structural (interactive) openness. All self-referential systems are organizationally closed in the sense that one or more of the major relations characterizing these systems must be circular, a relation between the system and itself (Mingers, 1995, 1997). On the other hand, all systems are structurally (interactively) open, because some of their actual components interact with an environment. "The notions that autopoietic systems are organizationally closed and have no inputs and outputs have often been misinterpreted. That has been taken to mean that such systems are completely isolated and have no interactions with their environment. This is not at all the case. Such systems are organizationally closed but interactively open. They interact with their environment through their structure" (Mingers, 1995, p. 33).

Conclusion: The analysis of autopoietic system principles indicates that openness and closure are not only simultaneous phenomena but they necessitate each other.

Appendix 5: Arthur Andersen (Business Consulting)

Arthur Andersen at a Glance (in 2001)

Founded: 1913 by Arthur Andersen and Clarence DeLany.
Ownership: Privately owned by worldwide partners.
The fiscal year that ended August 31, 2001:
Arthur Andersen, total:
                     Revenues: US$ 9.3 billion.
                     Growth: 10% in net revenues expressed in U.S. dollars.
Arthur Andersen Business Consulting Practice:
                     Revenues: US$ 1.7 billion.
                     Growth: 6% in net revenues expressed in U.S. dollars.
Employees in 2001:   85,000
Headquarters: Chicago, Illinois.
Offices: 390 offices in 84 countries worldwide.
                     Correspondent relationships with other firms in 78 cities and 62
                     additional countries (in 2000).

The Knowledge Enterprises Unit includes the Global Best Practices® Group and the Next Generation Research Group. They facilitate organizational learning and develop knowledge-related issues.

Services

The services provided by the offices in various countries vary according to their relevance to clients. The services of Arthur Andersen include:

- Assurance and Business Advisory services
- Tax, Legal, and Business Advisory services
- Business Consulting
- Global Corporate Finance

Interviews (1997–1998)

Interviews

Carsten Dalsgaard, Partner. Arthur Andersen Business Consulting, Copenhagen, Denmark.
Robert J. Hiebeler, Managing Director, KnowledgeSpace[SM], Arthur Andersen LLP, Chicago, USA.

Sanne Prestegaard, Management Consultant. Arthur Andersen Business Consulting, Copenhagen, Denmark.

Ruth L. Williams, Research Project Director, Next Generation Research Team, Global Best Practices[SM]. Arthur Andersen LLP, Chicago, USA.

Discussion

Christina Schultz, Experienced Manager, Arthur Andersen Technology Solutions (AATS), Arthur Andersen LLP, Chicago, USA.

Frederick T. (Toby) Bell, Director, Arthur Andersen Technology Solutions (AATS). Arthur Andersen LLP, Chicago, USA.

Demonstrations

By Robert J. Hiebeler, Managing Director, KnowledgeSpace[SM] unit, and Ruth L. Williams, Research Project Director, Next Generation Research Team, Chicago, USA. The demonstrations covered The KnowledgeSpace[SM] and AA Online.

Selected Company-Related Material

Dutta, S., & DeMeyer, A. (1996). Knowledge management at Arthur Andersen (Denmark): Building assets in real time and in virtual space. Fontainebleau, France: INSEAD.

Hiebeler, R. J. (1996). Benchmarking knowledge management. *Strategy & Leadership*, March/April, *24* (2).

Hiebeler, Robert, Arthur Andersen Knowledge Enterprises. (1997). *The Arthur Andersen knowledge journey.* Presentation material.

Hiebeler, Robert, Kelly, Thomas B., and Ketteman, Charles. (1998) *Best practices. building your business with customer-focused solutions.* Arthur Andersen. Simon & Schuster Books.

Williams, R. L., & Bukowitz, W. R. (1997) Knowledge managers guide information seekers. *HRMagazine*, (January), 77–81.

Appendix 6: Arthur D. Little (Europe)

Arthur D. Little at a glance

Founded:	1886 by Arthur Dehon Little and Roger Griffin.
Ownership:	Private, employee-owned company. The ownership is arranged mainly through the Memorial Drive Trust, set up in 1950.
Legal structure:	A corporation with a Board and CEO.
Revenues:	About US$ 0.6 billion (in 1997).
	Growth percent in 1997–1999: more than 3% annually.
Employees:	More than 3000 (in 1997).
Headquarters:	Boston, Mass.
Offices:	52 offices in 30 countries worldwide. The firm has more than 100 research laboratories.

Arthur D. Little has two technology centers. *Acorn Park* has numerous laboratories in Cambridge, Mass. *Cambridge Consultants Limited (CCL)* in Cambridge, UK, is one of Europe's leading multidisciplinary innovation companies. The company has also established an office in Palo Alto, California. In 1995 Arthur D. Little acquired *Innovation Associates (IA),*[1] because of its strong traditions and the emerging market needs. It provides organizational learning tools and methods particularly for the USA market. In Europe learning organization services are integrated as a part of management consulting. *Arthur D. Little School of Management*, founded in 1964, is an accredited and relatively independent management school. The teachers consist of leading Arthur D. Little consultants and professors from institutions such as Harvard University and the Massachusetts Institute of Technology (MIT). It offers a one-year Master of Science in Management degree, executive education programs, and short professional programs. More than 3200 managers from over 115 countries have completed the program. Examples of other specified organizational units are Pyxsys (creates high-performance turnkey solutions for customers in the Internet and e-commerce market segments), SciRox (an incubator that brings technologies and product concepts to the marketplace), *Arthur D. Little Enterprises (ADLE,* commercializes ADL's own inventions and assists clients in licensing technologies), *Arthur D. Little Program Systems Management Company (PSMC)* that manages large, complex projects, and *The Joyce Institute* that provides ergonomics planning, consulting, and training services.

Services

Arthur D. Little operates in one business, consulting. The services are:

- Management consulting
- Technology and innovation
- Environment and risk consulting
- Incubator services

In Europe, the distribution of services is organized by markets. The activities are organized along two collaborating practices: (1) *Industry practices* (18 in Europe), and (2) Five *functional practices,* such as Strategy and Organization, Technology and Innovation Management, Supply Chain Management, and Information Management.

Arthur D. Little has created and acquired services that help clients to implement organizational learning and change. Examples of them are the 'Five Disciplines' (Peter Senge, Innovation Associates, Inc.), Unwritten Rules of the Game (Peter Scott-Morgan), Ambition Driven Strategy, Cornerstones of Learning Organization, The High Performance Business Model, Pathway to Performance Model, and the three-level Model of Managing Learning (the helicopter model).

List of Interviews (1997–1998)

Philippe Alloing, European director Human Resources, Arthur D. Little International, Inc., Paris, France.

Boudewijn Arts, manager, Arthur D. Little International, Inc., Brussels, Belgium.

Ralph Baron, director, Public Services, Arthur D. Little, Inc. Berlin, Germany. (Phone discussion, comments).

Jean R. Becker, managing senior manager, Arthur D. Little International, Inc. Copenhagen, Denmark.

Frederick Bock, vice president, Global Strategy and Organization Practice Leader. Arthur D. Little International, Inc., Wiesbaden, Germany.

Nils Bohlin, director, Arthur D. Little International, Inc., Copenhagen, Denmark; Gothenburg, Sweden; London, UK.

Larry Chait, the global director of Knowledge Management, Arthur D. Little International, Inc., Boston, USA (Phone interview).

Jacques Hurkmans, market manager, Arthur D. Little, Inc. Rotterdam, Netherlands, (Phone discussion, comments).

Maurice Olivier, senior vice president Europe and Middle East. Arthur D. Little International, Inc., Wiesbaden, Germany.

Serge Pegoff, principal, Arthur D. Little International, Inc., Information Management Practice, Brussels, Belgium.

Kamal Saad, senior director, Arthur D. Little International, Inc., Brussels, Belgium.

Suzanne B. Thompson, principal, Innovation Associates, Inc., Gothenburg, Sweden.

Alexander de Wit, Arthur D. Little International Inc., Strategy and Organization Practice, Brussels, Belgium.

Selected company-related material

Arthur D. Little. (1991). In *Management Consultancy. The Inside Story*, C. Rassam and D. Oates. Mercury.

Arthur D. Little, Inc. (1994). In: *Management Consulting 1994. Harvard Business School career guide*. Harvard Business School.

Arthur D. Little, Inc. (1995). Teaching Case 9-396-060. Rev. February 15, 1995. Harvard Business School.

Arthur D. Little, Inc. (1996). Management consulting 1996. In: K. Speicher & S. Stump (Eds), *Harvard Business School career guide*. Harvard Business School.

Internet address

http://www.arthurdlittle.com

Notes

1. Innovation Associates was co-founded by Peter Senge and Charles Kiefer in 1976.

Appendix 7: Ernst & Young (Management Consulting)

In this text, the name Ernst & Young (Management Consulting) will be used because that was the name in use during the interviews, before the merger with Cap Gemini.

Ernst & Young (Management Consulting) at a Glance

Ernst & Young (Management Consulting)[1] was previously a part of Ernst & Young and merged in 1999 with Gemini Consulting and Cap Gemini IT Services. The resulting company, Cap Gemini Ernst & Young, is today one of the largest management and consulting firms in the world. It combines the resources of Gemini Consulting, Cap Gemini IT Services, and Ernst & Young Consulting Services.

Ernst & Young (Group):

Founded:	1989 with the merger of Ernst & Whinney and Arthur Young.
Ownership:	Private. The national member firms are privately owned by local partners.
Offices in 2002:	84, 000
Employees in 2002:	In more than 130 countries.

Revenues worldwide in the fiscal
Year ended June 30, 2001:xUS$ 9.9 billion.

Ernst & Young (Management Consulting in 1997–1998):

Revenues in 1997:	US$ 2.7 billion.[2]
Growth percent in 1997:	29% (1996: more than 38%).
Employees in 1998:	Nearly 10,500.
	Including alliance with Tata Consultancy: 15,000.

Ernst & Young has established Centers for Business Knowledge[TM] (CBK) on various continents in order to facilitate knowledge management.[3] The Ernst & Young Center for Business Innovation[TM] (CBI) is a 'thought leadership' unit, the Center for Business Transformation (CBT) develops methodologies, and the Center for Technology Enablement (CTE) facilitates the use of information technology. Ernst & Young Technologies Incorporated (EYT) maintains, for example, EYT StoreFront[4] for the subscribers of Ernie[SM]. It is a virtual information technology store for IT systems, peripherals, and other items. Clients have access to more than 60,000 IT products, such as computer components and peripherals. They benefit from low purchase prices, easy comparisons, purchasing, configuring, and shipping. They can make reseller and service integrator agreements around the world and get access to EYT's after-purchase services.

In 1996, Ernst & Young established Global Client Consulting (GCC) groups in Europe, Asia Pacific, and Latin America in order to serve selected global clients. These groups, along with the aforementioned knowledge centers, were developed with the purpose of reducing the US focus of the firm.

Services of Cap Gemini Ernst & Young (in 2002)

The three core business areas are:

- Management consulting
- Systems transformation
- Information systems management — outsourcing.

Professionals with a Specified Role in Knowledge Management

The following list presents the professionals with specified roles in knowledge management at Ernst & Young in 1998 (Ralph W. Poole):
Chief Knowledge Manager (CKO)
Knowledge centers (9)

- Center for Business Knowledge CBK/Cleveland, Ohio
   - Knowledge Services Group (KSG) = Information Resource Center librarians and 'cybrarians' (= Information Professionals)
- Other knowledge centers

COINS Communities of Interest Networks (Knowledge networks)

- 80–100 networks a 12–20 core group Subject Matter Experts
- Coordinators/facilitators/transnational knowledge managers

National Chief Knowledge Officers (CKO)

- Europe
- Other regions

Knowledge Managers in management consulting practices[5]
Knowledge Stewards (in the engagements)
Knowledge Based Businesses (KBB) Practice (Service line)
Other development centers:

- Ernst & Young Center for Business Innovation™ (CBI)
- Center for Business Transformation (CBT) (methods development)
- Center for Technology Enablement (CTE)
- Ernst & Young Technologies Incorporated (EYT)

Interviews, etc. (1997–1998)

Interviews

Knud Musaeus, knowledge manager, Ernst & Young Management Consulting, Copenhagen, Denmark.

Michel Constant, managing director, Ernst & Young International, CKS Center for Knowledge and Support, Paris, France.

Ralph W. Poole, director, CBK Center for Business Knowledge, Cleveland, Ohio.

Anker Nielsen, managing director, Ernst & Young Management Consulting, Copenhagen, Denmark (Phone discussion, comments).

Kristian D. Ambeck, senior consultant, Ernst & Young Management Consulting, Copenhagen, Denmark.

Company Visit

CBK Center for Business Knowledge on 29.10.1997, in Cleveland, Ohio.

Presentations

John G. Peetz, The U.S. Chief Knowledge Officer CKO, Ernst & Young LLP.

Ralph W. Poole, director, CBK Center for Business Knowledge.

Dick Loehr, E&Y Partner and Director in charge of Knowledge Networks, CBK Center for Business Knowledge.

Sameer Bhide, CBK Center for Business Knowledge.

Giovanni Piazza, CBK Center for Business Knowledge.

Tim Green, Knowledge Services Group, Business Research manager, CBK Center for Business Knowledge.

Demonstration

By Knud Musaeus, knowledge manager, Ernst & Young Management Consulting, Copenhagen, Denmark.

Selected Company Related Material

Davenport, T. (1996). Ernst & Young Champions knowledge management. *Knowledge Inc. The executive report on knowledge, technology & performance. 1*(3), July, 1–4.

Digrius, B. (1997). *Knowledge Management Consultants: Ernst & Young.* External Services Providers (ESP). Research note. Gartner Group. May 13.

Emerson, J. C. (1997) Ernst & Young LLP: Setting The new knowledge sharing standard. *Emerson's Professional Services Review.* March/April.

Ernie — your online business consultant. Answers to Subscriber Questions. (1997). Ernst & Young LLP. Entrepreneurial Consulting. Revised 3/1997.

Ernst & Young United Kingdom. (1995). Teaching Case Description A. Harvard Business School 9-495-061. Revised, June 23.

PowerPack Man. (1997). Fast Company. August/September.

Internet Addresses

Cap Gemini Ernst & Young: http://www.cgey.com/
Ernst & Young: http://www.ey.com/

Notes

1. Ernst & Young Consulting Services.
2. Source: Consultants News (1998).
3. In Cleveland, Toronto, Paris, Sydney, Sao Paulo, London, Stuttgart, Rotterdam, and Singapore.
4. This service did not belong to the Ernst & Young Management Consulting practice, but is presented here to depict the scale of Ernst & Young's IT-based services.
5. This figure includes only the management consulting practice knowledge managers. The other practices have knowledge managers as well.

Appendix 8: The KaosPilots and KaosManagement

The KaosPilots and KaosManagement at a Glance

The KaosPilots

Founded:	1991. The origins in 'Frontrunners', starting in 1982.
Ownership:	The KaosPilots 'owns itself' ('selvejende organisation', A Danish organizational form). The KaosPilots has in Denmark the status of a private educational institution, and it is structured as an autonomous business entity.
Budget in 2000:	US$ 1.2 million (DKK 8 million). The KaosPilots is funded by the Danish Ministry of Education in Denmark, student fees, and self-generated income.
Employees:	Permanent employees in 2000–2001: 12 in Aarhus, Denmark, 1 in Durban, South Africa. In addition, a relatively wide network of teachers from universities, companies, and consulting firms.
Locations:	Based in Denmark. Outposts in California and South Africa.
Services:	The three-year 'kaospilots' education program for students. Lectures, workshops, etc. for firms and other organizations.

KaosManagement

Founded:	1993
Ownership:	In the beginning, KaosManagement was an association. Starting in 1999 it is a private, independent consultancy and project company.
Annual revenues 2000:	About US$ 1 million (6.5 million DKK).
Employees:	A nucleus of 14 full-time employees and some freelancers. A wide network of trendsetters, resource persons, and collaborating partners.
Offices:	Aarhus and Copenhagen in Denmark; Oslo in Norway.
Services	Workshops, conferences, and development programs.

Key concepts, defined by The KaosPilots and KaosManagement

Chaos: confusion, or confused mass of formless matter and infinite space, supposed to have existed before the ordered universe; any mixed mass, without due form or order — (from Greek chaos, empty space, abyss).

Kaos: Danish word for chaos.

Pilot: steersman; specifically, a person licensed to steer ships into or out of harbor or through difficult waters; a guide; a director; a person who flies an airplane, airship, or balloon — (from Italian pilota, from Greek pedon, an oar) — Webster's Dictionary.

Kaospilot: A person who has successfully completed the management-training program offered by The KaosPilots (The KaosPilots ... Crossing the Atlantic, 1996).

Interviews (1997–1998)

Marianne Egelund Siig, CEO of KaosManagement
Uffe Elbaek, the Principal of The KaosPilots
Ørjan Jensen, Coach of The KaosPilots
Rasmus Gejl, Project leader at Ungdomsklanen
Alfred Iversen, Contact person, guide, and problem solver
Vibeke Johansen. Daily leader of the Future Library
Patrik Liljegren, Student at The KaosPilots
Gitte Madsen, Head of Information at The KaosPilots
Heidi Meier Pedersen, Freelancer consultant at KaosManagement
Wickie Meier Pedersen, Consultant at KaosManagement
Toke Paludan Møller, member of The KaosPilots Educational Council. Former Chairman
     of the Danish Entrepreneurs' Association.
Henrik Nitschke, Coach of The KaosPilots
Max Samuels, Student at The KaosPilots
Ulrik Schiøtz, Anthropologist, observer in the event in San Francisco.
Morten Teisner, Student at Aarhus University, Institute of Information and Media.
Jørgen Thiele, Administrator and Second in Charge, The KaosPilots (Phone discussion,
     comments).
Erik Wingren, Student at The KaosPilots

The KaosPilots POP-event in San Francisco, California, on July 10–13, 1997

The objective of the event was to formulate the purpose and principles for The KaosPilots in order to transform it into a self-organizing, 'chaordic™' organization. Altogether 74 persons attended the event, including Mr. Dee W. Hock, Chaordic Alliances™, CEO emeritus of Visa USA and Visa International.

Selected Material

Deichman-Sørensen, Trine (1997). *KaosPiloterne i tidens tendenser.* AFDIs rapportserie
     nr. 3/97. Oslo: Arbeidsforskningsinstituttet.

Elbæk, Uffe (1998). Kaospilot- en personlig beretning om en skole, en uddannelse og et miljø. Copenhagen: KLIM.

Langager, Søren (1995). The KaosPilots — Evaluation of a Course of Training. (English summary) April. (The evaluation was published in 1993 and 1994.)

The KaosPilots. A Scandinavian Management University crossing the Atlantic. (1996). Description.

Internet Address

http://www.kaospilot.dk